Teaching Critical Thinking

Prentice Hall Studies in Writing and Culture

Series Editor
Nancy Sommers
Harvard University

PRENTICE HALL STUDIES IN WRITING AND CULTURE captures the excitement of an emerging discipline that is finally coming into its own. The writers in this series are challenging basic assumptions, asking new questions, trying to broaden the inquiry about writing and the teaching of writing. They not only raise challenging questions about the classroom—about teaching and building communities of writers—they also investigate subjects as far ranging as the nature of knowledge and the role that culture plays in shaping pedagogy. Writers in the series are particularly concerned about the interplay between language and culture, about how considerations of gender, race, and audience shape our writing and our teaching. Early volumes will be devoted to the essay, audience, autobiography, and how writers teach writing. Other studies will appear over time as we explore matters that are critical to teaching writing.

Nancy Sommers is Associate Director of the Expository Writing Program at Harvard. She has also directed the composition program at the University of Oklahoma and has taught in the English Department of Rutgers University where she was a Henry Rutgers research fellow. She has published widely on the theory and practice of teaching writing. She has received the National Council of Teachers of English Promising Research Award for her work on revision and the Richard Braddock Award for her work on responding to student writing.

Books in This Series

Nancy Kline, *How Writers Teach Writing*
James E. Porter, *Audience and Rhetoric*
Kurt Spellmeyer, *Common Ground: Dialogue, Understanding,*
and the Teaching of Composition
John H. Clarke & Arthur W. Biddle, *Teaching Critical Thinking:*
Reports from Across the Curriculum

Teaching Critical Thinking
Reports from
Across the Curriculum

John H. Clarke
University of Vermont

Arthur W. Biddle
University of Vermont

Prentice Hall, Englewood Cliffs, New Jersey 07632

Library of Congress Cataloging-in-Publication Data

Teaching critical thinking: reports from across the curriculum /
[edited by] JOHN H. CLARKE, ARTHUR W. BIDDLE.
   p. cm.—(Prentice Hall studies in writing and culture)
   includes bibliographical references (p.).
   ISBN 0-13-917410-9 : [price]
   1. Critical thinking—Study and teaching. 2. Interdisciplinary
approach in education. I. Clarke, John H., [date]. II. Biddle,
Arthur W. III. Series.
LB1590.3.T4   1993
371.3—dc20   92-45226

Acquisitions editor: *Alison Reeves*
Editorial/production supervision: *Edie Riker*
Prepress buyer: *Herb Klein*
Manufacturing buyer: *Bob Anderson*
Editorial assistant: *Kara Hado*

© 1993 by Prentice-Hall, Inc.
A Simon & Schuster Company
Englewood Cliffs, New Jersey 07632

Printed in the United States of America

10 9 8 7 6 5 4 3 2 1

ISBN   0-13-917410-9

Prentice-Hall International (UK) Limited, *London*
Prentice-Hall of Australia Pty. Limited, *Sydney*
Prentice-Hall Canada Inc., *Toronto*
Prentice-Hall Hispanoamericana, S.A., *Mexico*
Prentice-Hall of India Private Limited, *New Delhi*
Prentice-Hall of Japan, Inc., *Tokyo*
Simon & Schuster Asia Pte. Ltd., *Singapore*
Editora Prentice-Hall do Brasil, Ltda., *Rio de Janeiro*

Contents

Chapter 3
EXAMINING IDEAS AND RELATIONSHIPS: THEORY TESTING PROCESSES

Chapter 4
APPLYING PLANS TO PROBLEMS: DATA GENERATING PROCESSES

Preface

Teaching Critical Thinking: Reports from Across the Curriculum presents innovative strategies for teaching students to think critically in a broad variety of disciplines. Critical thinking has emerged as a dominant concern in pedagogical journals, workshops, and conferences. Teachers want to know how to improve cognitive skills in content areas. We believe that critical thinking is not a faddish add-on to already crowded courses, but the central means of introducing learners to the ways we perceive and interact with our worlds.

Teaching Critical Thinking offers its readers a sound pedagogical-epistemological basis from which to develop personal instructional approaches, plus dozens of specific suggestions from teachers around the country showing how they teach their students to think critically. The contributing authors have all published articles in the leading discipline-based journals.

PLAN OF THE BOOK

The plan of the book is simple. Our introductory essay explains briefly the learning theory behind the work. The rest of the book is divided into four chapters that reflect the aspects or parts of the thinking process as we see it. Each chapter begins with an explanation of that particular mode of thinking, followed by reports from the field. These reports are the heart of the book. Each report

- describes concrete assignments for a particular course
- explains intellectual skills presented
- gives samples of students' responses
- tells how these assignments complement course goals.

Some reports describe strategies that are discipline-specific, but many are adaptable to other courses in other areas of the curriculum.

AUDIENCE

Our audience is the practicing teacher. College instructors of introductory-level courses across the curriculum and their high school counterparts will find many useful ideas here. Teachers of college composition courses will discover a rich source of ideas for writing assignments. Teachers-in-training will gain a sound way of thinking about their subjects and their students.

Our interest in critical thinking does not end with the publication of *Teaching Critical Thinking: Reports from Across the Curriculum*. As we travel around the country leading faculty development workshops, we hope to meet many of our readers and share your experiences. We would like to hear from you.

JOHN H. CLARKE
ARTHUR W. BIDDLE
University of Vermont
Burlington, Vermont

Introduction:
🙰 *Critical Thinking*
Across the Curriculum

TEACHING THINKING ACROSS THE CURRICULUM

Critical thinking has emerged as a priority for the high school and college curriculum in most of the core subject areas. While knowing a subject area remains the primary goal of most secondary and college teaching, knowing how to use information to discover further information or to solve problems has become increasingly important. In this age of information, access to knowledge is both general and immediate. Both print media and electronic media have brought complete libraries into the hands of any person who would want to read. How can any of us find what we need to know? How can we make sense of the expanding pool of knowledge in any area? How can we use what is known to ask further questions and generate new ideas? How can we put knowledge to work in solving human problems? How can we think critically in this tumultuous intellectual environment? The challenge in today's curriculum is to teach students to manage the work of their own minds.

As you will note in the articles that fill this book, thinking across the disciplines puts the student at the center of classroom study. What all our writers have discovered is that thinking strategies cannot be taught by a teacher standing at the front of the room. Instead, thinking strategies must be learned by individual students, working cooperatively or alone, to make sense of course material. This shift in classroom focus from "teacher-work" to "student-work" has a profound effect on student morale and motivation. It puts them in the driver's seat. More often than not, the products they create and the processes they devise to make sense of what they are learning also become the subject of study in the classroom. "Depend on it, Sir," Samuel Johnson observed. "When a man knows he is to be hanged in a fortnight, it concentrates his mind wonderfully." Students who walk into a classroom knowing that they, rather than someone else, must climb the intellectual scaffold, also experience a similar tightening of focus.

When a teacher is only a purveyor of information, high school and college classes fall into a monotonous pattern. Teachers talk; students listen. Teaching thinking across the curriculum does not relieve the teacher of responsibility for knowing the subject. In fact, greater knowledge is required because student inquiry, once unleashed, knows few limits, not even those polite conventions that divide the subject areas. Teachers who include thinking strategies in their courses must prepare for unpredictable questions: What does it mean? What difference would it make? How does this connect? What would Marx say? How does this work? How can we change things? What if? What if? What if? Questions such as these change the nature of what teachers must know.

These questions also radically change the character of classroom teaching. The teachers who wrote articles for this book have all developed facets or roles that conventional teaching leads us to neglect.

> *Teacher as researcher*:   In teaching thinking, we have to devise questions that guide students through a vast pool of potentially useful information.
>
> *Teacher as designer*:   To support student inquiry, we have to design materials that guide students reliably from questions toward possible answers.
>
> *Teacher as consultant*:   With inquiry in motion, we have to provide direction for students who are not familiar enough with different methods of inquiry to recognize their virtues and limitations.
>
> *Teacher as referee*:   Because contention, confusion, and uproar are not uncommon effects of thinking about the subject areas, we have to know when to settle disputes and when to use questions to drive further inquiry.
>
> *Teacher as analyst*:   Because the thinking process, rather than the information, leads different students in different directions, we have to be ready to represent processes of thought as the subject of study.
>
> *Teacher as judge*:   How much do students know? The question is relatively simple. How well do they know the subject? This question makes us judges of their thinking processes as well as their content knowledge.

First and foremost, this is a book about teaching—a celebration of ingenuity in the classroom. Second, this is a book about critical thinking as a purpose for teaching. The teachers who wrote articles for this book have used their classroom work to develop and refine ways to help their students manage intellectual processes that make learning meaningful.

THINKING: A PURPOSE FOR TEACHING

Thinking! What are we talking about? As you continue through this book, you will notice that our definition shifts constantly, toward greater and greater specificity, we hope. For the time being, we refer to thinking as *the process by which the human mind manages information to understand established ideas, to create new ideas, or to solve problems.* We have chosen this definition, not because it is perfect from a psychological or philosophic point of view, but because it can help organize and clearly describe a range of options useful in all classroom teaching. A method used by a history teacher to show students how to gather and interpret facts may be adapted to the business management classroom. A technique for teaching students to use the scientific method may be adapted to the writing classroom. To support learning in the age of information, teaching in all the disciplines should have the purpose of helping students manage a particular body of information using particular strategies that they can then adapt and transfer to use with more content or work in life itself. We believe, and the articles in the book demonstrate, that students acquire content knowledge more effectively when teachers make critical thinking a dominant purpose for study in their courses.

The kind of thinking this book illustrates cannot be reduced to a single paradigm, protocol, or catalog of heuristics. Lauren Resnick, a psychologist and past president of American Educational Research Association, has focused much of her attention on the kind of thinking required for success in modern life. She sees a need for teaching thinking skills adaptable to different demands. From her perspective (1987), the thinking we seek

- Is nonalgorithmic; the path of action is not fully specified in advance.
- Is complex; the total path is not mentally "visible" from any single vantage point.
- Often yields multiple solutions, each with costs and benefits, rather than unique solutions.
- Involves nuanced judgment and interpretation.
- Involves uncertainty; not everything bearing in the task is known.
- Involves the application of multiple, sometimes conflicting, criteria.
- Involves self-regulation of the thinking process, not regulation by others.
- Involves imposing meaning, finding structure in apparent disorder.
- Is effortful.

At first glance, Resnick's definition would seem a prescription for chaos in the classroom. As in the articles from the field that fill this book, however, the words *purpose, structure, path, solutions,* and *self-regulation* all point to the need for careful planning and organization in thinking strategies instruction.

CRITICAL THINKING AS PLANNED MOVEMENT IN THE MIND

We believe that the central feature of critical thinking is not skill in any particular kind of thinking strategy, but the planned use of different strategies to fulfill different purposes. To think critically about a subject, a student must first develop a purpose for thinking and then devise a method for moving toward that purpose. Critical thinking requires deliberate movement through planned steps toward some outcome. When we say that thinking strategies involve movement from one kind of thinking to another, what are we talking about? At the broadest level, thinking can move between concrete experience and abstractions that explain that experience (see Figure A.1).

We may use specific observations of one black bear (experience), for example, to assert generalizations about all bears (theory), if we dare. We may use a survey of student opinions (experience) to identify more abstract trends in American values (theory). We may use selections from a poem (experience) to assert beliefs about a poet (theory). In most subject areas, drawing inferences from facts is necessary to critical thinking.

Moving in the other direction, we may use established theories to plan, predict the future, or solve problems in experience. We may use the abstract idea of hibernation (theory) to predict what one bear may do in

FIGURE A.1   One avenue for movement in thinking

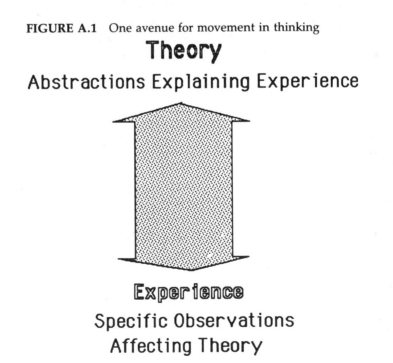

Theory

Abstractions Explaining Experience

Experience

Specific Observations
Affecting Theory

FIGURE A.2   A second avenue for movement in thinking

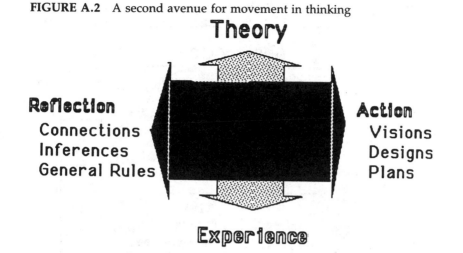

November (experience). We may use a trend observed in survey data to forecast election results next year. We may use the theme of isolation to search Frost's poetry for specific imagery that reveals the source of isolation. Using theoretical constructions to explain, predict, or plan is the source of enormous power. Movement between the abstract and concrete is the one intellectual facility favored by virtually all academic disciplines. It is also the facility young people most require—and often resist.

Movement in thinking also involves interaction between reflection and action. In reflection, we try to make meaningful connections between parts of our experience—sometimes widely scattered (See Figure A.2) In action, we try to manage or change the experience we have. Through reflection, we may grow to believe that hibernation among bears is a response either to food shortage or failing light. In action, we may then test our beliefs by trying to feed a bear all winter or by setting up lights in a bear's den. By reflecting on old survey results, we may come to believe that Americans were once more confident in democratic institutions. Then, in action, we might conduct the same survey and compare results. Our reflections on Frost's use of nature imagery might lead us to reformulate our own writing to include commonplace events or imagery. We reflect to adjust our actions; our actions then give us further cause for reflection.

From the interaction of abstract/concrete thinking and reflective/active thinking, we propose the four quadrants that organize the articles in this book (see Figure A.3):

> *Data analysis processes*:   Movement from observed experience to re-
> flection, selecting information, making connections and developing
> ideas that describe general patterns

FIGURE A.3 Critical thinking as continuous movement among processes

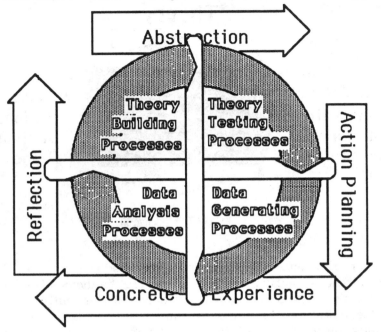

Theory building processes: Movement from reflection to abstraction, using observation, concepts, and generalization to propose cause-effect relationships

Theory testing processes: Movement from theory to action, clarifying and synthesizing ideas as a basis for creating new ideas, planning, predicting, or designing

Data generating processes: Movement from action planning to experience, developing processes or procedures for solving problems

The cycle we have used has four main quadrants or phases in which different kinds of thinking can be demonstrated and enacted by students: a data gathering and interpreting phase, a theory generating phase, a theory testing or creative phase, and a data generating or problem solving phase. (Costa, 1985; Clarke, 1990) We do not believe that thinking strategies instruction should aim solely for facility in any one of these areas. Instead, we believe critical thinking instruction should teach students to use one strategy as the beginning point for another, in a purposeful effort to make sense of information or devise new ideas. Thinking strategies instruction requires teaching students to move purposefully from one kind of thinking to another in an endless cycle of refinement and adjustment.

In this general conception, and in the organization of articles in this book, thinking is a process of managing information that depends on different constructions of reflective and action-directed thinking strategies, aimed at developing reliable abstractions or changing experience. Kolb's studies of learning style among various disciplines showed that some subject areas favor beginning inquiry from different quarters (1976). Physics and mathematics, for example, usually begin with an abstraction, a law, principle, or theorem and then move toward confirmation in concrete experience. History and literature often begin with a verifiable record and then move toward abstraction of trends or themes. The social sciences, such as psychology or sociology, usually begin reflection from some established vantage point, then devise research techniques that promise to refine reflection. The professions or technical areas, such as health science, education, or computer science, may begin by favoring an action plan aimed at solving a problem. Carrying out that plan generates information that provokes more reflection and a new conception of the problem, provoking in turn a variation of their original plan. In teaching thinking, we are teaching movement on a self-correcting cycle.

Figure A.4 includes examples of specific critical thinking strategies in each of the four quadrants of the cycle.[1] Critical thinking in different realms may begin at different points. Medical diagnosis often begins with a search of patient history, for example, and then moves toward physical findings (data analysis), interpretation of findings (theory building), some hypothetical diagnoses (for theory testing), and a plan for treatment (data generating). Other kinds of scientific thinking may begin questioning with clarification of assumptions, synthesis of findings, and a prediction (theory testing processes) and then move from a stated plan (data generating process) through data analysis and theory building again. Many disciplines, such as English literature and history, emphasize the inductive side of the cycle, using facts to develop or propose a theory. Other subject areas, such as physics and engineering, emphasize the deductive strategies in which some abstract principle or law is applied to a specific case. Most high school and college students need to see and practice the kind of thinking professionals do in a subject area in order to build a flexible repertory of critical thinking strategies.

We have organized articles in this book to show how different teachers may share a general framework for critical thinking, but design courses to

---

[1]This conception of the thinking wheel is adapted from David Kolb's *Learning Style Inventory (Manual)* (Cambridge, MA: McBer & Associates, 1976); an analysis of inquiry in Art Costa's first edition of *Developing Minds: A Resource Book for Teaching Thinking* (Association for Supervision and Curriculum Development, Alexandria, VA, 1985) attributed to Ben Strasser in a letter from Art Costa to John Clarke (1989); and John Clarke's thinking wheel in *Patterns of Thinking: Integrating Learning Skills in Content Teaching* (Boston: Allyn & Bacon, 1990).

FIGURE A.4 Thinking as a wheel with four quadrants

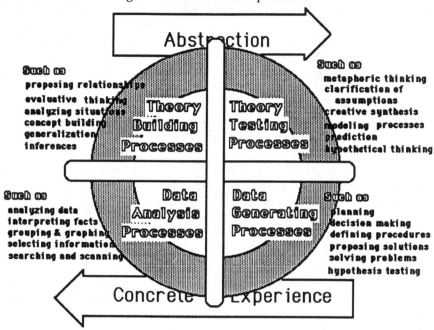

fit their own purpose and content. In this circular conception of thinking, all intellectual strategies bear some relation to each other (Clarke, 1990; Kolb, 1976). In different content areas, inductive thinking strategies, such as data gathering and theory generating, may begin creative thinking or problem solving. In other subject areas, problems or creative thought provide the beginning and data gathering follows as a result. We see the circular model or thinking wheel as a vehicle for teaching very simple strategies, such as drawing inferences from facts, and more complex multistage strategies for deep analysis or design. As the rest of this introduction explains, the purpose of the wheel is to let students and teachers recognize and apply aspects of critical thinking as they learn any subject.

TEACHING CRITICAL THINKING IN A CIRCULAR FRAMEWORK

The challenge in teaching critical thinking is to show students how to manage their own learning. For teachers, a circular conception offers many advantages:

1. Focus on content: The learning cycle proposes a general process for organizing inquiry, allowing content area teachers and students to focus on their subject.

2. Flexibility: The learning cycle allows teachers to sequence instruction in almost any order and still emphasize one thinking strategy as the basis for another.
3. Coherence: The learning cycle allows teachers to develop a coherent language they can use to describe the evanescent processes of thought guiding inquiry in the disciplines.
4. Ubiquity: The learning cycle describes a pervasive pattern of thought, as reflected, for example, in the scientific method, meditational poetry, medical diagnosis and treatment, legal argumentation, and many rhetorical conventions.
5. Movement: By refusing to recognize an endpoint, the cycle proposes that all learning is part of a continuous, self-correcting process in which deepening and broadening are possible—but finishing is not.
6. Community: Used across the subject areas the cycle can show students that learning and thinking in many subject areas are related, allowing them to adapt and transfer learned strategies across realms.

We see aspects of thinking—reflective and active, abstract and concrete—as inextricable in the ordinary life of the mind. We see them as one process—a cycle. Reflective thinking, as we use the term, is the process of generating theories from more specific bits of information in experience. Creative thinking is the process of using theories to analyze a situation, predict future events, or solve problems in experience. In teaching reflection, we are teaching students to organize established information in a way that lets them propose theories about how things work. In teaching creative thinking and action planning, we are teaching them to organize principles, processes, or procedures in a way that lets them predict the future or solve problems emerging in experience. Most of us—when driving a car, speaking with friends, or shopping for groceries—can draw information from the experience, compose a brief theory or plan, and take steps to redirect our experience within a matter of seconds. We do it without conscious control. Others may focus a lifetime of work refining one theory to explain a narrow range of experience or planning a technology that may alter microscopic events. The cycle or wheel is a useful metaphor on the small and large scale; in both contexts, it makes evanescent processes more palpable. The metaphor of the wheel is an instructional device for showing students how their minds can work, so they can gain further control over their own intellectual powers.

LEARNING TO THINK CRITICALLY

In a journal entry on the first day of a class on thinking across the disciplines, we asked 25 college juniors to define thinking as they understood it. "What is thinking?" we asked. Figure A.5 contains phrases from those journals that were selected to illustrate different aspects of the think-

FIGURE A.5   How undergraduates define thinking: sampler from an in-class 3 minute journal

ABSTRACTION	→
On Theory Building Processes	**On Theory Testing Processes**
It's more or less a love for questing ideas around us in our environment. (Biology)	The process involves a concentration on the IDEA, developing an understanding as to the importance of the IDEA. (Biology)
Thinking is the creator of the "why" question. It inspires us to find answers. (English)	Sometimes thinking is based on one major thought, with several tangibles. (Health)
Like putting together pieces of a puzzle to get a final result or answer. (Health)	Once an idea is created, thinking becomes the development and connecting of ideas. (Biology)
Thinking. I am thinking? to wonder to consider probabilities, memories in the past. (English)	Uh? The mind shoots ahead and jumps from thought to thought and comes to conclusions on something, some sort of information. (French)
Circumstances, books and everything cause us to form opinions and redesign in our mind what was placed before us. (French)	The ability to write down or put together a coherent argument for a Point of View. (History)
Taking information, analyzing and using it in everyday situations. (Health)	There is also creative thinking. For instance, daydreaming is one form of the mind creating a fantasy world. (Physical Education)
Thinking allows a person to move from the concrete to the abstract. (Biology)	We also imagine or predict what will happen in the future. (Health Professions)
On Data Analysis Processes	**On Data Generating Processes**
To look at something or someone, and draw conclusions. (Political Science)	The ability to plan, to see into the future and hypothesize. (Political Science)
Processing and storing information so it is available for later use. (Art)	Thinking is using knowledge to solve problems, or more often than not, come up with more questions. (Earth Science)
A cognitive process of receiving ideas, facts, figures. (English)	Thinking is being able to make decisions responsibly about occurrences in life. (English)
Understanding facts . . . putting together ideas. (History)	A Process used to obtain a goal—steps taken after receiving input to produce output. (Mathematics)
A response to outside stimulus—categorizing, labeling, remembering . . . (History)	The student who understands and uses critical analysis can create well thought-out art productions. (Art)
Even while we sleep, we are experiencing new things and remembering past events. (Art)	
All sensory skills go into thinking. (English)	
←	EXPERIENCE

ing cycle. Taken as a whole, the student definitions express with some elegance the many different ways we work with information. Virtually all the students saw thinking as a flexible process in which a great deal of individual choice was possible. Virtually all students implied that thinking requires using one kind of thinking as a basis for another. Collectively, the assembled definitions represented a comprehensive view of thinking as a continuous, self-correcting process.

Taken one student at a time, however, the student definitions were wildly idiosyncratic and incomplete from a practical standpoint. Different students emphasized different strategies, different structures, and different conceptions of purpose. Apparently, our students developed different strategies to meet their needs for critical thinking. If we were to ask these students to think about a single subject, could we expect coherence among their responses?

Data Analysis Processes

Some students who emphasized data analysis processes recognized some formal steps in the process of making sense of information. "Processing and storing information so it is available for later use," an art major asserted. "A response to outside stimulus," a history major wrote, "categorizing, labeling, remembering." "A cognitive process of receiving ideas, facts, figures," an English major said. All of these responses are defensible and interesting, but these student responses and others contain a perceptible gap between having an experience and making meaning from it. "Understanding facts . . . putting together ideas," a history major wrote. "Even while we sleep, we are experiencing new things and remembering past events." True! None of the students described a strategy they could actually use to analyze data and draw meaningful conclusions.

Theory Building Processes

On theory building processes, some students gained further eloquence. "Thinking is the creator of the 'why' question," an English major wrote. "It inspires us to find answers." "Like putting together pieces of a puzzle to get a final result or answer," another said. One French student described the transforming effects of learning on information. "Circumstances, books, and everything cause us to redesign in our mind what was placed before us," she wrote. Despite the reverence students felt for theory making processes, "questing ideas around us in our environment," the same absence of reliable process is evident in their writing. "Thinking. I am thinking?" one English major groped, "to wonder, to consider probabilities, memories in the past." Yes, "Thinking allows a person to move from the concrete to the abstract," as one biology student expressed it, but how can we traverse that distance and achieve reliable, interesting, or novel results?

Theory Testing Processes

With reference to theory testing processes, many students recognized the importance of reformulating what they learned to explore important relationships, "developing an understanding as to the importance of the *idea*," as one biology student explained. "Once an idea is created, thinking becomes the development and connecting of ideas," another biology major said. Several saw the practical implications of theory testing processes, "the ability to write down or put together a coherent argument or point of view," "We also imagine or predict what will happen in the future." Still a failure to recognize reliable creative processes is evident. "Uh, the mind shoots ahead and jumps from thought to thought," a French major explained, "and comes to conclusions on something, some sort of information." How can we show students how to test relationships among ideas and create new ways of seeing?

Data Generating Processes

Some students recognized the potential power of data generating processes, "the ability to plan, to see into the future and hypothesize." Students who referred at all to problem solving or data generating processes tended to anchor their descriptions in their own content area. "The student who understands and uses critical analysis can create well thought-out art productions," one said. "A process used to obtain a goal," a mathematics major wrote, "steps taken after receiving input to produce output." An English major observed that thinking "is being able to make decisions responsibly about occurrences in life." Another recognized indeterminacy in solving problems: "Thinking is using knowledge to solve problems, or more often than not, come up with more questions." None of them tried to describe how they would use information to solve problems or ask new questions.

MANAGING THE WORK OF THE MIND

Students in our class recognized the importance of strategic thinking in the content areas. Few described techniques for managing their own thinking in a self-conscious way. If thinking strategies were taught explicitly and demonstrated in the academic disciplines, as the essays in this book suggest they may be, high school and college students could better use them to make sense of classroom experience. They could also use the same strategies to make sense of experience at large. Thinking strategies are useful control mechanisms for the critical and creative work of the mind. They allow educated people to control and direct intellectual work. Instructors in the academic disciplines can teach them as surely as they teach the subject knowledge those strategies have produced.

From the same first-day journals, we selected sentences and phrases which describe ways of managing these processes of thinking, what psychologists call metacognitive control (see Figure A.6). What is most apparent in student comments on managing the mind's work is that some students felt personal control—and some did not. In compiling this list we were also struck by the observation that students who implied that they

FIGURE A.6 Thinking as directed movement in the mind: An organizing conception

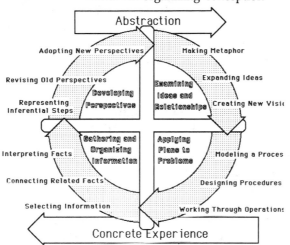

managed their own thinking were largely successful in their academic classes. Students who felt little control over what their minds were doing were more susceptible to a variety of academic ills—such as withdrawal, low GPA, or academic probation.

Students who wrote little about controlling the work of their minds had a variety of poetic expressions for the roiling mental tumult that all of us experience at one time or another. "It just sneaks up on you, and suddenly it's just with you," one English major wrote. "A flow, a stump, a block, a flow, a block," another said. "Sparks flying in your brain that let people know you are not a vegetable." "Thinking, thinking boggled mind," an art major agreed. "Why did I think of that?" Such is the stuff of sleepless nights. Some of us delight in the roiling wash of unmanaged thought. What is distressing about these student comments is the announced failure to direct the work of the mind in some desired direction. "You can't think on command," one asserted. "Thinking is a process of the brain, just as pumping blood is a function of the heart." Managing such an organ as the brain means "gritting your teeth and running your hand down your face, grimacing in time consuming thought." None of us can stop the mind from turning. Some of us can intervene and direct thought more easily.

The more successful students in this class referred to self-conscious control and a variety of tricks for directing mental work. "You back yourself off from doing things mechanically," one said from objective distance, "then try to improve the process." "Being deliberate in the consumption of knowledge," using "certain structural patterns" to organize mental work, approaching "a problem from different perspectives"—all of these are tricks of metacognitive control. With them, change becomes possible. "I can do different things now," a junior in computer science said, "and other things that used to seem easy now seem hard." These students had recognized some "devices of the mind" that made academic study possible. None of us would want to live our lives by means of those devices alone. All of us, we presume, would want a hand on the lever that activates different ways of thinking.

TEACHING STUDENTS TO MANAGE THEIR MINDS

We have used the wheel or thinking cycle as a metaphor to hold this book together and to represent ways in which teachers can embed thinking strategies in content instruction (see Figure A.7). The wheel or cycle is our metaphor for thinking. How is thinking like a wheel?

First, and most important, a turning wheel implies destination or purpose. Where do we want to go? We see thinking strategies as inherently purposeful. Purposeful activity can be planned and evaluated. It can be taught.

Second, thinking requires motion. Yes, a wheel is an object, but it achieves meaning not as much by "being" but by "going." Learning to think effectively requires directed movement.

Third, the wheel suggests reliability. It moves us forward by rotating around a stable center. It leaves tracks. It let's us check on where we have been—our assumptions, our design, our data, our analysis—so we can increase reliability through revision.

Fourth, the wheel suggests that thinking is *recursive*. It turns once, then turns again. It implies reflection, turning back to look again, from a new perspective or with new data in view.

Finally, the wheel is a simple machine, adaptable to many more sophisticated devices. Simplicity is a virtue in any new task. The wheel is commonplace. It is essential to human work. As a metaphor, the wheel is initially accessible to our students, who may change it to meet new needs.

When baffled by complexity, we can use a metaphoric wheel to return to simplicity, to look for a central organizing thought, to try another track, to play out implications, or to check our progress. Stuck? Turn again, the wheel suggests. Thinking in any discipline can give students intellectual practice in setting direction, moving from one idea to the next, applying strategies, testing beliefs against facts—getting somewhere. We believe that we can teach students to turn the wheel of their own minds.

As you read the essays in this book you will see that the skills of thinking are further specified by the writers who describe their teaching. You will also recognize that the practices described by the authors do not fall as neatly into quadrants as we have suggested. In fact, each of the articles in this book describes movement from one set of skills to another. Some articles describe movement within one of the quadrants we have proposed. Others move between quadrants. Some have designed their classes to move students full cycle—once and then again. After all, it is movement that most signifies the active mind. We have organized the articles to illustrate quadrants of the thinking cycle to reflect what we saw as a basic interest of the author, rather than an exclusive interest. We have used the articles first because the thinking strategies being taught are ingenious and interesting, and then to illustrate specific strategic movement in the cycle. We hope that the labels and general model used to organize the book do not distract our readers from our main purpose: to show how different teachers include thinking strategies in content area classes. If high school and college teachers are to collaborate in teaching strategies for thinking, we must share a conception of thinking in which all may play a part. We believe the authors of articles in this book represent our profession in two important ways: Individually, they have designed instruction to meet the needs of their own students; collectively, they represent the central purpose of teaching—to show students how to use specific information to manage the work of their minds.

WRITING TO THINK

As you read these descriptions of innovative teaching, you will notice the prominent role that writing plays in the teaching of critical thinking across the curriculum. Each of the strategies described here employs writing to support the process of learning. Writing is the most powerful tool we have for making thought visible. In their own writing, students can recognize their own thought processes and amend those processes to better suit their aims. Writing slows the tumult of the mind, making the mechanics of thought susceptible to change. With thought represented in physical form, we can help them exert greater control over its development. Used for informal exploration of facts, theories, relationships, and procedures, writing serves to help students gain control of their own mental work.

The purpose to which teachers apply student writing assignments shifts throughout the book. Used informally in classroom and homework assignments, writing can illuminate the structure of thought and open thought processes to questioning and revision:

data gathering processes: Writing helps students link factual information and try out their interpretive skills;

theory building processes: Writing helps students weigh alternative perspectives and arrive at defensible theories;

theory testing processes: Writing helps students extend the ideas they discover toward their implications, raising questions that need to be answered;

data generating processes: Writing provides a vehicle for planning, imagining steps in a procedure, and working through problems with attention to detail.

Most important of all, writing puts students at the center of their own learning, representing what they know and how they know it. In writing, each student directs the path of his or her thought, but also makes it available to others. With writing at the center of classroom work, thinking and learning become social events; knowledge evolves through interaction. Perhaps it is the social nature of written inquiry that brings such energy to classroom learning and teaching.

Chapter 1

Gathering and Organizing Information: Data Analysis Processes

ໄ

Students often try to consume information the same way they might consume fast food. They may try to stick a straw in it and suck it down like soda, or pick, dip, and eat it one piece at a time. The results of this kind of learning are rarely satisfying, either in the short or longer term. Still, much of what students have learned about learning puts them in the passive consumer role. They may sit in class regularly, take copious notes, follow directions with care, and even pass examinations without really making much sense of the material presented to them. The purpose of articles in this section is to describe ways some teachers have discovered to show their students how to select, organize, and interpret factual or text-based information so their learning becomes more meaningful and long lasting.

MEANINGFUL LEARNING: GATHERING AND ORGANIZING INFORMATION

What does it take to make meaning from any subject area? For better or worse the human mind does not work quite the same way the human stomach does. For one thing, the human mind is not particularly good for bulk storage. We remember new information best when we can attach it to meaningful information we already understand. At the end of a college course on thinking across their subject areas, we asked students to describe the processes that bring meaning to study in their own academic areas. One English major described the difficulty of converting data from external sources into a personal representation of the information:

> Data is concrete. It comes in the form of dates, measures, names, rules and numbers. In every subject area there are certain necessary groups of data to be learned in order to have a complete experience of that subject. For some, memorizing data and regurgitating its exactness comes easy. For others, it is impossible for it lacks reason and meaning. In many cases, rote memorization

> is a useless process, because without a meaningful connection between the material and the learner, nothing will be remembered. (Karyn Burtt [English])

Making connections between the material and a class full of unique individuals is the main challenge in classroom teaching.

How does meaningful learning happen? Meaningful learning occurs when we connect new information to what we already know. "The most important single factor influencing learning is what the learner already knows," David Ausubel wrote in *Educational Psychology: A Cognitive View* (1968). "Ascertain this and teach him accordingly." One of our students used the metaphor of a sand castle to reflect on the relationship between the bulk of prior knowledge and the task of adding new pieces.

> Is a piece of sand more than a piece of sand? No. In this instance, a piece of sand itself seems to hold no value. When you put pieces together, you may get a whole—a sand castle. Then, it is hard to understand the single piece of sand without referring to the castle. (Dan Frazer [English])

As this student observed, at some point a single grain of sand may cause a slide that changes the whole structure. In meaningful learning, each piece of information finds its meaning in relation to a large whole. The whole of what we know changes shape with each added grain.

All new learning is guided by prior knowledge, Ausubel insists. Ausubel's axiom and advice seem simple enough, but they lead almost immediately to perplexities.

- Students who already know a lot find it easy to learn more.
- Students who know little have little basis for learning more.
- Students who have included errors in their learning may only confirm those errors in trying to learn new information.

Paradoxically, students who know very little, and thereby have the greater need, find it very hard to make sense of new information. Students whose prior knowledge is riddled with misconceptions, some of which may be held widely as common knowledge, may only extend their basic errors in trying to reconstruct their ideas. All new learning is guided by prior knowledge, whether we know a little or a lot, but students who know little are more easily misled by the little they know.

Are we doomed to fail with all but our most successful students? Recent research in learning suggests that students who lack systematic strategies for thinking about a subject learn more when they practice using a strategy taught explicitly with the content (McKeachie, 1984; Meyer, 1989). Low achieving students taught to visually represent relationships among ideas in their reading, for example, may raise their test scores significantly in a course over the period of one semester. Students who are already learning well, using whatever strategy they have devised for themselves, do not benefit from instruction in new thinking strategies.

Teaching data analysis strategies in the subject areas may require development of a general approach that teaches low achieving students to organize and interpret what they see, but lets successful students continue to refine their own techniques.

PURPOSE, STRUCTURE, AND STRATEGY IN MEANINGFUL LEARNING

The game of chess has given psychologists a field on which they can observe the effects of prior knowledge on memory—and consider new ways to teach. Curious about the nature and effects of prior knowledge on new learning, psychologists have conducted experiments with chess players of different ages and levels of ability (Simon, 1979). When researchers showed a game-in-progress to both experienced and inexperienced chess players, the experienced chess players were far more able than new players to reposition the pieces accurately after leaving the game. Experience supports long-term memory, researchers concluded. When they showed a chess board with pieces placed in no particular pattern, however, neither the experienced nor inexperienced chess players showed better memory. Researchers then concluded that memory depends on recognizing patterns among the pieces, rather than on raw quantity of prior experience. Even when the experienced chess players were ten years old and the new players were adults, the findings still favored the experienced ten-year-olds. Aha, the researchers concluded, long-term memory depends on having enough experience in a particular field to see patterns of organization in the content in terms of a clear strategy with a defined purpose. Purpose, structure, and strategy are aspects of the accumulated wisdom of experienced chess players. Purpose, structure, and strategy may be necessary to effective learning in any field.

"Why can't my students remember any of the milestone events I described?" the expert historian complains. The answer may lie in the effects of prior historical knowledge on the learning of historians and students:

Purpose: The expert historian has a destination, the sense that one event leads to the next.

Structure: The expert has also constructed a mental model on which new facts can hang, a vision of historical time that brings contextual meaning to almost any event.

Strategy: The expert has learned to interpret facts in terms of related events and the general themes or trends that historians use to group information.

What the expert sees as milestones the novice sees as road rubble. "Will it be on the test?" the student asks. Lacking better alternatives, students turn to passing the course as a purpose, exam questions as a guiding structure, and rote memorization as the only available strategy they can use.

Under most conditions, purpose, structure, and strategy in any content area are not easily taught from the lecture podium. They must be discovered by students struggling individually to make sense of new content. This struggle requires as much personal commitment as cold technical skill, as one of our students recognized.

> Data analysis is synonymous with self discovery as I see it—the discovery of style and voice in both the reader and the writer. Discovering individuality in all voices of all readers and all writers is a data analysis process that comes when students learn why someone has chosen to write about the subject in the style that they use. (Sarah Rutledge [English])

Learning new information makes sense in the context of a personal quest. Paradoxically, teachers may need to reduce their dominance from the lecture podium to increase student engagement with the substance to be learned.

TEACHING STUDENTS TO MAKE SENSE OF THE FACTS

Allowing variability in process and outcome changes the way we teach. How can teachers design a course so individual students actively pursue a meaningful purpose, organize basic content into meaningful units, and learn to use interpretive strategies to make meaning? How can we find out what students already know? Will what students know make new learning easier? What kind of teaching lets students access and reconstruct what they learned earlier? How can a teacher struggle successfully with the many individual quandaries that fill seats in an ordinary classroom? To hold on to new information in academic classes, students need a purpose for seeking it out, a structure for holding it in place, and interpretive strategies for finding meaningful patterns among the pieces.

Teachers of the content areas face an audience whose prior knowledge may be thoroughly idiosyncratic. Even when talented teachers distribute information with painstaking attention to delivery, they may not activate the active processes that make learning meaningful. The teachers who wrote articles in this section have all designed ways to guide students through intellectual processes that make meaning from facts. It is not enough to exhort our students to be purposeful, organized, and strategic in their learning. They often lack sufficient background information in the disciplines to make even those prompts meaningful. In any content area, teachers can engage students actively in a process of inquiry that represents interpretive learning and then use what students have done to point out the role of purpose, structure, and strategy in data analysis. We will use three terms to represent teachable aspects of information gathering:

1. *Selection:* Students become purposeful when asked to select a limited amount of information from a broad array—in order to answer an important question. Having to choose narrowly requires development of a purpose for choosing.
2. *Connecting:* Structure becomes visible when students have found some relationship among selected facts and explained the connection. By naming and explaining relationships, students create categories they can then use to select more information and connect further facts.
3. *Interpreting:* Strategy becomes visible when students assert a meaning for facts they have selected and grouped. In asserting meaning, they can see that they have either affirmed or changed their original purpose.

As Figure 1.1 shows, selecting, connecting, and interpreting can be taught as a continuous cycle of revision. Data gathering and analysis usually proceed in a seamless flow, with selection of facts, regrouping, and interpreting all following from each other in continuous regeneration. We have chosen somewhat artificial labels for parts of this process to help teachers define their own teaching strategy. As a matter of convention each discipline may use different terms to describe intellectual processes that are similar. In any case, because we cannot teach processes that we cannot recognize, we have chosen these labels to create a visible path from concrete information toward abstraction.

FIGURE 1.1 Data analysis processes

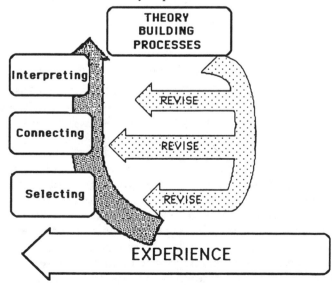

Teaching students to search and interpret information must allow for considerable individuality. The teachers who wrote articles in this section have all developed ways to show students how to set a purpose for their intellectual work, design a structure for holding information in place, and apply interpretive strategies to the material they have collected. The teachers who wrote articles for this section do not teach data selection, connection, or interpretation as discrete skills. On the contrary, they all recognize that meaning comes not in the facts, connections, or interpretations, but in moving recursively through interpretation and reformulation. We have grouped the articles in a way that highlights one or two aspects of data gathering or analysis only to freeze temporarily the evanescent dance of teaching so its strategies become visible and known.

Selecting Information

Students can interpret aspects of a photograph more easily than they can interpret extended text. Michael Smith shows his students how to use what they see to develop an original idea about what they read, and then expand or change that idea during their reading of an author's work.

How can students learn to see, really see, objects that come into their vision? Julie Springer recognized that representational art often confirms student misconceptions about art, for example, that the painting is the same as the object. To make her students see and interpret, she must help them see how their minds create meaning in response to a work of art. Looking at non-representational art, her students have to control what they choose to see. A non-representational artist may not tell them anything. Instead, through careful observation and reflection, they learn that they make meaning from what they see.

Making Connections

How can students learn to recognize the power of data organization in the development of ideas that guide the study of economics? Working from general principles to specific instances may confuse students, who want to see all such abstract principles as immutable laws. Jannett Highfill and William V. Weber designed an introductory course in economics as an inductive process in which students graph specific events using real data and then construct abstract graphs from the specifics. A graph may hold nicely for specific events. How well does it hold when they eliminate specific referents and try to assert a more general idea—a trend or prediction or rule? By working with concrete and abstract graphs, her students see how they can organize information to make meaning and how tentative the process of generalization must be.

Robert Zeller begins an extended exercise in data gathering and analysis with a familiar object, a photograph of the author E. B. White sitting at his typewriter. What patterns can students perceive in the photograph? What ideas about the author come to mind? As they look at essays and biographies for further evidence, their initial perceptions change. Of course, simple conceptions become more elaborate as the evidence accumulates. By working from a relatively simple medium toward more complex literary works, he shows his students how to use simple interpretive tools to develop more sophisticated interpretive strategies.

Interpretive Strategies

A strategy may defined as a series of steps carried out in behalf of some clear purpose. When there are many steps in a strategy, students may easily lose their path, and then lose heart. Robert Cannon finds that he can show his students how to summarize research articles in microbiology and teach them to watch for signs of strength and weakness in what they read. By summarizing articles within an established frame, students learn how to see indicators of good and bad research. Over time, they also accumulate the basis for interpretation of research findings. Interpretive skill lets them look critically at any research article, or assess the weight of several studies in the same area. It also prepares them to design and carry out their own research projects.

Ken Holland has designed a process for showing his students how to construct a legal brief for the Supreme Court. Careful and selective study of one case is essential, but so is study of related cases and the decisions which followed them. What kind of argumentation will link a specific case favorably to the right precedents? In writing briefs, Holland's students gain respect for the place of facts and findings in legal decisions, but they also recognize how important a coherent and complete legal strategy can be.

REFERENCES

Ausubel, D. (1968). *Educational Psychology: A Cognitive View*. New York: Holt Rinehart and Winston.

Simon, H. A. (1979). The information storage system called the "human memory." In H. A. Simon (Ed.), *Models of Thought*. New Haven, CT: Yale University Press.

MICHAEL W. SMITH

Interpretive Strategies
in Literature Study

The power of literature resides in large measure in its ability to provide us with the opportunity to come to know men and women we would never otherwise meet, to participate in their lives, indeed, to use their lives as rehearsals for our own. In *The Call of Stories* (1989), Robert Coles gives dramatic evidence of this power. As one of Coles's students explains:

> When I have some big moral issue, some question to tackle, I think I try to remember what my folks have said, or I imagine them in my situation—or even more these days I think of [characters in books I've read]. Those folks, they're people for me . . . they really speak to me—there's a lot of me in them, or vice versa. I don't know how to put it, but they're voices, and they help me make choices. I hope when I decide "the big ones" they'll be in there pitching.

Teachers of literature accept as an article of faith that literature has the power to change lives. Unfortunately, they also recognize that some students are unaffected by this power. I know literature did not speak to some of my students, especially the younger ones. Instead of making the voices of characters part of their lives, some rejected the stories that we read: "That story was boring, Mr. Smith. Why'd you make us read that one?" As I listened to my students' complaints I began to understand that, at least to some extent, their feelings were informed by their failure to care about the characters they encountered. Instead of characters' being people to them, people worthy of care and concern, they were only ink on a page. I began to realize that my students would never care about literature until they created characters they cared about based on the hints and clues stories offered. And I discovered that giving students conscious control of interpretive strategies to create characters was an effective way to meet my goal.

IDENTIFYING THE PROCESS OF INFERENCE FROM DETAILS OF CHARACTER

Because students are able to make sophisticated inferences about the people they encounter in their lives, I begin my unit of instruction by having them examine the sources of implication on which they base those judgments. I do this by simulating an argument with one of my students.

The student and I work out that he or she will comes into my class a minute or two late and that I will then begin to yell at the student. The student is free to play his or her part however he or she chooses. After several minutes of increasingly heated discussion, I turn to the rest of the class and ask, "Now, how am I feeling? How do you you know?" After the giggles that accompany the draining of tension from the class, students easily recall the details that helped them understand that I was extremely angry: "You shouted," "You poked your finger," "Your face was all red," "No one would look at you," "Your arms were folded." We then move from these specific details to generalize about the kinds of details they represent. "You shouted" becomes "A character's language." "You poked your finger" becomes "A character's actions." "Your face was all red" becomes "The physical description of the character." "No one would look at you" becomes "the reaction of others." "Your arms were folded" becomes "A character's body language." After completing this list, we talk about other sorts of clues that can be the source of inferences about characters, focusing on clues to which students don't have access in their lives but which might appear in literature, for example, a character's thoughts.

DIRECTED PRACTICE IN MAKING INFERENCES FROM OBSERVATION

Once they generate their list of the sources of implication that can give rise to inferences about characters, my students move on to practice making inferences on the basis of these details. To help them focus on one detail at a time, I wrote little scenes designed to reveal a character on the basis of only one type of detail. For example, among the scenes designed to give them practice making inferences on the basis of a character's actions is this one:

> It was a cold and rainy day. Joan heard a whimpering from behind the dented, empty garbage can. She walked over to the sound, unsuccessfully attempting to avoid the muddy puddles that were in her way. She saw a small dog, its hair filthy and matted. Quickly she scooped it up, hugging it against her newly dry-cleaned coat. She took the dog home. The next day she took off from work to take it to the vet.

It doesn't take students long to realize how rich a single source of implication could be, even in so short a scene. "I think she must be really caring. Look at all she did for that dog" was a common response. And as students talk more about Joan, they make more inferences: "She's got money, I'll bet. She didn't care that her coat got dirty. And she missed work and paid for the vet." Occasionally students go even further in their analysis: "She's independent. Either she lives alone or she doesn't care what the person she lives with thinks because she doesn't ask anybody if it's OK."

In their discussions students have to recognize key details, but to understand the significance of those details, they have to apply their knowledge of the world, something students are reluctant to do, perhaps because they are so seldom asked to do it. One benefit of using such short scenes is that students have to push hard to make use of the few details available to them. For example, students often use an analogy from popular culture to help them understand the following scene, one that they discussed when they made inferences on the basis of the reaction of other characters:

> Honey, you won't believe it. We're going to be rich. I've got a chance to get in on the ground floor of a company. . . . Will you stop cooking and listen!
> I heard, Larry, "The ground floor . . ." Oh, I forgot to get butter; would you run next door and borrow some?
> I said the ground floor. We'll be rich.
> That's great, dear, but we still need butter. Do run and borrow some.

Often students say, "Hey, this guy's like that guy on 'The Honeymooners.' A real dreamer." Through their discussions students begin to understand the benefits of using their life, literary, and cultural experiences to understand the characters they meet.

In most of my classes it becomes something of a game for students to figure out as much as they can about the characters in each scene. Many students focus exclusively on the plot of the stories and the novels that they read, so working with the scenes not only heightens their attention to important kinds of details, it shows them how rewarding character analysis can be. And focusing on one source of implication at a time helps students secure the sources of implication in their minds, giving them a heuristic they can apply when they read.

PRACTICE INFERENCE IN THE READING OF LITERATURE

Of course, reading literature is much more complex than reading the little scenes that I composed. No story presents details one type at a time. The length of stories puts demands on students' memories. They have to add up the details to some end. To help students transfer their knowledge of how they understand characters to their reading of literature I use questions to model the sort of considerations I make as I read. Because any good reader is an active reader, I interrupt the stories to highlight important details and to ask students to speculate on the implications of those details. I always begin with "The Lament" by Anton Chekhov, a beautiful and very short story that nonetheless involves all six of the sources of implication explained above.

The first paragraph of the story introduces readers to the main character:

> It is twilight. A thick wet snow is slowly twirling around the newly lighted street lamps, and is lying in soft thin layers on roofs, on horses' backs, on people's shoulders and hats. The cabdriver Iona Potapov is quite white, and looks like a phantom; he is bent double as far as the human body can bend double; he is seated on his box; he never makes a move. If a whole snowdrift fell on him, it seems he would not find it necessary to shake it off.

After reading this paragraph, I ask: "On the basis of this physical description, what do you expect Iona to be like?" The question highlights important details and labels those details in the language the students had been using. My students call out predictions, "He's tired," "He'll get sick," "I think he's sad," and I list them on the board. As we note details of other sorts, some predictions are confirmed and others contradicted. Others offer new insights into Iona or give rise to new predictions. When we finish the story, we talk about what we know about Iona and how we feel about him. We talk about the details we found evocative and those that didn't work so well for us. Such a lesson helps students put the principles they have practiced into action. And more than that, it models how rich a reading experience attending to details can provide.

Moving Students to Independence

Answering questions is much different from posing them oneself. Recognizing key details is much different from making inferences on the basis of details others have highlighted. Because my goal is always to have students transfer their knowledge to new reading situations, I conclude the unit by having students apply what they had learned without the aid of my questions. This application could have many forms, both oral and written. I might ask students to debate whether a character is admirable. Following a suggestion of Elizabeth Kahn, Carolyn Walter, and Larry Johannessen in *Writing about Literature* (1984), I might ask them to take a character from the context of a story and make judgments about how that character would behave in a new context. For example, I might say "We know that Gatsby was a bootlegger. If he were alive today would he be a drug dealer?" I might ask students to write analyses of characters we hadn't discussed, portraits of others, their own autobiographies, or stories in which they created their own characters. All of these activities involve students in transferring what they have learned to new situations.

In general, my instruction is designed to help students consciously apply the techniques they use to understand people in their lives to their understanding of literary characters. Our students bring to literature a wealth of knowledge about human behavior and a highly developed capacity to make the inferences most critical to creating characters. I am often surprised at how well my students "read" me. I hear, "Watch out; he's in a bad mood," on the basis of a quick glance into the room during a passing period. Every election year I have students predict, usually very accurately, the candidates for whom I will vote. I hear high school freshmen make judgments about my teaching colleagues after a week or two of classes that very closely approximated the judgments I had made after knowing them for years. Quite clearly, students are able to make judgments about people's feelings and their characters with only subtle clues to guide them.

TRANSFERING INDUCTIVE SKILLS FROM LIFE TO LITERATURE

Throughout the unit, then, I work to help students transfer the knowledge they so readily employed in their lives to literature. My work is guided by the principles David Perkins and Gavriel Salomon articulate in the September 1988, issue of *Educational Leadership*. They note that two very different mechanisms for transfer exist: low road transfer and high road transfer. Low road transfer is the automatic triggering of well-practiced routines to new contexts that are very similar to the original learning situation. One possible explanation for the popularity of young adult literature is that it addresses situations sufficiently similar to the life situations of adolescent students that it allows low road transfer to take place. However, students are unlikely to experience low road transfer between their lives and much of the literature they are asked to read, from canonical texts like *The Great Gatsby* to contemporary masterpieces like *Beloved*, because they believe that such literature is unrelated to their lives. Because I want to prepare my students to read about people and cultures removed from their experience, I cannot presume that low road transfer will take place. High road transfer, on the other hand, involves mindful abstraction of skills and knowledge from one context to another. With high road transfer comes the possibility of "far transfer," that is, transfer of learning to situations substantially different from the context in which the learning took place. Because I want to promote the "far transfer" of skills and strategies students developed in their personal interactions to their reading of a wide range of literature, I had to develop a unit of instruction designed to promote the mindful abstraction of those skills and strategies.

EFFECTS OF TEACHING
INFERENTIAL THINKING

One of my colleagues who taught the unit explains its effects this way:

> The greatest strength of this approach to character study is that it applies life skills to literature instead of applying literature to life. As we examined each scenario, students had no trouble drawing conclusions about what these people were like based on what they looked like, what they said, what they did, etc. They recognized that this is the normal process that human beings use every day in interpersonal relations.
>
> Because this approach to characterization is so simple and so easily recognizable, it takes away some of the mystique of literature. Students are so often afraid that they will interpret a symbol the wrong way or misunderstand a theme that they are afraid to venture guesses. This approach to characterization gives them confidence.

Instead of writing papers in which they qualified and undercut their judgments, students began to assert their interpretive authority in the judgments they were making. One student, for example, concluded her character analysis of Nick in *The Great Gatsby* as follows: "The only compliment Nick made through the entire book was directed to Gatsby, but should have been directed to himself, 'They're a rotten crowd, you're worth the whole damn bunch put together.' " Another student concluded his paper on Daisy this way:

> F. Scott Fitzgerald introduced a universal character type when he created Daisy, the dream girl of the period. Daisy is a capricious young woman. Her love of money and pleasure lead her into many rash actions and makes her vulnerable to disaster. In one word, Daisy could best be described as superficial.

These papers may not be remarkable for the insights they offer, although both writers did a fine job supporting their claims. And what's more, they seem to have a stake in the points they make.

Literary critics are becoming increasingly aware that any meaningful reading requires that readers be active meaning-makers rather than passive recipients of information. Unfortunately, students too often stay in that passive role, perhaps because they doubt their abilities, perhaps because they don't realize what they can accomplish when they transfer what they know from their lives to the literature they read. And as a consequence, many students fail to experience the transforming power of literature. By helping students make that transfer, by giving them conscious control over the interpretive strategies they employ, teachers can make available to more students the unique and powerful way of knowing what literature provides.

Author's Note

I would like to thank Jane Fraser of Elk Grove High School, Elk Grove Village, Illinois, for her help on this chapter.

REFERENCES

Perkins, **D.N.** and **Salomon, G.** (1989) Are cognitive skills context bound? *Educational Researcher* 18(1), 16–26.

JULIE SPRINGER

Object-Based Study in Art

Traditionally, art museums have always found an eager audience for their resources among studio art teachers and elementary school teachers. The connection between the art museum and their particular classroom activities is, obviously, rooted in content. Studio instructors typically bring their students to study the techniques of great artists or learn something about the history of art. Elementary teachers likewise withstand the logistical headaches of group outings so their students gain early exposure to art.

Teacher usership of the art museum is beginning to change, however. More and more it is the specialist in language arts, the humanities, or social studies that you're likely to encounter in the museum. Why are they there? Most often these new museum users are there to practice the skills involved in analyzing works of art. They're in the galleries not to learn art "facts" (such as they exist) but to use art objects as provocative stimuli for thought, inquiry, problem-solving, and imaginative speculation. Through art, they are presenting their students with challenges in both creative and critical thinking. In short, the primary goal of these teachers is to build higher order thinking skills through the medium of art.

The skills, or "steps," involved in analyzing art are listed below in order of increasing complexity. Note that these do not occur in a strictly linear manner, but are recursive, and mutually influential:

1. observation/description
2. reaction/analysis/reflection
3. synthesis of data
4. hypothesis/informed speculation
5. conclusions/evaluation

My objective here is to share an exercise I have successfully used with high school and college students at the National Gallery and to highlight the learning skills involved. Through repeated use I have found this activity helps students articulate their ideas about art and develop their thinking skills as they examine and defend their ideas. The activity is designed for use during the typical 1½ to 3 hour class visit. It is most successful when coupled with the pre-visit and follow-up activities.

FOCUS THROUGH STUDY SHEETS

I'm a big advocate of using study sheets to establish focus and facilitate thoughtful study of works of art. The natural tendency in museum visits is to try to see as much as possible. Students end up tramping along endless corridors, overwhelmed by the sheer number of things, but "seeing" nothing (studies show that the average novice visitor to a museum spends about two seconds looking at a picture before moving on to the next!) I'd like viewers to sacrifice the amount of information experienced, for greater depth of insight. In-depth study of a single work has the additional advantage of requiring students to model the behavior of experts (art historians, critics, aestheticians), thereby introducing them to the procedures used by those with more sophisticated skills.

Why Modern Art?

When teaching thinking skills, I prefer to work with modern objects. My reason is simple. Modern art is difficult for novice viewers and requires thorough engagement. Non-representational art or art made of unorthodox materials poses unique problems of interpretation. Such works challenge our ingrained (and perhaps unconscious; at least unarticulated) notions of what *"Art"* is, and what impact it should have on us. Modern art is not only difficult for novice viewers to accept on a cognitive plane, but on the affective level as well. More often than not, it is "the art you love to hate!"

But the negative emotional response in this case works to an educator's advantage. The important thing is that students *have an opinion*, the stronger the better. At least they are not complacent! Working with twentieth-century art, students can be expected to have doubts, opinions, questions—all of which makes for lively discussion.

Getting Started: What Students Already Believe and Value
(Cognitive and Affective Values)

Study Sheet I is an introductory exercise designed to tap students' existing assumptions about modern art. It is a first step in the process of getting students to explicate, understand, and critique their ideas and values. It is useful in the classroom as a pre-visit activity to get students thinking about issues they will pursue once at the museum. Students should record their responses as a preliminary for discussion. They should also save their written responses so they can refer back to their "starting point" and monitor any changes in their thoughts about modern art.

FIGURE 1 Modern art study sheet I

When you hear the words, "Modern Art," what thoughts come to mind?
(Jot down random words, or phrases.)

Cognitive	Affective
Abstract; no recognizable subject	Meaningless
Difficult to understand ("I don't get it.)	Difficult to like ("Wow, is this ugly!")
Colorful; bright	No apparent skill involved in making ("easy to make," "messy")
Big	
	Alienating
Bold brushwork; paint texture emphasized ("lots of gloppy paint")	
	Viewer is being tricked or deceived by the artist (It's all a big joke.)

The question asked (When you hear the words, "modern art," what thoughts come to mind?) is intended to be as divergent as possible, requiring students to supply their own mental imagery. Equally important, the question is phrased to encourage both cognitive and affective responses. Practical experience has shown me that people of all ages often need to express their affective response to art before they are willing to tackle the object on a cognitive plane. Also, affective factors are often the strongest stimulus to curiosity and motivation needed to explore an issue further. If only to defend their existing values, students are often motivated to pursue the issue further.

Typical student responses have been charted on the sheet as either cognitive or affective (Figure 1). As a follow-up activity, teachers may wish students to re-examine their responses and classify them as either cognitive or affective, in order to direct their attention to their own thought processes.

For this activity to be successful, the instructor will need some general knowledge of modern art and its theoretical base.* The instructor will need to facilitate dialogue and channel student responses in a constructive direction. For instance, many students' misgivings about modern art will stem from applying traditional criteria to evaluate it. The instructor will need to interject new considerations for them, such as, the need for artists to invent new forms as a way of expressing something new. Analogies are helpful. For students puzzled over how a non-representational painting can "express something," the teacher needs to pose a question like: "Does a musical composition require lyrics to be expressive?"

---

*If an instructor feels uncomfortable leading such a discussion, he/she might pass out the sheet in class, but arrange to postpone discussion of student responses until the museum visit when an educator or guide might act as facilitator.

The responses given during discussion can also help the teacher identify different developmental, or learning stages, of students participating. For instance, sometimes the insistent refrain of "what does it *mean*?" identifies the student who thinks of the art object as possessing meaning of a very narrow and explicit kind. On the lookout for "right" and "wrong" answers such learners are not aware that works of art require *interpretation*. At the opposite extreme is the "subjective" thinker who believes that the act of interpretation is entirely personal and therefore all interpretations are equal—equally valid or pointless! The next step for both types of thinkers is to recognize that although interpretations vary, some are more persuasive because they are more reliably grounded in the visual evidence of the work of art. Study sheet II is designed to accomplish this goal, as it revolves around students' abilities to argue and defend a position.

ELLSWORTH KELLY . . . "LESS IS MORE"

Of all the twentieth-century works on view in the National Gallery, the large, spare canvases of Ellsworth Kelly are perhaps the most problematic for novice viewers of all ages. My colleague, Judy Landau, recognized this several years ago and drafted the opening sequence of Study Sheet II (Figure 2). I have since added items 2–4, based on questions and issues raised by students in discussions of Kelly's work.

FIGURE 2 Look and learn study sheet II. Ellsworth Kelly *White Curve VIII*

---

1. Study the painting. Choose one word from the list below that *best* indicates, in your opinion, what the artist is concerned with in this painting. *Streeeeetch your mind!* Don't go for the obvious. Select other words that are significant or add your own.

BALANCE	EDGES	DEPTH	SURFACE	SHAPE
TENSION	FLATNESS	MOVEMENT	STILLNESS	
EMOTION	GESTURE	PRESSURE	WEIGHT	ANONYMITY

2. A student once noted that Kelly doesn't sign his paintings; then asked (teasingly?) how we knew we had it hung right side up. Would *White Curve VIII* be as effective (More???) hung differently? Why did Kelly choose to orient the painting this way?

3. Speculate on why Kelly refrains from signing his canvasses in the traditional way. Would a signature "sabotage" his goals as a painter? Does the lack of signature sabotage our habits of thinking about art?

4. Look around the room at the other paintings by Kelly for similarities to *White Curve VIII*. How do you think Kelly would define the aims of his art? Are these aims legitimate, do you think? Why or why not?

Written by Judy Landau, Asst. Director, Museum Education Program, George Washington University, and Julie Springer, Coordinator of National Teacher Institute, National Gallery of Art.

FIGURE 3 Ellsworth Kelly, *White Curve VIII,* 1976. Oil on canvas, 96¹⁄₁₆ x 76¹⁵⁄₁₆ inches. Gift of Mr. and Mrs. Joseph Helman, *National Gallery of Art, Washington, D.C.*

At first encounter students will groan in disbelief that they are charged with spending the next forty-five minutes to an hour analyzing *White Curve VIII* (Figure 3) and other paintings by Kelly that hang nearby. "I'll be done in a minute!"; "there's nothing to look at!" they typically complain. An hour later they'll willingly admit, "there's a lot more here than I thought," or, "he proves the saying, 'less is more!'"

Working in pairs, or small teams, students must first choose from the group of words they think best apply to the painting. They must think creatively and fluently first, identifying as many words that apply, and coming up with their own. Then they must think critically, in terms of which of the words is most applicable. The strength of rationale—the "why"—comes out in dialogue.

Typically, students will begin by circling the words *flatness, edges, shape, stillness*—the more obvious terms that apply. As they consider words remaining, however, they will find that others also fit, some which mitigate against previous choices. A longer look will show that depth is as applicable as flatness, or surface. Someone will note that the contrasting areas of black and white establish themselves spatially; optically appearing to recede and advance in alternation. Another student will note that this optical illusion of push-pull (black against white) establish movement—as does the slight arc bisecting the canvas. This gentle curve implies both ascending movement (at the center) and downward thrust (at the outer edges). A perceptive eye will generally note that, in addition, this curve lends the illusion of alternatingly convex and concave surface planes in both upper and lower registers.

As discussion evolves, students will see that the work embraces contradictory visual features—that the work entails flatness as much as it does depth, stillness as well as movement. At this point, someone will suggest that perhaps balance—or even better—*tension*—is the most operative word for a work in which opposites are held in check. As students progress through the study sheet, they will return to the word list as they discover other visual features, they wish to "name" or verbalize. About the only word on their list most students agree has no relevance whatever to Kelly's art is *emotion*.

Step two on their study sheet again requires students to think, first, creatively, then critically. They must first employ *flexible* thinking and imagine alternate orientations for the picture, and why a different hanging would, or wouldn't work. From these possibilities students must then reconsider why the given orientation of the painting was decided upon by the artist. After discussing alternatives, someone will generally conclude that the painting derives much of its excitement (yes, by this point some students will think Kelly's work is exciting) from the black shape being on top. Another student invariably adds that this is because the black is the "heavier" color, so there's an element of tension, as the black shape hovers weightlessly over the white field below. This will prompt some students to launch into discussion of the psychological and perceptual associations we attach to different colors.

Step three requires students to focus on a specific "problem"—the absence of a signature—and make educated guesses based on what they've already discovered about Kelly's art. After preliminary jokes that the artist doesn't want it *known* that this is his creation, students address the matter seriously and eagerly, and will volunteer ideas with a little prodding from me as facilitator. They are generally quick to say it has something to do with "anonymity" (referring back to the word list); that the artist seems to be at pains to eliminate all signs of handcraftsmanship from his work, as evidenced by the crisp edges and the even, matte surface devoid of any trace of autographic brushwork.

More interesting is the *divergent* thinking that takes place as students address the next question: "Does the absence of signature sabotage our habits of thinking about art?" Here they must extrapolate from the specific (Kelly's art) to a broader conceptual plane (art in general). They must also consider issues we generally take for granted when dealing with the arts— issues of "authorship," "originality," and "uniqueness," each of which are implicit in a signed art work in *any* medium. Students gradually begin to realize that the lack of signature on Kelly's paintings is probably *intended* as a challenge to traditional notions of artworks as irreproducable, one-of- a-kind objects.

Item four, the last matter for discussion, requires students to think both creatively and critically. They must synthesize what they've learned, draw some conclusions as to what the artist's larger aims might be, and then make some judgments as to the validity of these aims. These are by no means easy tasks, even after an hour or more discussing Kelly. To some extent, the sophistication of response will depend on an individual's prior exposure to modern art and knowledge of its theoretical base. Still, with encouragement from the facilitator, students will generally offer the follow- ing insights: "His art is about visual concerns, and optics; not emotional issues." Or, "He wants you to see art as a thing of *visual matters*—size, shape, color; he wants you to experience the power of these, and subject matter can get in the way . . ."

When asked to assess the legitimacy of Kelly's artistic goals, classes offer very mixed responses. Sometimes a group will cite "freedom of ex- pression" as a basis for an artist's doing anything he or she wishes, but otherwise act reluctant, or feel unqualified, to pass any critical judgment. Other times I've had students react strongly one way or another, generally drawing upon their personal set of "likes and dislikes" to challenge the premise of Kelly's minimalist, emotionally-neutral canvases.

Realistically, there's generally little time left at the close of this exercise to do more than raise issues of judgment, and to follow-up on them back in the classroom.

FOLLOW-UP: "BUT IS IT *ART*? AND IF SO, IS IT *GOOD* ART?"

Asking students to grapple with matters of aesthetic judgement is asking them to do what the experts do, and this should be made clear to them. They should be made aware that: 1) it is no easy task! 2) it is a highly speculative and theoretical endeavor! 3) critics and philosophers of aesthetics often disagree among themselves and have debated aesthetic issues and definitions of art for centuries!

One way of approaching issues of judgment is to have the class try to come up with a collective definition of art. This activity will help students realize that experts who pass qualitative judgements have a *set of criteria* against which to judge to work. Students should ask themselves: "What is Art?" "What should it be?" "What criteria should an art object meet?" As a starting point, students might return to the pre-visit activity and re-examine earlier assumptions implicit in their comments on modern art. Students should work in teams on this, sharing their definitions and then critiquing other team responses until the class as a whole has agreed on a pared-down set of criteria.

An alternate approach addresses the frequent student question "Why is this considered *good*?" The method, again, is for students to try to define for themselves who might make a qualified judge of art. Ask them: Who should decide if an object is of good or poor quality? Are all judgments of equal persuasiveness? Have student teams discuss the matter and list the skills an art expert would need. Specifically, what skills and experience would he or she need to possess? Getting back to Kelly, what would the expert need to know about Kelly's work and the context in which it was made, in order to assess the quality of *White Curve VIII*? These follow-up activities, being highly abstract, should challenge students to employ higher order thinking skills to the greatest extent of individual ability.

WORKING IN YOUR LOCAL MUSEUM

If you'd like to develop similar activities around objects in a local art museum, your first step should be to call and explain your goals to the staff responsible for education. The museum staff will be able to recommend specific objects that best meet your teaching objectives. They might also be able to provide background information on your chosen objects and perhaps reproductions for classroom reference.

When framing your study sheet questions, pick one or two issues you wish students to explore, but make sure they are "big" issues, that is, central to the artist's work or to your larger teaching objectives. Also, questions should be divergent, so that students' responses radiate outward like ripples in a pool. Above all, structure your study activity, and your museum visit, to allow for the random, and unexpected. Allow students ample freedom to pick and choose among art objects, to provide their own visual evidence, and to express their personal likes and dislikes. In sum, allow for spontaniety and self-directed discovery—critical, I believe, to fostering higher order thinking skills in any discipline.

WILLIAM V. WEBER AND
JANNETT K. HIGHFILL

Economics Graphs:
From Concrete to Abstract

Graphs have become an inevitable part of basic economic analysis. The use of graphs is not intended to keep economics a mysterious or highly-mathematical subject, nor do graphs simply give us "something to teach" in order to make the principles course especially difficult. Economists use graphs because they are a useful tool for organizing our thoughts and ideas about how the economy works. In fact, graphs serve two distinct purposes in economic analysis. Graphs provide us with a simple and convenient method for organizing both concrete economic data and abstract economic concepts.

Instructors of introductory economics principles commonly teach graphing skills, and such skills are typically covered in textbooks. We have found, however, that this coverage usually ends prematurely. All too often, while the graphing section does a good job explaining concrete graphs (those graphs which are designed to present concrete economic data), it either altogether ignores abstract graphs (those graphs designed to communicate and manipulate abstract concepts) or does not provide students with adequate transition from concrete to abstract graphs. This omission is particularly unfortunate because once students have mastered concrete graphs, relatively simple techniques can be used to facilitate their learning of abstract graphs.

In this article we suggest ideas to help students build on their knowledge of concrete graphs in order to master the use of abstract graphs. The lessons begin with a set of data from which the students will construct a concrete graph. Students then use this concrete graph to construct an abstract graph by a process of "erasing the numbers." Finally, students learn how to construct abstract graphs and manipulate abstract concepts without the intermediate step of relying on an initial concrete graph.

Such lessons in graphing are essential to any instructor's objectives for the economics principles course. For students to understand economics, they must learn about a multitude of statistics which describe the economy, such as real and nominal GNP, the Consumer Price Index, the federal budget deficit, and the foreign trade deficit. But to learn *how* the economy works, students must also learn about some of the abstract economic concepts (like the law of demand, the law of supply, the law of increasing costs, and the law of diminishing marginal returns) which help to describe the causes-and-effects that rule our economic system. Graphs facilitate the learning of both types of knowledge. Concrete graphs provide a convenient method for summarizing the large amount of descriptive numerical data used in economics, while abstract graphs are an excellent tool for manipulating the abstract concepts which are at the heart of economics. It is not an exaggeration to say that one or both types are used every day in an economics course. Thus these lessons, designed to acquaint students with both types of graphs, are essential to the student's mastery of every other topic in an economics course.

THE TRANSITION FROM CONCRETE TO ABSTRACT GRAPHS

We begin our graphing unit with a very traditional exercise.

Exercise 1

(a) Construct a concrete graph showing the relationship between disposable income (i.e., income after taxes) and consumption spending. Place disposable income on the horizontal axis and consumption spending on the vertical axis. Base your concrete graph on the following data:

Year	Disposable Income for the U.S. (trillions of dollars)	Consumption Spending in the U.S. (trillions of dollars)
1965	0.49	0.44
1970	0.72	0.64
1975	1.14	1.01
1978	1.55	1.40
1980	1.92	1.73

(b) Draw a trend line through the data points on your concrete graph. Calculate the approximate slope of this trend line. What does this slope tell you about the relationship between disposable income and consumption spending?

The objective of this exercise is to provide a review of basic graphing skills. Part (a) is the traditional "plotting points," and students should have no difficulty obtaining the concrete graph of the data in Figure 1.

Part (b) is simply a standard exercise in slope. By applying the "rise over run" formula to any two points on the concrete graph, students

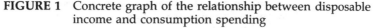

FIGURE 1   Concrete graph of the relationship between disposable
income and consumption spending

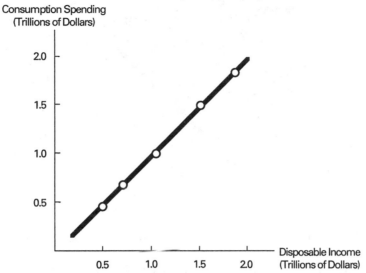

should obtain a slope in the range of 0.9. The interpretation of this slope is
straightforward; an extra $1.00 in disposable income will cause consump-
tion spending to rise by $0.90. Once students have mastered these basic
concepts, we are ready to help them make the transition to abstract graphs.

Exercise 1 (continued)

(c) On a new diagram, "erase the numbers" from your concrete graph
to construct an abstract graph of the relationship between disposable
income and consumption spending.
(d) When you compare the two graphs, what information is common to
both? When you contrast the two graphs, what information is contained in the concrete graph that is not contained in the abstract
graph? Since the abstract graph contains less information than does
the concrete graph, why would anyone ever want to use an abstract
graph?

When we ask students to "erase the numbers," we want them to dispose
of both the numerical axes they constructed and the data points they plotted
in the concrete graph. This procedure leaves them with the abstract graph
shown in Figure 2. The heart of this exercise, of course, is part (d). We
want students to realize that graphs without numbers like the above (abstract graphs) are as useful as graphs with numbers (concrete graphs) and
that these two types of graphs are simply different tools with different
purposes. Furthermore, although the abstract graph looks almost naked in

FIGURE 2   Abstract graph of the relationship between disposable income and consumption spending.

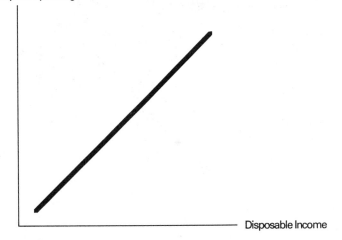

comparison to the concrete graph from which it was derived, we want students to notice in this exercise that much of the meaning of the original concrete graph remains behind in the abstract graph. As one student, Debby Allen, said in response to part (d),

> The two graphs both show that consumption spending and disposable income are directly related. In the concrete graph we are given precise numbers that illustrate how the disposable income and consumption spending were in certain years. It gives us specific factual instances. People would want to use the abstract graph because it allows us to grasp a whole concept. We take hold of the abstract economic concepts without having to mess with numbers. We can use these abstract graphs to help us to see the cause-and-effect, so that we can manipulate many situations, instead of concentrating on numbers in one instance.

RULES FOR INTERPRETING
AND MANIPULATING ABSTRACT GRAPHS

To this point we've shown students that abstract graphs free us from the limitations of data and allow us to concentrate on the abstract concepts which are at the heart of economic analysis. The students' next step is to realize that abstract graphs not only allow us to *visualize* abstract economic concepts, but they also provide us with a tool to *manipulate* those concepts to help us understand the cause-and-effect which occurs in the economy. Just as concrete graphs require that certain rules must be followed (such as the construction of accurate scales for the axes), the interpretation and manipulation of abstract graphs also obey some basic rules. Students' intuition for abstract graphs will develop throughout the principles course as they deal with economic graphs, but to get them started we give them the following three rules for interpreting and manipulating abstract graphs.

Rule #1—The slope of the curve in an abstract graph is used to illustrate a basic economic relationship.

The slope of a trend in a concrete graph becomes self-evident as you plot the data points. In contrast, the slope of a curve in an abstract graph must be *chosen* in order to illustrate the economic relationship between the variables on the axes. For example, the upward slope of the graph from Exercise 1 illustrates the Keynesian idea that consumption increases as incomes increase. If we had chosen a downward-sloping curve for the graph, this would of course say that consumption spending falls as income increases, which goes against our intuition. (The magnitude of the slope of this income/consumption relationship is known to economists as the marginal propensity to consume and plays a key role in understanding the demand side of the economy.)

In general, whenever we introduce students to a new abstract graph, we want them to first apply Rule #1 to determine whether an upward slope (i.e., a direct relationship) or a downward slope (i.e., an inverse relationship) is appropriate for the economic relationship being graphed.

Rule #2—Concave and convex shapes of curves in abstract graphs are often used to illustrate economic concepts.

Abstract graphs in economics often have two possible shapes: concave and convex. "Concave" means "bowed-out" or "hill-shaped," while "convex" means "bowed-in" or "bowl-shaped." Concave or convex shapes, like the slope, are used in abstract graphs to illustrate abstract economic concepts such as "the law of increasing costs" and "the law of diminishing marginal returns." For example, consider the following exercise which we give to our students.

Exercise 2

Consider Figure 3, the accompanying abstract graph showing the relationship between the number of hours spent studying and the score you receive on an exam.

(a) What does the upward slope of this curve tell you about the relationship between the hours you spend studying and your exam score?
(b) What does the concave shape of this curve tell you about the relationship between the hours you spend studying and your exam score?

Part (a), of course, simply asks students to apply Rule #1 and recognize that the graph indicates that increased studying will raise one's exam score. Part (b) asks them to distinguish this upward slope from the concave

FIGURE 3 Abstract graph analyzed in Exercise 2.

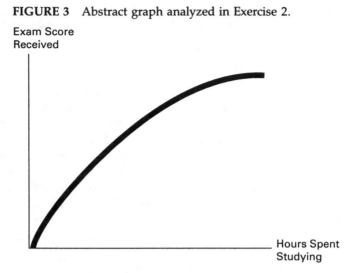

shape and its implications. Students will easily see, as Scott Sudkamp noted, that the "concave shape signifies that it's not a steady, straight increase." From this beginning, we would ask students if it's not a "steady, straight increase" what type of increase is it? After some reminders about the meaning of slope, students will be able to arrive at an answer like Tanya Dartez's: "The concave shape shows . . . the score received does not improve as much with more studying." John Wright attempted a more formal reply: "The concave shape shows as the hours studying increases, the rate of increase of exam scores decreases. The first few hours sharply raise the score but, for instance, after studying for 32 hours one may only receive an extra ¼ point." We might slightly revise John's answer and say that the "32nd hour of studying" only contributed an extra ¼ point. (By the way, the economists' formal name for the idea that these students are discovering is "the law of diminishing marginal returns.")

Rule #2 dealing with concave and convex shapes is a bit more difficult than Rule #1. Very few students will grasp the implications of concave and convex shapes the first time around. Often students will overgeneralize and try to group all concave and convex shapes under a single economic concept.

Rules #1 and #2 deal with the interpretation of an abstract graph; Rule #3 focuses on the manipulation of the graph.

Rule #3—A shift of a curve in an abstract graph represents a change in some important underlying factor.

Not all factors affecting an economic relationship directly appear on an abstract graph. We only have two axes for the graph, and economic relationships are too complex to be summarized in only two variables.

Many important factors which affect an economic relationship will not appear on an axis in the diagram and must be kept in the background. We tell students that the important variables which do not appear on an axis are called "parameters."

The concept of parameters is usually new to students in the economic principles course, and it causes a conceptual problem in the reading of abstract economic graphs. When a change in the variable on the horizontal axis induces a change in the variable on the vertical axis, this situation is illustrated as a movement along the curve in the abstract graph. (In terms of the underlying concrete graph, we are simply moving from one data point to another.) On the other hand, a change in a parameter affects the entire relationship between the two variables in the abstract graph, and so the entire curve shifts when a parameter changes. Furthermore, economists frequently use different terminologies for the two situations (for example, "an increase in quantity demanded" refers to a movement along a demand curve, while "an increase in demand" refers to a shift in a demand curve), so it is essential for students to recognize the difference between them.

To provide students with an aid to help them master the idea of parameters, we like to use a "parameters diagram" to accompany an abstract graph. For example, a parameters diagram for the abstract graph in Exercise 2 above would look like the diagram in Figure 4. The dependent variable, "Exam Score Received," is at the center, and as the arrows indicate, many factors affect this variable. One of these, "Hours Spent Studying," is chosen as the most important and thus is selected as the independent variable in the abstract graph. These two variables are then circled in order to distinguish them from the other parameters ("Study Materials Available," "Difficulty of the Exam," and "Innate Ability").

The parameters diagram serves as an effective mnemonic to help students remember what factors will cause a shift in an abstract graph and

FIGURE 4 Parameters diagram for the abstract graph from Exercise 2.

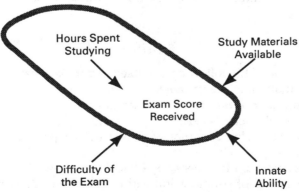

what factors will not. The circled area represents the relationship shown by the abstract graph. As shown by the parameters diagram, the "outside factors" affect the entire relationship in the circled area. Students are instructed that since the parameters or "outside factors" are not shown on an axis of the abstract graph, we must shift the entire curve to illustrate any changes in these "outside factors." If only the variables or "inside factors" change, those are both already shown on the graph and there is no shift in the curve.

For a beginning exercise on the difference between changes in variables and changes in parameters, we continue the previous problem.

Exercise 2 (continued)

(c) Suppose you decide to raise your exam score by increasing the number of hours you spend studying. Would this change be shown on the abstract graph by a shift of the curve or a movement along the curve? Explain.

(d) Suppose you attend a workshop on study habits and learn some ways to improve the effectiveness of your studying. Would this change be shown on the abstract graph by a shift of the curve or a movement along the curve? Explain.

After seeing a presentation on parameters diagrams and Rule #3, students generally have little difficulty arriving at correct answers. For example, Scott Sudkamp replied:

(c) This would be illustrated by a movement along the curve. Since hours studying is on the horizontal axis, increasing it would move the point on the curve right, and thus up along the exam score axis.

(d) The workshop has a parameter effect. Since it's not on either axis, it would have shift the curve. In this case it would shift the curve left, since less time would be needed to achieve the same effectiveness.

To require students to integrate this knowledge, we assign one final problem.

Exercise 3

(a) Choose one of the following variables and make a list of three or four factors that affect the variable.
- The number of unwanted pregnancies which occur in the U.S.
- A baseball pitcher's earned run average
- The dollar value of imported goods from Japan purchased in the U.S.
- The salary paid to the star of a television show
- The number of people volunteering to serve in the armed forces

(b) Of the factors you listed in part (a), which one do you feel is the most important? Construct an abstract graph based on your answer. Explain how you chose the shape for the curve representing the relationship between the two variables.

(c) Construct a parameters diagram to accompany your abstract graph. For each of your parameters, explain how changes in that parameter would shift the curve you graphed in part (b).

This exercise is purposely left open-ended, and students can be invited to add to the list in part (a). Lisa Vonderheide gave us one of the better responses:

(a) The salary paid to the star of a television show
  1. number of shows he acts in
  2. his experience
  3. his fame
  4. popularity of the TV show

(b) The most important factor is the number of television shows that he is in. I chose the upward slope because the more television shows the actor makes the more money he will earn. I used the concave shape because eventually his salary will level off because the company or producer will only want to pay him so much. The actor only has so much time to devote also. There is a limit to what one can physically do and what one can earn.

(c) Suppose the curve labeled A represents the original relationship. A shift from A to B represents if his fame would rise, if the popularity of his TV show went up, and if he is very experienced. A shift from A to C represents his fame falling, negative feedback from his TV show, and if he is not experienced.

FIGURE 5   Student's abstract graph for Exercise 3(b).

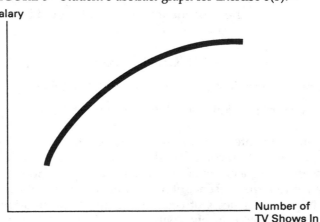

FIGURE 6 Student's parameters diagram and abstract graph for Exercise 3(c).

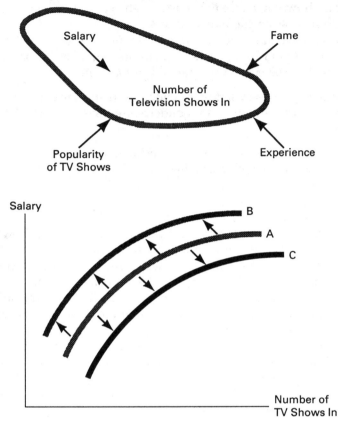

The only major change we would make in Lisa's reply is in her parameters diagram—the salary is the dependent variable and should be placed at the center.

CONCLUSION

This unit on graphing is designed to teach the following skills:

- Concrete graphing skills, i.e., definition and labelling of axes, plotting of points.
- Definition and interpretation of slope, i.e., how to find slope, and more importantly, recognizing the economic interpretation of slope.
- Interpretation of aspects of graphs such as slope and concavity/convexity without the presence of numerical data. Students learn that the most important aspects of economic graphs can be learned from a graph which is completely abstract.

- Identification and manipulation of parameters. Students are shown how to choose the axes (the quantity being explained and its most important determinant) and how to depict the effect of a change in one of the factors which is not shown explicitly anywhere on the graph (the parameters).

Our students must deal with concrete graphs throughout their adult lives. Business presentations, news broadcasts, and even the pages of popular magazines like *Consumer Reports* contain graphical presentations of data. The use of graphs in the popular media is only natural, because the human brain excels at picture recognition. Human beings, unlike computers, easily process information contained in pictures and graphs rather than in strings of numbers. Furthermore, human beings are also superior to computers in handling and manipulating abstract concepts. As we have seen in our discussion of abstract graphs, picture recognition and the manipulating of abstract concepts are related skills. This unit not only helps develop students' graphing and picturing skills (particularly with regard to economic concepts), but it also provides students with an outline of how to use abstract thinking to tackle complex problems.

ROBERT ZELLER

Drawing Inferences
in the Basic Writing Class

A recent trend in developmental English programs has been to move away from the use of grammar exercises and simple paragraph assignments to integrating reading and writing—to helping the students develop the critical thinking abilities that they are called upon to use in their other classes. Since the students in my developmental writing classes are already being assigned summaries, critiques, and research papers, I felt that I would be doing them a disservice by limiting them to simplistic writing tasks and by focusing merely on mechanical correctness.

Thus, over the past several years I have developed sets of assignments to help my students work on critical thinking in a controlled way. My object is to try to build on the thinking skills the students bring with them to the developmental writing class.

In each set of assignments, we concentrate on a single theme or figure. And in each set we work with a variety of sources, moving from photographs to written texts (and in some cases video). By choosing to work with a narrowly focused, usually unfamiliar subject and providing students with a limited number of sources, I hope to have them become aware of how they build their knowledge. Also, I have found that developmental students can get so overwhelmed by source material that they lose track of major ideas amid mountains of detail. In my approach, we work intensively with a few sources and try to extract as much knowledge as we can rather than skimming over a great deal of material.

I always start out with photographs because the students seem more comfortable working from visual details. Also, it is easy to use photographs to distinguish between observation and inference—between a detail, which they can point to, and a conclusion drawn from that detail. The students' writing serves as the primary means for them to begin constructing their own knowledge networks into which they can incorporate new ideas and inferences from their observation and reading. Eventually, the students move beyond inference to analysis and synthesis.

THE SEQUENCE OF ASSIGNMENTS

1. Observing Details/Drawing Inferences

The series of assignments I will describe begins with an exercise in which the class gets together in groups to draw inferences from photographs. At first I ask them simply to list the details they see in the pictures, but they usually very quickly start listing inferences. At that point we pause to discuss the difference between an observed detail (e.g., that the woman's dress looks worn and is frayed at the sleeves) and the conclusion they draw from that detail (that the woman is poor), and then the exercise continues with another photo. Eventually we discuss how this process of drawing inferences is something that they do all the time without being aware of it, and we talk some about how our views of people and events are shaped by the inferences we make on the basis of our observations. For instance, we can gauge a person's mood by his facial expression, tone of voice, and behavior; and we make inferences about someone's income, taste, and self-image by observing her clothes or the car she drives. (Of course, in these circumstances drawing unwarranted inferences can sometimes get us into trouble.)

After this warmup, I give the class a photograph (taken by Jill Krementz in 1982) of E. B. White at work. Again the students start by observing the details of the photo, in which White sits in his boathouse at his typewriter. Most of the students do not recognize White's name, so the conclusions they draw about him from seeing him at work are not influenced by familiarity with his writing. We also discuss how a photographer is like a writer in that she can select her point of view in order to convey a particular impression of her subject.

2. Using details to support conclusions

For the first writing project, I ask students to write a paragraph in which they draw a conclusion about White based on their observations and support it with specific details from the photo. The limitation to one source enables us to work on the concept of thesis and support before they have a larger amount information to deal with.

The usual types of conclusions students use as main points are that White is a writer, that he is old, that he is old-fashioned, etc. For example: "In the picture a man who seems to be in his early 80s is typing something in a very quiet place" and "Looking at this picture makes me think that E. B. White is a simple person." Some students are able to combine conclusions and come up with a thesis that links what White is doing to the place where he is doing it: "It seemed like a nice quiet place for the old man to get away and do something that he enjoys doing; typing" and "E. B. White seems content working in humble surroundings."

In the paragraphs, I try to encourage students to move back and forth between observation and inference, as in the following:

> Looking at this picture makes me think E. B. White is a simple person. He likes to work in places with no distractions. There's no phone, television, or radio. All he has on his table is the tools he needs to work with. His clothes are simple but they look comfortable. Maybe the room he sits in has no electricity, so he sits by the window for light and fresh air. The reason I think there is no electricity is because he is using a manual typewriter instead of an electric one. Everything in the room leads you to believe he is a simple person.

In working on revising this paragraph, I might suggest to the writer that she could include a few details to show what the "tools" are, what sort of work he seems to be doing, and what makes his clothes look "comfortable." Ideally, the paragraph should be neither simply a list of observed details nor pure inference without supporting illustrations.

3. Working with Texts

After doing some group work and revision with the paragraphs, we then move on to the readings. The first one I give them is the brief essay "Education," in which White tells about how his move from New York to Maine has affected his young son's schooling. White describes both schools—the private school in the city and the two-room public school in the country—and it is clear which he prefers, but he never explicitly states his main point. In notebook writings and class discussion, we focus on the clues in the writing that lead us to conclude which school White prefers and why, and to draw inferences about White and his attitudes towards city life versus country life and towards education. One student, for example, notes that "White describes the country community in a light and friendly tone. His trust in the community is shown when he tells us his son 'walks or hitchs all or part of the way home' from school."

I also ask the students to try to make connections between what they have read and what they have seen in the photo. I try to make them aware of how we are continually fitting our new knowledge into a framework created out of the knowledge we already have, with the new knowledge expanding or modifying our old framework. Another student writer does this by relating White's concerns in the essay to the place where we see him at work in the photograph: "He prefers casual over formal and you can see this in White's lifestyle also. He seems to need no luxuries around him when he is writing."

Another aspect of the essay we focus on is White's use of language, especially humor and irony, since it is the tone of the essay more than anything else that conveys the author's attitudes. For instance, in poking fun at the private school, White says that his son "soon learned to read with gratifying facility and discernment and to make Indian weapons of a semi-deadly nature." The reference to the weapons baffles some of the students, but by having them think back to some of the classroom projects of their elementary school days, I can usually clear up that confusion. More difficult is sensitizing the students to White's use of inflated language—as in "gratifying facility and discernment"—to satirize the pomposity of the private school and those (including himself and his wife) who send their children there. One thing we do is to list the terms White uses in describing each of the schools and compare them; the students begin to become aware that words are not simply neutral markers for things.

This leads us to our next brief reading, "Democracy," in which White defines the term in a series of metaphors. I have the class try to paraphrase the ideas about democracy that the metaphors convey (e.g., that democracy is "the mustard on the hot dog" means that it adds something to our lives that makes them more worthwhile and more enjoyable), and we then talk about what is gained or lost in such paraphrasing. Part of one student's response is as follows:

> [I]n the essay he wrote on "Democracy" E. B. White states, "Democracy is the stuffed shirt through which sawdust slowly trickles." To me, this quote means someone who thinks and acts as if he is more important than he really is, but the way they act makes them look stupid because they really arn't what they put on to be.

Also, we focus on the reading process—on places where students have run into difficulty with either of the essays, and on how we make sense out of what we read. Another issue this piece raises is the importance of understanding historical context; we talk (and/or the students write) about how knowing that White wrote the editorial in 1944 affects our interpretation of what he says. Again I ask the class to respond in a notebook entry about how what we learn in the new essay connects to what we already have learned about White. This time, because of our attention to language, students can say something about White as writer in addition to focusing on biographical details.

The last source I provide the class with is William Smart's introduction to a selection of White's essays in *Eight Modern Essayists*. In it, Smart gives a brief biography of White and offers some critical assessments. The students are usually gratified to learn that the sorts of inferences they have been drawing from the limited evidence available to them are valid—that White preferred living in the country, for instance. Again the students write in their notebooks, this time about connections between Smart's introduction and the other sources and about what new they learn about White.

4. Putting it Together: The Synthesis

The next assignment calls on the students to write an essay in which they synthesize the knowledge they have gained from the various sources. Their first task is to formulate a main point about White or his writing. As the class is doing this, we talk about the thinking processes involved whenever they are called upon to do writing based on sources: how they use the sources to build a network of facts and inferences rather than simply a collection of discrete pieces of information; how they then can draw an overall conclusion about their subject; and how they can then use that conclusion as a main point which they can support by using the knowledge they have gained. We also talk about the forms the thesis-support essay can take in their other courses.

Most of the students' main-point sentences focus on the idea of simplicity, especially since that idea comes across strongly in "Education," and it is one that Smart emphasizes in his introduction. Typical examples would be the following: "Equipped with only a little knowledge of E. B. White, I have discovered that he must have liked the country life with its simple surroundings"; and "E. B. White seemed to be a man who preferred things to be simple, both in his writing and the way he lived his life." Note that in the second example the writer is able to set up an essay in which she will discuss the biographical details she has picked up from the photograph and from Smart as well as the conclusions she has drawn about White's writing. Another student takes a more adventurous approach: "White's life shows us why he uses his particular style in writing." The effort to connect biography to writing style turned out not to be altogether successful, but it shows the writer growing in an attempt to come to terms with a rather sophisticated idea. A few students choose to focus primarily on White as a writer. One such thesis reads, "In conclusion of the writing style of E. B. White, I feel that he is an open-minded writer who expresses his thoughts and emotions in a down to earth somewhat satirical way."

After having formulated a working thesis, the students produce a writing plan in which they list the points they want to cover and the material from each of the sources that they will use to develop those points. Often students start to organize their essays by discussing each source in turn. I try to discourage them from doing that if possible, since taking that direction tends to lead them away from synthesizing their material. (However, sometimes that turns out to be the most effective way to organize the essay.)

Prior to having them produce a draft, we do some preliminary work on the conventions and mechanics of incorporating quotations into their writing. We also review the distinction between a quote and a paraphrase. Then I have them begin their drafts.

We work with the drafts in groups in class and in my individual conferences with the students. Since everyone has worked with the same sources, students are often able to point out places where another writer could add a piece of evidence from one of the sources to illustrate a point. The paper goes through at least two revisions before they submit the final draft.

The following is the final copy of one of the essays produced for the synthesis assignment:

E. B. White

E. B. White is a man who tried to live a simple life in a complicated world. This attitude is visible in his writing and in the way he lived his life.

White's views on big-city living can be seen in the essay "Education." He describes the school his son goes to in the city as being a, "medium-priced private institution with semi-progressive ideas of education, and modern plumbing." White goes on to say that "His days were rich in formal experience." The two key words in these sentences are "institution" and "formal." When White describes the private school his son went to, he doesn't call it a school he calls it a "institution" or in the next paragraph he calls it a "private seminary." These words give more of a feeling of a semi-elite, rigid, serious place for children to go and learn.

This is very different from the way he describes the school in the country. As soon as he starts to describe the country school you get a feel of a more relaxed atmosphere. White states, "In the country all one can say is that the situation is different and somehow more casual." In the next paragraph White tells us what the children do on their unsupervised play. He goes on to say that "It seems to satisfy them." When he describes the school in the city, he never gives the reader the impression that it satisfied his son.

White's writing in "Education" only reflects his own life. White himself grew up in a small town and graduated from a public high school in 1917. White never forgot his lazy childhood and relaxed early adulthood, and the sensible laid-back attitudes instilled in him at this time in his life are usually visible as themes in his writing. William Smart best sums up White's attitudes for writing and life when he says "The themes that White came back to in essay after essay are, first, that the natural is preferable to the artificial or mechanical, and, secondly, that even though time moves on apace and things constantly change, the larger patterns of Nature are recurrent."

White was a very versatile writer who used a standard of nature and common sense to judge life. In most of White's themes their is a message of equality and an emphasis on the natural.

How does student writing highlight important elements of observation and inference?

Paragraph 1: The main point synthesizes conclusions drawn from all of the sources. The second sentence focuses the reader's attention on where the writer's supporting evidence will come from (White's writing and biographical details about White's life).

Paragraph 2: The writer uses language as evidence here, something I want students to become comfortable with doing. The last sentence amplifies the assertion made in the first sentence in the light of White's language use in "Education."

Paragraph 3:   Here the writer integrates paraphrase with quotation, setting up the conclusion in the last sentence referring back to paragraph 2.

Paragraph 4:   The writer includes biographical details as well as an extended quotation that help to connect White's writing to those details.

Paragraph 5:   The writer returns to the point he is focusing on without simply restating his opening paragraph.

Overall, the essay follows a logical plan of organization, and the writer effectively integrates his own anyalsis with the supporting material from his reading. The only notable problem lies in the closing, where he moves off into generalizations not discussed earlier in his essay.

In their last notebook entry, I have the students write about which of the sources they learned the most from and why. That leads us into a final discussion about how we learn from our observation and reading and how the production of a piece of writing can enable us to see connections and learn new things that we would not have seen or learned from reading and observation alone.

CONCLUSION

I would like to call attention to two major features of this sequence of assignments:

1. The arrangement of assignments builds on the thinking skills the students bring with them to the class. The problem most of them face as basic writers is not that they are cognitively deficient, but that they have not yet developed the ability to apply their inferential reasoning abilities in academic settings. My job is to get them to see how this process of drawing conclusions from observed detail is a natural human activity. Then we can move on to how they draw inferences in creating knowledge from their reading and how they can use that knowledge in an original piece of writing.

2. I continually direct the students' attention back to the thinking processes involved with what they are doing. My purpose in so doing is to attempt to demystify those processes and to get them to see how they are used in their other academic courses: this could include doing a lab report (requiring observation and inference) for biology, a critique of an article (reading, writing about a text) for psychology, or a research assignment (synthesizing source material) in history.

This is not to overemphasize the service aspect of our basic writing course or to deny the validity of using assignments that call for expressive writing. However, writing is itself a mode of thinking, and in these assignments students are learning that good writing isn't just making sure the grammar and punctuation are correct. They are also learning that the real work of academic writing is in creating knowledge and making it their own.

SOURCES

Smart, William. Introduction. *Eight Modern Essayists*. Ed. Smart. 5th ed. New York: St. Martin's, 1990. 76–79.

White, E. B. "Democracy." *The Norton Reader*. Ed. Arthur M. Eastman et al. 7th ed. (shorter). New York: Norton, 1988. 514.

————. "Education." *The Little, Brown Reader*. Ed. Marcia Stubbs and Sylvan Barnet. 3rd ed. Boston: Little, Brown, 1983. 178–80. "Education" is excerpted from "Education," which appeared in the collection *One Man's Meat* (New York: Harper's, 1942). The entire essay covers pp. 63–70. The portion that is excerpted covers pp. 63–66. (The part that is omitted is not of a piece with the part that is included.) "Democracy" appears in the collection *The Wild Flag: Editorials from The New Yorker on Federal World Government and Other Matters* (Cambridge: Riverside, 1946), p. 31. The Krementz photograph appears in *The Little, Brown Reader*, 3rd ed., 1983.

ROBERT E. CANNON

Summary and Analysis
in Microbiology

How do you get to Carnegie Hall?—Practice, Practice, Practice.

Before I begin to explain about the techniques, tricks, strategies, etc. that I employ in my General Microbiology class to lead students toward thinking critically in this discipline, I thought I should begin by writing about my view of critical thinking. Critical thinking in microbiology is probably not a lot different from critical thinking in any academic discipline. Since I am a scientist and we tend to abbreviate, from now on critical thinking will be abbreviated as CT. Also, as you can see from the format, I've decided to write the paper in the sections that might appear in a scientific journal.

Why CT? Why not just Thinking? In large classes where we lecture to students to provide them with a body of knowledge based on our expertise, we may actually do little to bring to students our enthusiasm for the discipline. Lecture and formal tests and possibly even term papers may do little to expose students to the excitement of learning. It is easy for students just to learn a body of knowledge and regurgitate it on tests. The trick is to get them to learn the material and then move to a higher plane where they can develop new thoughts and ideas based upon previous knowledge.

CT takes a lot. A lot of what, you ask? It takes *practice, time, energy, and compromise*. It also takes *critical reading*.

Reading and thinking are intimately related; and reading is the foundation for the writing exercises in my class that lead toward CT. I am sure that I don't have to convince this audience of the importance of reading so I'll say no more.

If you have a class of Descartes, Nietzsches, and Bertrand Russells, you don't need to worry about *practice*. However, the rest of us must have the students do a number of exercises to learn to think critically. Writing critically takes *time* for the students; reading and critiquing their writing takes me time, more time than if I were lecturing and testing without the writing component. The time is worth it, I'm convinced, for both of us. They learn more and teaching satisfaction has increased for me. CT through writing takes *energy*. Both my students and I expend it through the work of doing the assignments and trying to improve their CT. Fortunately our campus writing center is available to help students as needed.

Students are learning more through their writing; they are thinking more because they are spending more time with my course (at least I hope they are). These efforts on their part will translate into making them better students and potential scientists.

MATERIALS AND METHODS

Dr. Cannon, how long do these writing assignments have to be? What form do we have to use for references?

Long enough to show me what you know, any form you'd like.

I use three major writing assignments in my microbiology course to help students develop critical thinking in addition to essay type tests, which play a CT role. One writing assignment is called "biweekly writing." For this assignment I placed on library reserve a variety of books about major people or events in the field of microbiology. These include Watson's *The Double Helix,* S. E. Luria's autobiography *A Slot Machine and Broken Testtube,* Dubos's *Louis Pasteur, Free Lance of Science,* Black's *The Plague Years, A Chronicle of AIDS,* Jones's *Bad Blood—The Tuskegee Syphilis Experiment,* Desowitz's *New Guinea Tapeworms and Jewish Grandmothers,* and Eron's *The Virus That Ate Cannibals* to name a few. The assignment is for students to read a few chapters from any of these books and then write a 2 page typed (or 3–5 pages handwritten) summary/critique of what they have read. A goal of this assignment is obviously to get students to read more widely in the discipline as well as to practice summarizing, finding important points in literature, and putting ideas, concepts, thoughts written by others into their own words. When I read their assignments, I am interested in seeing them support their statements, use scientific language and a scientific style of writing, and continue to develop a scientific perspective. Students do six or seven of these assignments over the semester giving me an opportunity to evaluate improvement in their writing and thinking skills. I do not grade the first assignment that they turn in. I try to help by pointing out errors of both commission and omission in such areas as paragraph development, logic, grammar and style—anything that jumps out at me as a serious thinking/writing problem. If the weaknesses in their thinking and writing are causing them great difficulty with this assignment, I will call students to my office for individual conferences to go over their writing assignments in detail. With these biweekly writing assignments, I believe that I can have the most impact on their CT skills, since they practice and receive feedback from me on a regular basis.

A second writing assignment to encourage CT is a detailed analysis of a research paper from a recent issue of a journal related to microbiology, such as *Journal of Bacteriology, Journal of General Microbiology, Virology, Applied and Environmental Microbiology, Cell, Canadian Journal of Microbiology*. Students are expected to read the article, study it, and become intimately familiar with it. Then they are ready to extract the most important elements from it: purpose, key materials and methods, results, significance, controls, statistical analyses used, and relationships to previous work. The students learn that science is based upon the experiment, and that there is a logical progression from what has been learned to new knowledge through experimentation. I must approve the research paper chosen, and I am available to help them as much as they need on this assignment. By summarizing and analyzing the information in the research article in their own words, students come to understand it well, identifying the crucial points in the research. Sometimes they must refer to previous work and go to their textbook or other sources for clarification, and these activities bring them even closer to the realization that science is an active process that builds upon previous work, not a process that resulted in knowledge springing *de novo* into their textbook or out of my mouth in lecture. This assignment is due about a month before the draft of their term paper. Since some students choose an article that is related to their term paper topic, this assignment can serve as the beginning of their efforts with the research term paper. My evaluation of their work gives them clues as to how to proceed with further analyses of research papers. I try to stress that scientists do this kind of thing all the time. It is this kind of analysis that leads to new questions, new experiments, more data, new conclusions, and back again to new questions, which moves scientific thought forward.

The third potential CT assignment is a research term paper with a required draft. From a list of over seventy topics, the students are expected to write a research paper based, as much as possible, upon primary research literature. The topics cover the breadth of microbiology: virology, immunology, microbial ecology, biochemistry, microbial genetics, and microbial biotechnology. I expect my students to study primary research literature, though they may begin with a review article. Their efforts when writing the research paper will involve summarizing research in their own words, presenting experimental evidence while minimizing methodological detail, and presenting conclusions. I also encourage them to identify, as best they can, the questions or hypotheses that are being tested by the experiments presented in the literature. The rough draft, due about four weeks before the final copy, is the key part for encouraging them to think critically because it is through the draft that I can give them feedback about their thinking and writing. Evaluating, (though not grading) the draft permits me to help them identify problems and difficulties with scientific content, organization of their thoughts, presentation and organization, grammar, paragraph development, analyses, and clarity. A common problem for many students is to "fix" only what I mark on the draft. Better students take a wider view of their work, going beyond my comments and criticisms to really improve their papers. I stress that re-writing, however painful, is something that all scientists do. Also, I try to convince students that incubating their paper, i.e., putting it away for a while to think about it, can help make it a better. The lag period between draft and final copy can give them an opportunity to be more critical of their own writing. Finally, I am not compelled to mark everything that I think is wrong or try to fix everything for them. I will make comments such as "unclear" or "awkward," leaving it up to them to do the re-writing. When they turn in the final copy of their papers, they also turn in their rough drafts so I can see the changes that they have made.

As you can see, the three writing assignments, though different, are asking students to do similar things: to analyze, to summarize, to write in a scientific style, to go beyond what they learn in class or lab or from reading the text.

RESULTS

Through cosmic interactions, the earth was created. It began when the stars in the sky collided. This is known as the Big Band. (from biweekly writing assignment)

Although we have recently established a writing-intensive course requirement on our campus, our students still have little experience with writing in biology, because we still have few writing intensive courses in the major. In addition, they have even less critical thinking experience. But no matter what people say about today's students, most of them can learn both to think critically and write effectively with practice. The key word in the previous sentence is practice. Without it, there can't be improvement. The tasks for the students to learn in microbiology are: to read critically, to summarize, to digest complex ideas, then translate them into understandable written form, to show relationships to previous knowledge, and to build a knowledge base in the area of microbiology. Does this approach work? Let's look at examples from writing samples of my students. They get to the point and proceed to write good paragraphs.

Here is the introduction to one student's biweekly writing assignment. I consider it to be a good example of a how to digest and summarize. The writing is concise and clear, and is presented in an interesting way, showing that the student understood what she had read.

To many healthy people, cancer is a frightening word. It carries connotations of strange growths, pain, and all the severity of chemotherapy treatments. To the molecular biologist, however, cancerous cells are the product of an interesting phenomenon. They result from a mutation in one or more genes on the cell's strands of DNA which causes the growth of the cell to go haywire. Fundamental to understanding tumor cell processes is the comprehension of a normal cell's translation of DNA to protein. This puzzle has been the focus of Bob Weinberg and his associates at the Whitehead Institute of Biomedical Research. It is also one of the bases for Natalie Angier's book *Natural Obsessions*.

Now let's look at two examples from concluding paragraphs of bi-weekly assignments. These demonstrate differences in ability to analyze and summarize from literature as well as a variation in critical thinking abilities.

This discovery (of Kuru) proved to be a major breakthrough in medical science. It had linked a plague in stone-age-like people to some rare, but very western neurological disorders, to a common type of slow developing virus that invades and degenerates the central nervous system. Many unexplained neurological disorders could be contributed to this type of of slow virus. It would change the way scientists would perceive other dementias like Alzheimer's Disease, by suggesting that they could be consequences of a slow viral infection masked or interrelated with heredity and genetics. The author used actual quotes from Koch's letters and papers which was helpful in realizing how it really was for the biologist of the 1800s. The book is basically a history of bacteriology and microbiology with an emphasis on Robert Koch.

The first sample is excellent, despite the out of control second sentence. It demonstrates that the student has understood the reading and shows how connections between areas of science can be made. The second sample shows me that the student didn't get much from the reading. This exemplifies the superficial "book report" style that some students use. The student fails to analyze the reading in any detail.

The second type of writing assignment, analysis of a research paper from a scientific journal, tests the student's ability to comprehend a complex report and then to explain its main points. Here are some excerpts from several student papers.

Previous work has shown that HIV LTR is trans-activated by immediate early proteins of DNA viruses such as HSV, CMV, and Adenovirus. These experiments show that PIE, which is functionally similar to immediate early proteins of other DNA viruses, transactivates the

HIV LTR. This work also suggests that PIE-responsive sequences are located in the Spl binding region of HIV LTR, supporting previous evidence that PIE trans-activation may involve interaction with host transcription factors.

The effects of two MAbs targeted for specific epitopes of gp120 during attachment to the CD4 antigen of T lymphocytes were studied. One Mab was specific for a neutralizing epitope on gp120 and the other recognized a second epitope on gp120 that reportedly inhibited viral binding but not replication. Also, the researchers investigated the binding of a gp120 construct lacking a 44 amino acid sequence within its carboxy terminal region.

Results suggest that human RBC's contain O-acetylated sialoglycoproteins on their surface that interact specifically with the HE glycoprotein on the influenza C virus. The high sensitivity of influenza C virus for O-acetylated sialic acids provides a sensitive probe for the presence of this sialic acid on cells and may help assess the importance of $Neu5,9A_c$ in the biological role of sialic acids.

These exemplify effective writing. They show technical detail and scientific sophistication. They are concrete and concise. Students have analyzed the research papers critically putting ideas into their own words. It is via scientific literature that scientists communicate. Being able to understand the literature leads to more questions leading to more experiments—the *raison d'etre* for a scientist.

DISCUSSION

The writing really wasn't a problem, I enjoyed it and feel that it is important to develop skills in writing in any area.

The writing assignments were helpful in exploring topics peripheral to micro. It is important to learn to summarize.

There should be less writing assignment.

The writing assignments: well, I hated doing them, but I feel that I have benefited from them. I think that I have learned to better organize my thoughts now and produce a logical summary. (from selected General Microbiology course evaluations, Fall, 1989)

The purpose of the discussion in a scientific paper is usually to draw conclusions from the experiments that have been designed and the results (data) that have been generated from carrying out those experiments. What do the data mean and how do they fit into the body of biological knowledge? How successful was I in testing a particular hypothesis? I cannot discuss hard data here because I don't have a truly quantifiable assessment of the critical thinking ability of my students, but I do have feeling about it. A problem with an article like this one is that you, the reader, are only reading the few, judicious examples that I have picked to support my views about the value of writing to learn or refine critical thinking. You are not seeing the writing examples that demonstrate the shades of gray, the continuum, between good, average, and poor writing and thinking. My personal bias must be factored in to the assessment equation of critical thinking by my students. Maybe if I had a nationally standardized critical thinking examination to test my students at the end of the semester, I'd know for sure how they are doing. I hope that we never have one or we'll start teaching to the test rather than teaching critical thinking in microbiology.

In the short term, I believe that the critical thinking abilities of my students improve throughout the semester. As I look over their biweekly writings, I can see changes, usually improvement, which indicate that they are benefiting from the practice of doing the assignments. Both the biweeklies and the detailed analysis of a research article help them cope with the term paper, which serves as the writing capstone for the course. The term paper at the end of the semester gives students an opportunity to summarize and organize knowledge and information that they have drawn from scientific literature. Critical thinking develops when they can draw parallels and new ideas based upon the knowledge that they have gained. They will have had some experience with the vast literature in microbiology, and as I've written before, it is practice that helps make anyone a better thinker, writer, microbiologist, or anything.

The long term evaluation of the success of my efforts to help students become critical thinkers is almost impossible to assess. One of the goals of the liberal education for students is that they will develop CT skills. We tell students that they will be better able to handle new learning situations with the "skills" that they have learned in college. For the students who have taken my microbiology courses and my advanced courses, which are also writing-intensive (and I hope thinking-intensive), I cannot assess their long term value. The students may not have been out of school long enough to appreciate or see the value of the education that they received. I plan to survey my former students in the next few years to ask questions about the value of my course in microbiology to them. Then I may know better and more concretely how much they may have benefited from their efforts at critical thinking and writing in my course.

Can I know intuitively that my students are developing CT skills and improving their writing? Hell, *yes*. Or, at least I hope that they do, but as I noted earlier, simply one course or even a few courses is not enough; students must get the opportunity to work on critical thinking in different courses. Before closing, I'd like to make a pitch to those teachers who haven't tried using writing in their classes to help students think. Try it, you'll like it. Once you get the hang of evaluating their writing, you can't help but be pleased at the fact that students are learning and thinking more about your discipline because they are doing considerably more thinking about it outside of class.

ACKNOWLEDGEMENTS

I would like to thank Janne Cannon, Karen Meyers, and Walter Beale for their expert editorial assistance. This paper is dedicated to my students who have been willing guinea pigs in my experiments with writing in my courses, and to Mr. Ambrose Short, my ninth and tenth grade English teacher, who showed me that reading, writing, and thinking go together.

KENNETH M. HOLLAND

Briefing the Supreme Court:
Summary and Analysis

In *Ohio v. Akron Center for Reproductive Health*, the United States Supreme Court upheld state laws requiring physicians to notify parents of minors before performing abortions on them. These are the key facts of the case as presented by Anne, a student in Law and Politics, an upper-division political science course:

> Rachel Roe sought an abortion from Max Pierre Gaujean, M.D., a physician at the Akron Center for Reproductive Health. Rachel Roe is an unmarried, unemancipated minor woman who has not obtained parental consent. Given the Ohio statute, House Bill 319, a person cannot perform an abortion on an unmarried, unemancipated minor woman without parental notification, with certain exceptions.

The students in this course must summarize, or brief, a Supreme Court decision in no more than 400 words. The assignment's format is highly structured, consisting of six parts, each of which must be numbered and labeled:

1. Case name and official citation (10 words).
2. A summary of the key facts in the case (125 words).
3. The constitutional issue presented by the case, stated as a one-sentence question answerable only by "yes" or "no" (25 words).
4. The Court's resolution of the issue (the "holding"), the breakdown of the vote, and the name of the justice who wrote the majority opinion (10 words).
5. A summary of the Court's reasoning justifying the holding (200 words).
6. A list of which justices, if any, wrote separate opinions (25 words).

WHAT THE ASSIGNMENT DEMANDS

1. Case Name and Citation

Ohio v. *Akron Center for Reproductive Health,* 111 L Ed 2d 405 (1990).

2. Summary of the Key Facts

Note that Anne has expressed her summary of the facts in the form of a syllogism:

A. Rachel Roe is an unemancipated minor who has asked a physician to perform immediately an abortion without her parents' consent.
B. An Ohio statute prohibits physicians from performing abortions on minors without first notifying their non-consenting parents.
C. Therefore, Dr. Gaujean may not perform an abortion on Rachel Roe.

The syllogism enables her to see which facts must be included in the premises in order to reach the conclusions.

3. The Constitutional Issue

Part three demands that the student recognize and express the constitutional issue addressed by the Court. Just as there are typically numerous nonessential facts in a lawsuit, there are often a series of questions of legal substance and procedure raised by the Court. Which *one* determines whether the appellant or the appellee wins? The issue in the *Akron* case, according to Stacey, can be stated this way: "Is the statute, HB 319—which makes it a criminal offense for a physician to perform an abortion on an unmarried and unemancipated woman under eighteen years of age—in violation of section 1 of the Fourteenth Amendment, which states that no State shall deprive any person of liberty without due process of law?" Stacey is keenly aware that whether Rachel gets her abortion hinges on the answer to this question. The survival of the statute depriving her of that freedom depends on its compatibility with the Fourteenth Amendment's guarantee of due process. Stacey now sees the debate over parental notification as a legal, or constitutional, question, and not just in terms of what her personal preferences might be.

4. The Holding and Vote

No (6–3) (Opinion by Justice Kennedy)

5. Summary of the Majority's Reasoning

The biggest challenge presented by the assignment is part five, where the reader must reduce the judge's effort to justify the Court's holding (an effort which may consume a dozen closely printed pages) to two-thirds of a typed page, double-spaced. Paraphrase and extensive quotation are out of the question. There is only space for a thorough rewording, in the reader's own language, preceded by digestion of what is being said and discernment of which portions of the author's argument and evidence are essential to support the conclusion. The difficulty of this undertaking is revealed in Rob's comment: "I wasn't sure exactly what was important to the justices' conclusions until I had read and reread the decision several times." Sarah's effort, which she described as "picking out the meat of the opinion and weeding out all the nonessentials," resulted in this summary of Justice Anthony Kennedy's opinion for the Court in *Akron Center*:

> We have set precedent in five cases addressing the constitutionality of parental notice or parental consent statutes in the abortion context, and HB 319 is consistent with them. HB 319 provides an opportunity for the minor to show that she is mature and well-informed enough to make her own decision regarding the abortion. HB 319 also authorizes a juvenile court to allow a minor to make the decision herself if parental notification would not be in her best interest. Also, the statute "takes responsible steps to prevent the public from learning of the minor's identity" and for expediting the juvenile court procedure. Each of these provisions of the statute satisfies the dictates of minimal due process. Also, we find that requiring physicians to notify parents provides benefits of disclosed medical information that the physician could not obtain from the minor herself. Thus, HB 319 does not "impose an undue, or otherwise unconstitutional, burden on a minor seeking an abortion." And it is the opinion of this court that the Ohio legislature acted in a rational manner in enacting HB 319.

Omitted from Sarah's list of the virtues of the parental notification requirement is one which Stacey thought critical in her version of part five—the law's alleged salutary effect on the family:

> In addition [to the statute's concern with the girl's health], the law's intention is to improve the parent-daughter relationship, which seems to be negated when she seeks an abortion without their knowledge. The state of Ohio is entitled to assume that, for most of its people, a child's decision concerning abortion should be made within the family, "society's most intimate association."

6. Listing of Separate Opinions

(a) Justice Scalia wrote a concurring opinion.
(b) Justice Stevens wrote a concurring opinion.
(c) Justice Blackmun wrote a dissenting opinion, which was joined by Justices Brennan and Marshall.

STUDENT RESPONSES

Students find the exercise unusually "challenging and exciting," in the words of Jennifer, who concluded in her assessment, "the Supreme Court brief is certainly not the norm for undergraduate writing assignments." Students, when asked to comment on the assignment, stressed the intellectual skills it helped them acquire.

(1) Discrimination.   Kevin spoke for many when he said it helped him "to find the important facts of the case and separate those facts and reasoning from the extraneous information in the opinion." On first reading, the material facts and key arguments are obscure, concealed in a sea of words. Discernment, or "picking the essentials out of the opinion," in Sarah's words, and separating the "important" from the "superfluous," in Biria's words, is a key skill taught.

(2) Inductive reasoning.   The reasoning peculiar to the common law system is inductive, which requires the inquirer first to identify the key facts in a case, find previously decided cases presenting similar facts, then to infer the general rule that was applied in each of the similar cases and, finally, to apply the rule to the facts found in the instant case. Thus Sarah reported that she "learned how to pick the essentials out of the opinion [and] the overall holding [so as] to apply it to similar scenario cases that may in the future come before courts." Matt as well as many other students in the class discovered that the rule governing the constitutionality of parental notification was made by judges in the course of more than a half-dozen cases and not all at once by a legislature.

(3) Interpretation.   One of the virtues of the case method of legal instruction, captured by the briefing exercise, is that it teaches students "to think like a lawyer." When asked in a law school class to identify the facts, issue, and holding in an appellate court decision, memory, even a photographic one, is of no use. "This assignment tested my skills of analysis and interpretation, things rarely challenged in college today," reported Steve. As Patrick put it, "it would have been easy just to regurgitate the information, but to really do the assignment one had to really *think*." Matt observed, "it made you read the case over and over again until you felt like you were a judge yourself. It was not something you did without thinking."

(4) Teaches students how to summarize.   One of the best techniques for transforming passive into active readers is to require them to summarize what they read. Thus, Virginia reported, "I think the main new skill I acquired which I found difficult was to condense specifically key facts and reasoning into the allotted number of words allowed per section." Michael "learned how to read and break down a legal document into more under-

standable terms." The assignment calls upon skills tapped by neither traditional multiple-choice nor essay examinations: "I am used to being forced to *expand* on thoughts," says Jon, "through essay examinations and papers. It was good to learn how lawyers must be concise and limit their wording to give brief synopses of opinions."

(5) *Teaches students how to analyze.*   Analysis is the separation of a whole into constituent parts for individual study. Separating a Supreme Court opinion into six constituents is a classic example of analysis. The student must construct an outline, the skeleton on which the flesh of the full opinion rests. The analyst reverses the process followed by the opinion writer, who begins with the holding and an outline of an argument, which may or may not be written. The student/analyst thus is able to see the main points of the argument as the writer saw them. In Michelle's words, "I found that having to choose certain parts of the decision helped me break the decision down and understand the entire reasoning behind it." "By reading a case," discovered Shawn, "you can see how the process works by breaking it down in the brief."

(6) *Teaches students to improve their writing skills.*   Surprising to many students is the revelation that briefing a Supreme Court decision helps them become better writers. Good writing is clear, coherent, and concise. "I feel I improved my writing technique," confessed Michelle, "by being forced to be *concise* and to pick out the important statements from the more subjective statements." One of the most common defects in student expository writing is the lack of a clear thesis. Of particular value, then, are parts 3 and 4, which require the writer to identify the issue to be resolved and the Court's resolution of it.

(7) *Provides a foundation for valuative thinking.*   Although the chief skill reinforced by this assignment, analysis is not the highest form of thinking. The ultimate aim of undergraduate teaching involving Supreme Court decisions is to equip the students to think for themselves, to assess whether the Court decided rightly or wrongly. It is essential, however, that the students not be permitted in the brief itself to comment, otherwise their opinions will color their analysis, a necessary prerequisite to sound evaluation. To Justin, "the most difficult part was discussing the Court's reasoning without allowing your own personal feelings on the case to show through." On the other hand, the summary provides the student and the class with a solid foundation on which to build a discussion of the merits of the decision.

Right opinion must be based on knowledge. As Cathy found, "I learned that my previous views on parental notification were based on a lack of knowledge of the issue." Michelle "learned more about the requirements of judicial bypass and parental consent or notification as a whole" and reached the conclusion that, her previous views notwithstanding, "depending on how you looked at it the issue could have gone either way." The brief is an excellent springboard not only to class discussion of the merits of an important issue of public policy such as parental notification in particular and abortion in general but can also be a prelude to another writing assignment, the argument, in which the writer must take a position on a contemporary controversy in law and politics and make the strongest possible case in its behalf (Biddle and Holland, pp. 76–78). The argument requires the student to explore the correctness of a judicial opinion in three dimensions: as a matter of law, as a matter of public policy, and as a matter of morality.

(8) Helps students improve their reading skills.   Patrick found that "one skill this kind of exercise certainly refines is the ability to read a case/excerpt, and be able to indicate the major points. This in turn helps students refine their comprehension skills." In Donna's words, "I practiced my skills of reading for important points rather than extra details." Many readers shared Ernie's discovery that "Court decisions are hard to follow and must be read more than once to fully understand what is going on."

In their evaluations, students pointed out virtues of the briefing exercise in addition to the intellectual skills it helps to hone:

(9) Demythologizes judicial opinions.   Several students including Jon reported "this exercise was my first encounter with reading anything published by the Supreme Court." As Steve put it, "the greatest asset of such an assignment is that it exposes you to an actual Supreme Court decision. For most students, this is probably a first." Most college students' knowledge of the Supreme Court is obtained through television, radio, and, to a lesser extent, newspaper accounts of significant Supreme Court decisions. Even if the reporter has legal training, which is rare, reports by journalists typically are oversimplified or distorted. The students learn that if one really wants to understand what the Court said one must read the opinion itself. Thus, Kim observed "usually when one hears about a decision of the Supreme Court, you just hear what the vote was and which way the justices ruled. Reading the decision, one gets to understand how and why they voted the way they did."

(10) Reinforces lectures.   Close analysis of a Supreme Court opinion reinforces and adds to lecture and textbook descriptions of how the Court operates as the third branch of government. The passive learning of listening and note taking is supplemented by the active process of analysis and summary. Thus Michael found that the brief "reinforced my class knowledge about how the Supreme Court reaches its decisions and how it expresses the views of the various justices." "By reading and analyzing decisions," discovered Jennifer, "there is a certain understanding of the

Supreme Court that, for me, can be achieved in no better way." The specific lesson about the judicial process most frequently mentioned was, in Biria's words, "how the Supreme Court makes its decisions using past decisions," i.e., the rule of precedent.

(11) Helps prepare students for law school. Approximately fifty percent of the students enrolled in Law and Politics consider themselves pre-law. One of them, Kelly, thought "this exercise is very helpful for students planning to study law more in depth." Jeffrey said that he "got a taste of what some of the work might be like in law school." The Law School Aptitude Test is a skills rather than a knowledge test, and one of the central aptitudes measured is analytic thinking. The substantive knowledge gained—concerning judicial process, jurisprudence, and the Supreme Court—will also be helpful in law school. The exercise, which immerses them in the special language and customs of the law, also helps students decide whether law is really the career for them. It may also have the effect of recruiting into law school students who had not seen themselves as lawyers but who did well in this unusually challenging exercise.

CONCLUSION

The improvement in intellectual skill stimulated by briefing a Supreme Court decision, unlike that generated by many writing exercises, tends to be categorical rather than incremental. Students' capacity to grasp the issue, holding, and reasoning of court decisions can grow suddenly and dramatically. Learning to read a judicial opinion is analogous to a kindergarten pupil's learning to read narrative—one day she must still rely on Daddy to read *Three Billy Goats Gruff* to her, the next day, following months of phonics instruction, suddenly she can read the story to him. Part of the success of the brief is due to the tight structure within which the students must work. By providing them with a container for the information, they are better equipped to discover it. The dictate of brevity forces them to transform legal jargon and convoluted prose into language they can understand. Thus, students like Steve described what they were doing in the brief as "interpretation" rather than analysis.

Numerous variations are possible on the assignment as sketched above. Many students would have preferred to have done a series of briefs, agreeing with Sarah that "the only way to improve this exercise is with practice and repetition." Susan suggested "allowing us to include a section on the opposing side." In Rahim's opinion, "if the writer were able to include a section in which he/she gave his/her own opinion the assignment would be somewhat improved." Damon also wanted "an opportunity to express an opinion." Another option, as suggested by Patrick, is "to require the student to go to the library and find their own case." Students might feel more vested in the exercise if they could "select an issue that they find particularly interesting and relevant to themselves," said Cathy.

Few tools are more useful to the student/reader and student/writer than the ability to discern the main point and outline of an argument. Few arguments are more authoritative and relevant to our daily lives than those found in the opinions of the U.S. Supreme Court. By briefing these opinions, students learn both to make better arguments and to become more discriminating consumers of political information.

WORK CITED

Biddle, Arthur W., and Holland, Kenneth M. (1987). *Writer's Guide: Political Science* (Lexington, MA: D.C. Heath).

Chapter 2

 Developing Perspectives:
Theory Building Processes

We can't help it. Our minds automatically draw inferences from facts. We observe, we infer, we assemble generalizations—we create theories to explain our experience—often without awareness. And that lack of self-consciousness can create problems for learners who need to control their theory building to ensure that the process remains flexible and self-correcting. In all the disciplines and professional areas, teachers can show students how to manage the construction of theories so their perspectives grow more sophisticated and their theories become more reliable for predicting, planning and higher level analysis.

THEORY BUILDING AS A TEACHABLE PROCESS

A theory is an explanation of how or why things happen, based on analysis of specific evidence. Theories are always somewhat tentative, but we use the theories we happen to have to manage the problems we face. If we believe that elves make the garden grow, we may invest more in charms than fertilizer. If we believe that good luck brings success, we may not put much time into studying for exams. The theories we hold exert tremendous influence on what we do. By teaching theory building, we can make students more purposeful and successful in academic learning.

What does it take to build a theory? What intellectual skills are required to develop a coherent perspective on events? In linear form, the process seems simple enough:

1. We gather a number of details that may have some relationship.
2. From the connection among details, we draw inferences explaining their connection.
3. From the inferences we have drawn, we propose some general rules or explanation—a theory.

4. We use our new theory to explain further details, adopt a fresh perspective, predict future events, or plan solutions to problems we foresee.

The first two steps in this linear scheme, data gathering and making connections, are data analysis processes, as described in Chapter 1. The last two steps add predictive power to simple interpretation and add fresh purpose to classroom learning. In subject area learning, of course, theory building hardly ever achieves a simple, linear form. In the accounts of scientists, politicians, and even young children, what is most notable about theory building is its circular self-correcting structure.

All of us are theory builders. We each spend a lifetime constructing a view of the world that seems coherent, justifiable, or simply useful. To a large extent, then, we each inhabit a world of our own making, a world imbued with values, beliefs, prejudices, and fears developed through years of exposure to details, years of ceaseless theory building.

The weather offers an example. Most of us theorize about the weather constantly, whether we are trained meteorologists or simply inveterate golfers. Each morning, we look to the sky. Are tufted grey clouds coursing in from the south? Many times we left home under these grey clouds and then came home wet. From the recurrent pattern in morning clouds and subsequent rain, we have developed an explanatory theory with some predictive power: Grey clouds from the south at dawn may mean early rain. We may check the newspaper, looking for more information to confirm or refute our theory. Or, we may just grab the umbrella and prepare for the worst. We develop such theories so we can manage our lives in comfort, in convenience—or simply in light of "truth" as we have constructed it. Theory building is a mental strategy that can put us one step ahead of events. From experience gathered from the past, we assemble an explanation that lets us predict, and then control, the future.

Interested in how students from different majors would respond, we asked a class of college students to define theory building in their own disciplines. Their responses reflect some variation, but general consensus around the central skills in theory building:

> Theory building processes . . . enable anyone capable of reading to draw some sort of general conclusion from an ordered group of words that make up articles, poems or narrations. Students can be encouraged to find key words or phrases that hint to the reader about the personality of the author. With these skills, readers can then draw more accurate and in depth meaning from the works. (Sarah Rutledge [English])

In focusing on the author's personality, Sarah has begun to devise her own theory of reading.

Theory building requires not only an ongoing collection of information, but continuous search for connections within the information. Some areas, such as history, take on an infinitely broad store of facts.

> Let's say we are learning about a desert region such as the Middle East. We find that the region is almost devoid of rainfall. The area is covered almost entirely by sand. The people generate their wealth in the trade of raw materials. They may infer that the area is covered in sand, so agriculture is not a major activity in the region. Since the countries there are selling oil, the student may induce that the countries that sell the most are also the richest. They may claim that the countries exporting the most oil import much of their food supplies. They may conclude that rich countries in desert regions are better able to feed their people. But is this true? Only theory testing will tell for sure. (Dave Thompkins [History])

Short cycles of theory making, such as this, may provoke a lifetime of further questioning and inquiry.

In some fields, such as creative art, the artist herself controls the source of "data" on a canvas. The product itself spurs further cycles in a theory making process.

> Thinking in art is not a linear process. The final piece creates new questions and provides new information. After the artist finishes the portrait of her father, she may make new discoveries about line, for example, the thickness of the lines gives her father's image a sense of strength. She now has a new hypothesis about lines and is ready to do more experimenting and practicing. A successful piece is one that generates so many new ideas that the artist may continue. Also, by making mistakes or even spontaneous marks, the artist can take off in a whole new direction, just like in science. (Amy King [Art])

Of course, theories may be more or less valid—and more or less useful in learning or in daily life. Teachers in any discipline can use the subject matter to teach students how to improve the reliability of their theory building. They can also use theory making to motivate the students to learn facts.

Because our minds make connections and draw inferences whether or not we direct the process, we sometimes use our inferential powers to build remarkably poor theories. All of us have met people who adopt personal theories:

- Learning is a passive act.
- Aspiration always leads to frustration.
- Authority must be distrusted (or trusted).
- Voicing opinions brings embarrassment.
- Mathematics is mindlessly mechanical.
- Science is a masculine province.
- Studying will always find a right answer.
- Writing is always painful.

These common theories are not necessarily wrong, but they are built inferentially on a narrow range of personal experience. What would it take to teach students to revise learned beliefs such as these? In academic subjects we have a chance to show students how to manage the process of theory building so they can revise beliefs that restrict their own capability or understanding.

All of this constitutes a reason to teach theory building in the academic disciplines. If we can show students how to construct a more reliable theory, they may gain a tool that lets them better manage their learning and their lives. If we can use the academic subject areas for the purpose of teaching theory making, they may gain respect for the kind of thinking that supports the construction of a discipline. If we teach theory making in class-sized groups, our students may gain respect for the perspectives of others and also develop skill in reasoning through problems in concert with other people. If we show students how built-in bias creates the possibility of error, we may prepare them to be steadfast, creative, durable, flexible, and persistent in their search for truth. Most of all, in making theories and changing them again, students may recognize a driving purpose for learning in the subject areas. They may get excited about what they are learning.

THEORY MAKING IN THE SUBJECT AREAS

As Figure 2.1 suggests, theory making requires openess to an endless process of revision, not dissimilar to the intellectual process that revolutionizes established ideas in the sciences. In *The Structure of Scientific Revolutions.* Thomas Kuhn showed how scientific paradigms or models may be finally overturned by the ceaseless flow of scientific research data. At first, most of the facts we assemble seem to support an existing theory: The moon, planets, and stars all circle harmoniously around the Earth, for example. More observations of further stars seem to confirm and extend this earthbound theory. When anomalies occur, such as the arrival of a comet, we push them aside as distractions. Then, we discover a pattern in the anomalies—that the comet may be circling the sun, for instance. What else might be circling the sun? The Earth? Suddenly, we perceive an entirely new pattern in all the circling skies. And the earthbound moon, once quite central to the universe, has become the anomaly. Such revolutions are not absolute, of course. After all, Copernicus had the circles right. It took Newton's discovery of gravity to find the center of those parabolic circles.

Our theories are never as rational or reliable as we would want them to be. First, our access to information is never complete. But, because we are automated meaning makers, we draw inferences nonstop from whatever details we happen to see. Our selection of details is largely controlled by

FIGURE 2.1   Developing perspectives: theory building processes

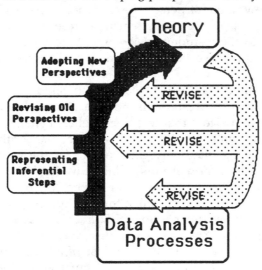

the preexisting ideas we already hold and use. In making connections, we tend to overlook evidence that runs counter to the theories we have already developed. In making theories we put far greater weight on the general truths we already hold than any inference we make up to explain a new instance. Bias exists in the awesome momentum of our own beliefs. Sometimes, we construct our theories with care and self-conscious control, but more often we leap at explanations with impulsive disregard for potentially useful alternatives. In theory making, these sources of bias guarantee our error.

Theory building requires endless recursion, endless reconsideration, endless revision. Sudden awareness, commitment, falling back from commitment, leaping out, falling short, exhilaration, and despair—all are part of the business of developing a perspective. No matter how persuaded we may be by our own theories, details from experience continue to flood our senses. We sort through details perhaps once, perhaps again, perhaps for years, searching for a hidden key. Among possible meanings, we may try three or four and then dismiss them all to search again though further details. With elation, we may strike upon a simple explanation of events, only to lose that explanation to one or two pieces of contrary evidence. We may hold a theoretical position for years, only to completely revise that position when a sufficient mass of contrary evidence has gathered.

All of this theory making can be tremendously exciting. As teachers, we often thrive on the excitement of making truth from facts. Because our students are seldom aware that their own learning is a kind of theory making that parallels the work of the disciplines and applied sciences, they are deprived of motivation to learn. Why not teach students how:

> Each discipline aims to define a body of knowledge, which can support the development of powerful new ideas.
> Each discipline is refining methods for locating and interpreting information to reduce the risk of error.

The excitement of learning is in the theory making, not the memorization. Still, it is up to the teacher to represent and explain the intellectual work that links facts, inferences, generalizations, and theoretical propositions. It is up to the teacher to lead students through the process again and again, until students sense the promise and risk in different paths through information.

TEACHING TO CHANGE PERSPECTIVES

High school and college students have a hard time coming to terms with the idea that making a theory or developing a perspective is the purpose of their labor in subject area classes. The facts and principles in a subject area look so palpable, so neat, so pleasingly finite, so manageable— we cannot blame even good students for seeing rote memorization as the task of learning. In contrast, the processes that generate these facts, inferences, and principles are circuitous, difficult, and frustrating. We cannot blame students for avoiding the task of building theories. The teachers who wrote articles in this section have all designed ways to teach students to recognize, adapt, and use reliable methods for theory making—and then revise their ideas in light of new information. We have organized their descriptions to emphasize three challenges involved in teaching theory building to high school and college students:

1. Representing inferential steps: The challenge of making an invisible process explicit to students so they can manage it
2. Revising old perspectives: The challenge of recognizing what students already believe as a basis for retheorizing or adopting new perspectives
3. Adopting new perspectives: The challenge of helping students extend their theories in light of their implications

The teachers who wrote articles for this chapter have used theory building in phases such as these to bring excitement to learning in the subject areas.

Representing Inferential Steps

How can we represent invisible processes to students who would prefer to stick with the facts? Jonathan Lewis uses his introductory sociology courses to teach theory building. He doesn't begin with social theory, however. Instead, he uses an old parlor game called Queen Anne to encourage his students to search carefully for patterns in what they see. Then, comparing new and old drawings of dinosaurs, he can help them see how an old paradigm is revised when new details are discovered. Finally, he can guide them in developing a new theory of social bias, based on new facts carefully examined. Professor Lewis has developed a computer program that lets students practice theory making from a base of facts in sociology.

Revising Old Theories

Because we infer automatically from daily events, we may be just as likely to build a bad theory as a good one. Howard Tinberg uses his writing courses to show students how to adopt a fresh perspective on their own behavior and values. He uses writing to show students how to sample their own lives for fresh data. With practice first in seeing themselves as "object," he prepares them to revisit their own culture, objectively gather new information, and propose a new explanation of their culture based on what they have newly seen. Having practiced revising a theory of the familiar, he casts them into the less familiar, where they again build a theory describing and explaining culture.

Kim King has developed exercises for her sociology students to complete together as they begin to devise theories explaining human behavior. She has developed a set of case studies that let students work through the process they use to assess human values. Early exercises help them define a process for valuing and decision making. Later exercises, involving a hypothetical people called the Eeks, force students to reexamine and explain the social dynamics of prejudice.

Richard Jenseth has developed techniques for teaching students to create a theory of language and bias. His students view language as an artifact, analyze that language, examine some restrictions on language and build theories of "symbolism" that explain stereotyping in several forms. He aims not to restrict language freedom but to increase awareness and clearsighted decision making

Elizabeth Stroble has aimed her religion class toward the development of new perspectives on religious conviction. Through a series of hypothetical cases, she shows her students how to locate theoretical inconsistencies in a specific event or instance. She then shows them how to describe beliefs from an objective viewpoint. Finally, she asks them to make and explain choices from a theoretical perspective which is not their own. Her students examine theoretically the choices that follow different patterns of religious belief.

Louis H. Henry wants his students to understand and use the constellation of ideas that organize the study of economics. How can he help them make connections among the abstractions that guide economic analysis? Clustering ideas in a relational map helps students see connections between ideas. Writing helps them apply ideas to current issues. Class discussion becomes a forum in which alternative ideas can be tested.

JONATHAN F. LEWIS

Theory Building in Sociology:
Queen Anne and the Dinosaurs

Students enrolled in my introductory sociology courses often wonder what specific skills or knowledge can be found there. Having indicated an interest in pursuing a degree in another area, they are anxious to learn just what practical benefits can be obtained from my course. While I would prefer to believe that all students are motivated by a thirst for knowledge, I realize that most have clear vocational reasons for pursuing higher education, so I point out both the availability of jobs to graduates having a social science degree and some of the skills they can acquire by successfully completing my course. Prominent among these skills is an ability to generate innovative explanations for a given set of facts. The capacity to see something unusual and novel in the everyday is to be capable of producing insight and generating insights is an invaluable component of any liberal arts education. The following exercise is one I often use to indicate exactly what I mean by generating insight and how important it has been in other academic fields.

INTRODUCING OBSERVATION
AND INFERENCE

Tell the class that you will demonstrate how training in sociology will help them develop critical thinking skills and that in order to do this, you would like to play a game of Queen Anne. You may wish to ask whether anyone is familiar with the game and, if so, for these individuals to please sit quietly and watch.

The premise of the game is very simple. You write a list of several words on the board and inform the class that these words are "Queen Annes," i.e., they have something in common. It is up to the class to figure out the common theme. In order to make this even easier, you write one word which does *not* share the theme, and describe it as *not* a "Queen Anne."[1] See Figure 1.

FIGURE 1

These Are Queen Annes	This Isn't	This Is What the Queen Annes Have in Common
QUEEN ANNE BOOK VACUUM	TOWER	Double letters
RED BLUE YELLOW	CORK	Colors
HORSE COW SHEEP GOAT	ROCK	Farm animals
PLOW TRAILER WATERSKIS	LAWNMOWER	Things that are pulled
906 1001 1691 1961	1492	Years that are the same if written upside down
2 3 10 12	4	Numbers beginning with the letter T

The first three of these are quite straightforward and are intended to lull the class into a sense of security, of a "this isn't so hard" frame of mind. Expect virtually all of the class to figure these out. The fourth one is a bit more difficult, as are the next two. You can easily devise several of varying difficulty, but make certain that the point gets across that, although some patterns are not immediately recognizable, nevertheless there is a sound reason for grouping the words in the selected fashion.

Having set up the students in this fashion, you can now proceed to the tricky section. This time, what the words have in common is not to be found in the words themselves, but in how you write them on the board. This is best set up by appearing to be deep in thought, trying to come up with another list of "Queen Annes." Scratch your head, pace around a bit, then stand to the left of the board and, reaching across with your right hand, write down the words in your list, saying "This is a Queen Anne, this is a Queen Anne, this is a Queen Anne, and" [stepping over to the right of the board] "this isn't" as you write the word that does not belong. See Figure 2.

If the students have not seen this game before, it is unlikely that they will catch on to the trick. They will proceed as if the list you have given them is no different from the others and will seek the solution accordingly. Reject any answers they devise as incorrect and tell them you will give them another chance. Proceed in the same manner as before, complete with the appearance of deep thought (which suggests to the audience both that the solution is complex and that it is perfectly appropriate to wander a bit back and forth in front of the board), and write up the next sequence. Because the obvious link is clearly incorrect, your audience will probably begin to fidget a bit at this point. They know something is going on, but they are uncertain as to just what. If you offer to give them one more

FIGURE 2

These Are Queen Annes	This Isn't	This Is What the Queen Annes Have in Common
WINDOW DOOR CAN	JOB	Written while standing on left side of board
UP SOUTH FALL	CHAIR	Written while standing on left side of board
2 4 8	10	Written while standing on left side of board
GREEN GREEN GREEN	GREEN	Written while standing on left side of board

chance and put the next list on the board, they will either see through it or be completely mystified.

In revealing the trick, point out that you did nothing to violate the rules of the game. The problem they had seeing the pattern stemmed from their preferred way of finding an answer. This is understandable given the previous success of that approach, but when facts fail to conform to theories, new theories are needed to generate insights into the facts being examined and their relationships.

OF PARADIGM SHIFTS AND DINOSAURS

What the students have just experienced is a shift in paradigms, the much over-used term from Thomas Kuhn's *The Structure of Scientific Revolutions*.[2] In that book, Kuhn argues that scientific research is guided by a dominant paradigm that helps make sense of data as it is uncovered. So long as there are no anomalies (research findings that the dominant paradigm has difficulty explaining), normal science continues its cumulative process. However, a series of anomalies increases the need for an entirely new way of comprehending reality.

By describing recent developments in the field of paleontology, you can convince students of the usefulness of paradigm shifts. Most adults retain knowledge of dinosaur trivia (names, appearance, diet, things of that sort) learned in childhood so it is quite likely that most of the class has a fair amount of knowledge about the creatures. What students may not be aware of, however, is the dramatic new interpretation of dinosaurs that has completely redefined the field of paleontology. Traditionally, for example, brontosaurs (misnamed due to a mix up of fossils, now they are referred to as apatosaurs) were portrayed as dim-witted and rather lethargic animals. Their enormous size and lack of sharp teeth suggested they preferred lakes (for buoyancy and safety, their long necks allowing them to trudge out into very deep water) and swamps (where the soft vegetation made for easy chewing). Other dinosaurs (the tyrannosaurs) were quite fierce and aggressive, but only for short periods of time. More often, the carnivores stalked the landscape, searching for victims to attempt to satiate their voracious appetites, dragging their thick tails behind them. Stegosaurs, usually portrayed as painfully stupid creatures, also tended to roam rather aimlessly about the Jurassic landscape. Triceratops, the three-horned tank, trudged about on short legs bent sideways at the knee. These and other images of dinosaurs are probably very familiar to the class. These images, like the dinosaurs themselves, are now extinct.

The revisionist perspective on dinosaurs has redefined dinosaur behavior by realizing that much of the old perspective was based on dinosaurs as ancestors of modern reptiles like snakes, tortoises, and crocodiles, all slow moving creatures with small and clumsy (or non-existent) limbs. Yet dinosaurs like the Archeopteryx were also the ancestors of modern birds, far more agile creatures. Consequently, making the assumption that dinosaurs were actually quite dexterous forces a reexamination of the existing

FIGURE 3   Stegosaurus (a) then and (b) now.

(a)

THEN

(b)

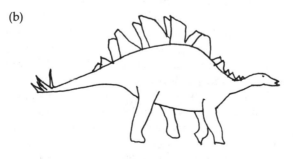

NOW

Adapted by the author from Robert T. Bakker, *The Dinosaur Heresies* (New York: Zebra Books, 1986).

FIGURE 4 The changing depiction of (a) Brontosaurus, now called Apatosaurus

(a)

THEN

(b)

NOW

Adapted by the author from Robert T. Bakker, *The Dinosaur Heresies* (New York: Zebra Books, 1986).

fossil record. Doing so has resulted in the new perspective, which sees tyrannosaurs as very nimble (their leg structure closely resembles that of an ostrich, renowned for its running speed), triceratops as more like rhinoceros (legs erect and beneath instead of bent and off to the side and, unlike rhinoceros, traveling in herds), and apatosaurs as capable of devouring rough vegetation (birds eat seeds with no teeth by way of a crop filled with stones that grind the food before it is digested; apatosaurs had crops too but until recently no one thought to look for evidence of them). Perhaps the greatest piece of rewriting involves stegosaurs, whose plated spines were a long-standing mystery (some saw them as defense against predators, others as radiator-like mechanisms for regulating temperature). The new perspective sees them as counterweights that facilitated the animal's erect posture, which it needed to reach the leaves of tall plants. For all the dinosaurs, pictures of tails dragging on the ground are gone, as the fossil record of footprints shows no signs of such a phenomenon.

The man most responsible for this revisionist approach, Robert Bakker, has in some circles taken on the role of a modern-day Galileo (and his book *The Dinosaur Heresies* by commutation the modern-day *Starry Messenger*[3]). The aptness of the analogy stems from the two men's ability to derive more elegant ways of comprehending both existing data and anomalies for which prior perspectives could only account in a cumbersome fashion. And, of course, these new perspectives led to the formulation of testable hypotheses the results of which tended to corroborate the new paradigms. Just like the Queen Anne exercise, entirely new ways of conceptualizing the data were necessary.

This contest of perspectives is not peculiar to contemporary paleontology. In the field of geology, tectonic plate theory (the theory of continental drift) was not widely accepted until the early 1960's, while the field of cosmology currently has several theories to explain the origins of the universe. Indeed, whenever new data is uncovered by spacecraft or earth based telescopes, many old perspectives are ditched in favor of new, a process familiar as well to those working in the field of particle physics. The legitimacy of a field of study has little connection with the number of perspectives it generates and herein lies one great advantage for students studying introductory sociology. Because the field of sociology deals with so many controversial topics (from homosexuality and drug use to abortion, from the persistence of poverty in wealthy societies to the presence of sexism in ostensibly egalitarian societies, from capital punishment to affirmative action), it has generated a wide range of perspectives on these subjects, many at loggerheads. Sociology is therefore filled with differences of opinion as to the proper way to understand a particular set of facts (witness debates in the field over the causes of wealth and poverty or the origins and functions of sex roles, for example).

DEVELOPING PARADIGMS IN SOCIOLOGY

I use various versions of what I have just presented in several sociology courses I teach. Introductory sociology classes react positively to the inclusion of unusual and unexpected material, and the lessons they learn from the lecture can be brought up whenever we cover a subject which is fairly controversial. In such cases, I present one perspective sociologists bring to the subject, then ask if that perspective seems to make sense of the available facts. If not, are the facts that cannot be explained serious enough to be considered anomalies which require a very different orientation to the subject? I can then introduce a very different perspective that other sociologists employ to analyze the subject and ask the same questions.

It may be useful at this point to present an example illustrating the way that the critical thinking skills described in the first part of this paper can be used to develop insight into a specific topic. Suppose we were to consider the subject of racial and ethnic prejudice and we are in possession of the following facts: (1) In a largely agricultural society, one group of people is legally free while another group is not. (2) Members of the group that is free have white skin and originally came from Europe. (3) Members of the group that is not free have black skin and originally came from Africa. (4) The white group has a higher standard of living than the black group. (5) The white group believes the black group to be not entirely human.

If the five bits of information are to make sense, to be made meaningful, they need some sort of interpretative framework or theory. This theory would have to explain both the existing observations and any subsequent ones. So the data are like Queen Annes and the theory is an explanation of what they have in common. A tentative idealist theory might be that this society has such inequality between groups due to the ideas that the dominant group has about the subordinate group. Such an approach ("inequality is caused by prejudice") can lead to testable hypotheses, e.g., *if* the dominant goup changes its ideas about the subordinate group, *then* inequality will eventually disappear.

The problem with this theory is that many of its testable hypotheses are not supported and thus represent anomalies requiring a shift in paradigms. In the case under discussion here (which is intended to describe the United States in the late 1700s and early 1800s), many whites recognized blacks as human beings yet inequality persisted. More recently, polls conducted in contemporary America find that the majority of whites reject the idea of innate black inferiority, yet inequality between blacks and whites persists. Looking at examples of inequality from other times and places, it seems clear that ideas do not cause inequality, although they seem to play some role in allowing inequality to persist.

An alternative materialist theory might be assembled which argues that inequality leads to ideas of inferiority which are used to justify the privileged position one group has over another. This general theory leads to such testable hypotheses as *if* one group has significant advantages over another, *then* beliefs arise which justify or support this situation. Studies can then be made of white–black, male–female, rich–poor, adult–child, or other such groupings to determine if the hypothesis can be supported. In the case described earlier, higher living standards for whites of European origin came directly from the cheap labor of black Africans. In order to justify this exploitation, a belief system of racial inferiority emerged that depicted black Africans as less than human. Remarkably similar belief systems emerged among Protestant Americans in the late 1800's to justify the low wages given to "racially inferior" (and largely Catholic) Irish and Italian immigrants.

SOCIAL THEORIES WITH FEET OF CLAY

In my social theory course, which focuses less on data and more on the theories themselves, I have supplemented the Queen Anne exercise with a more detailed look at theorizing in the physical sciences. This includes quotes from famous physicists which document the tentative character of any theory, for example, these two by Albert Einstein:

> The sense experiences are the given subject matter. But the theory that shall interpret them is man-made. It is the result of an extremely laborious process of adaptation: hypothetical, never completely final, always subject to question and doubt. It is the theory that decides what we can observe.

There are a variety of ways to develop critical thinking skills: this is simply the one I have chosen and found works best for my purposes. No course that I took as an undergraduate or graduate student employed such devices, falling back instead on the lecture–discussion format. That format works best when students have had the opportunity to develop the skills to examine lecture material in novel ways, something that Queen Anne has the potential to encourage.

ENDNOTES

1. I first became aware of the Queen Anne game in an excellent teaching workshop sponsored by the American Sociological Association. It was held at the University of Cincinnati by Prof. Theodore C. Wagenaar of Miami University of Ohio. I am not certain whether Prof. Wagenaar actually first invented the game, although his imagination and devotion to teaching make it possible that he very well could have.
2. **Thomas Kuhn**, *The Structure of Scientific Revolutions* (Chicago: University of Chicago Press, 1962.)
3. **Robert T. Bakker**, *The Dinosaur Heresies: New Theories Unlocking the Mystery of the Dinosaurs and Their Extinction* (New York: Zebra Books, 1986). For unusual insights into other aspects of dinosaur behavior neglected by the older perspective, see Sandy Fritz and Ron Embleton, "Tyrannosaurus Sex: A Love Tale," *Omni* (February 1988, pp. 64ff.)

HOWARD TINBERG

"Deep Play": Reading Culture
in the Writing Classroom

I recently devised a writing course at my community college that
encourages students to reflect on the extent to which we are "constructed"
by culture: How are we shaped, how are our choices defined, by the
traditions, beliefs, and values around us? To answer that question, students
must be able to see themselves through a kind of cultural frame. They must
view their beliefs and behavior within the context of their community's
beliefs and behavior. They must achieve a critical distance. The situation is
analogous to that of the anthropologist who must stand outside the culture
studied to read and interpret its larger structures and forms.

Enabling my students to interpret culture is not the only objective of
this course. I want them to come away from my class convinced that theirs
is a world ripe with meaning and significance. I should say that the majority
of the students at my community college are themselves immigrants or are
children of immigrant parents. By the time they arrive at the college, these
students have experienced some difficulty in negotiating between their
home or parent's culture and the mainstream or dominant culture around
them. Many have reacted to such difficulty by abandoning that home
culture for the success that assimilation into the mainstream can bring. I
see my course as an opportunity for them to explore the issues at stake in
such a process.

SEEING THEMSELVES AMONG OTHERS

Before attempting to define that difficult term "culture," I encourage
my students to see themselves as part of a group or community. It is a
necessary, early step. It also renders discussion concrete, since students
are encouraged to bring up in class and in their writing, examples of
groups to which they are affiliated: sports teams, work places, religious
institutions, and so on.

We begin by brainstorming the ingredients necessary for any community: people (naturally), a common purpose, a set or rules for its members to observe, a distinct language, and various roles or duties to be enacted. We then list various examples of communities from daily life: religious denominations or congregations, political parties, workers' unions, the family, nationalities, and so on.

In the assignment that follows, I ask my students to identify one community to which they belong (one of many, I remind them) and to describe the roles they and the other members play. I encourage them to reflect whether they consider themselves "leaders" or "followers" in the group, or indeed whether such terms are even relevant.

One student chose to write on her work community, the residents and nurses's aids of a nursing home. Early on, she turns to the role of the residents:

> The residents in this establishment are here for one main reason and that is personal care. They need to be here because they can no longer take care of themselves. They can no longer do as they please when they please. An example of this is each meal is served at a certain time everyday. Another example is they go to bed and rise in the morning at a certain time each day. And one more example is they are on a schedule for showers each week and you only get showers on your assigned day. In other words they have very little opportunity to make their own personal choices.

As contrast, the nursing aid's job (the student is an aid) is essentially to make those choices and perform the tasks that come with that responsibility: feeding, washing, cleaning and drying.

Yet in reflecting on whether she is a leader or follower, that is, when reflecting on her place within the context of this particular community, the student begins to see her role as rather complex. Although she has, in one sense, greater autonomy than the residents, she recognizes that when residents ring their bell she must respond quickly to their needs, thus yielding up something of her own freedom to choose. Moreover, as a nurse's aid, she is herself supervised by, and dependent on, nurses, who leave the dirty work for the aids to do.

In the end, the student comes to realize that for this community, the question of who leads and who follows becomes subsumed by the interest of the community as a whole:

> Altogether we all are a vital part in this community. We need the residents as much as they need us. For without them none of us would have jobs or fulfillment, and without us they would not have proper care. Who the leaders and followers are in this community I see as insignificant. The important thing is that these people are taken care of to the best of our ability.

Each member of the community pulls her own weight; each member is essential to the maintenance of the group.

FROM COMMUNITY TO CULTURE

Central to the maintenance of any community is that community's *culture*, the ceremonies and beliefs that are the glue of the community. It is to the idea of culture that I and my students now direct our attention. For assistance in understanding the concept, I ask my students to read Clifford Geertz's "Deep Play: Notes on the Balinese Cockfight." The essay begins anecdotally with the Geertzes' entrance into a Balinese village and their witnessing of an illegal cockfight, which is broken up by a police raid (the Geertzes flee along with the villagers and thereby gain acceptance in the village). Geertz then proceeds to describe the rules by which cockfights operate and the roles played by the participants. Eventually, the essay probes what the ceremony means for these villagers, that is, how it expresses the great themes: "death, masculinity, rage, pride, loss, beneficence, and chance" (Geertz 295).

We began our discussion of the essay by considering what it is like for someone to be amid a culture far different from her own, as is the case with Geertz. What are the obstacles that such a person faces in trying to observe and understand that culture? Geertz's experience as an "outsider," or, as one student put it, an "intruder," attracts my classes' attention early. In his journal, one student reacts to Geertz's dilemma by reporting a similar experience of his own:

> I have had the same experiment that Clifford Geertz and his wife . . . had. I was born in Portugal and immigrated to America when I was two years old. When I was 12 years old I went to Portugal to visit my family with my parents. I also felt that I was not wanted. When I walked in the street I felt that everybody was staring or talking about me. I don't know what they were talking about or why they were staring. I use[d] to always ask my parents why they stared and she replied because you are a new face in this town. She also said that not . . . many new faces come by here for years. One day my mother sent me to go out and get some milk. I really didn't want to go but I was glad I did because when I got to the corner to pay for the milk I didn't know how to count the money to pay for the milk. Some young gentleman help[ed] me count the money and from that day I knew how to count Portuguese money and felt more comfortable walking in the streets.

It is a narrative of estrangement and gradual adaptation. In retrospect, I am not surprised that this immigrant student would have reacted in this way to the Geertz piece, since the experience he describes is quintessentially the immigrants' story: the shock of entry into a strange culture; the fear of estrangement; the desire for, and achievement of, assimilation. The student must have experienced the very same feelings when first arriving in this country.

Reactions to Geertz's piece are certainly wide-ranging. Many students betray their own ethnocentrism when reading the rendering of a Balinese cockfight. They are appalled by the violence of the "sport," the callous treatment of the animals themselves, and are quick to condemn it. Yet others attempt to take the view that the ritual is exempt from criticism since "it is not part of our culture," as one student observes in her journal. But she goes further: "Cockfighting had a lot to do with the masculinity of the owners of the cocks."

That one observation prompted me to ask my students whether our culture contained rituals that "had a lot to do with . . . masculinity." By that I mean, Are there ceremonies that express and define what it means to be male in our society? In a brainstorming session, students are quick to list sports like football and hockey, whose combination of physical contact and fierce competitiveness seem to suggest cultural norms of "masculinity." For one student, the Balinese cockfight reminded him of boxing, but not merely because of the shared violence: "It reminds me of boxing in a way, in which a fan would call his bookie and place his bet on his favorite boxer and see who wins." He noted that, as in the Balinese cockfight, in boxing, "die hard betting fans stay round ringside, while the fans who are just there to see the event stay in the outskirts." This student was beginning to "read" his own culture. It was now time to go out "in the field" to engage in more thorough observation.

READING CULTURE: STUDENTS IN THE FIELD

As an assignment, I ask my students to identify a ritual for observation and interpretation. Specifically, I ask them to observe, with journal notebook in hand, the conduct of a particular ceremony with which they are familiar. I decided to have my students observe a ritual that they knew of or had experienced in large part because I did not want them to feel too ill at ease when observing. But, in retrospect, I now believe that familiarity breeds a greater challenge: to step back and see the ritual fresh is especially difficult.

Before sending the students out in the field I asked them to do more brainstorming, this time on the necessary ingredients of a culture's "ritual." A ritual, they decide, must have the following characteristics: repetition of action and a set or formal code of behavior or rules. In other words, rituals do not and cannot vary with each enactment. They must be predictable and the rules must be known by those who enact the ceremonies. The class then produced examples of rituals: a mass, a Thanksgiving meal, a bar-mitzvah, a wedding, a first date, and so on. Of course, there is a great deal of difference in the relative complexity and depth of meaning among these, but all fall under the category of ritual, as we define it.

One student, as an example of research that shows promise while coming just shy of achievement, produces an observant and amusing essay on the ritual of "hanging out" at the neighborhood mall. He describes the "mind games" that occur when boys and girls begin their flirting:

> We followed the two [girls] on the opposite side of the mall and we [both guys and girls] kept walking until we got to the end of one side. We made a U turn and switched sides and went the opposite way. Eventually we got to walk on the same side of each other, got to look at each other. We [the boys] said, "Hi." The girls did the same but they kept walking . . . .

Moreover, the student is able to distinguish the various duties of each member of "The Suicide Squad":

> First is me. I'm the sensible one who knows when we've reached our limit and say when we should back off. . . . Then there's . . . the gung-ho "bring 'em back alive" soldier . . . .

Each member of the "squad" has predictable traits and is called upon to behave in a certain way.

After carefully and humorously describing the behavior observed, the student is unable to go that last mile: to say what it all means. He is not able to comment on what "hanging out" says about being a teenager: about looking for some action on a Friday night and engaging in a rather confusing yet requisite mating dance. Perhaps if he could further explore the meaning of that label, "The Suicide Squad," the student might begin the process of interpretation. Nevertheless, he is able to capture the ceremony in considerable detail and does begin the process of framing the action, thereby gaining critical distance from it.

READING TV

As their next assignment, I ask my students to research a more narrow subject, yet one that speaks powerfully about our popular culture, namely, television advertisements. I asked them the following question: Is it possible that television ads may say as much about our popular culture as the cockfight does for the Balinese? Put another way, Is it possible that television may be selling more than particular products, but certain beliefs and values as well?

I invite my students to do a reading of a television ad, as they had done with a "live action" ceremony. First we read a sample critique, written by Mark Crispin Miller, of a soap commercial. In his essay, Miller argues that the commercial is selling an ideology or set of values as much as a product. Then I advise my students to select a commercial themselves and to describe patiently what they are observing, paying particular attention to seemingly peripheral images, such as clothing worn, background furniture. I invited them then to probe further what the images were saying: Who is the targeted audience? How exactly is that audience being appealed to? What, finally, does the advertisement say about our culture's values and beliefs?

The assignment produces some rather perceptive readings of television marketing. As an example, consider one student's observation and reading of a commercial selling headache medicine:

> We are watching a woman putting her earrings on. She is in a black dress and she gives the impression of going out somewhere special. She is walking around the room when suddenly she spots her husband (we presume). She says, "Bill, you aren't ready for the party yet. Put your tie on." She is very condescending to him. She cocks her head and exclaims that she didn't realize his head hurt him so badly. She takes out a box of Motrin IB and tells him to take it.

When the student begins to interpret the commercial, she arrives at the following reading:

> Watching the scene gives the impression that although "Bill's" wife is feminine she is in total control of her husband. She makes all the decisions from decorating the bedroom down to the fact that "Bill" will have a great time at this party.

The student goes on to suggest that the commercial offers a view of a relationship aimed directly at the housewives in the audience and that this advertisement purposely and cynically inverts the usual gender roles. What is being sold is a miracle cure, not merely for a headache, but for a dominating husband.

A NEW WAY OF SEEING

Much is gained from the kind of research into culture that I have described. To begin with, students, in reading their world, acquire a way of seeing that is reflective and critical. When students are able to view a television commercial as a construction of various cultural attitudes and values, they have arrived at a new and richer way of seeing.

That way of seeing, because it puts the observer in the position of making sense of the world, brings with it a kind of power, a power that students too rarely feel. In traditional classrooms, students are usually put in the position of receiving information from their teachers rather than seeking it out themselves. In the course that I have described, students go out "into the field," obtain information, and then return to "read" its meaning.

Finally, when students are asked to do research on traditions and ceremonies from their own communities (or television advertisements beamed into their own homes), they are being given a clear signal that something powerful and significant resides in their community's ways, and that those ways are fit for study even in the classroom. That is a message, we can all agree, is worth sending.

WORKS CITED

Geertz, Clifford. "Deep Play: Notes on the Balinese Cockfight." In *Ways of Reading*. Ed. David Bartholomae and Anthony Petrosky. 2nd ed Boston, 1990: 272–311.
Miller, Mark Crispin. "Getting Dirty." In *Ways of Reading*. Ed. David Bartholomae and Anthony Petrosky. 2nd ed. Boston: Bedford, 1990: 397–407.

KIM M. KING

Proposing Solutions to Social Problems

Although the discipline of sociology teaches students to "think socio-logically" as much as it teaches its basic set of facts, the typical introductory course usually emphasizes the facts over the processes. Introductory texts are chocked full of facts about the latest studies and make wonderful reference books but are generally not appropriate for the introductory student. Many students are turned off by a course where they have to memorize an overwhelming number of seemingly unconnected facts. Authors of introductory sociology books obviously see the connection between the facts and theories and the overall sociological perspective but first-time sociology students, especially those who are freshman or those never exposed to the social sciences, cannot. More importantly, I have found that the majority of my introductory students are what Kolb (1979) calls concrete experiencers (CE) who tend to be

> empathetic and "people-oriented." They generally find theoretical approaches unhelpful and prefer to treat each situation as a unique case. They learn best from specific examples in which they can become involved . . . and benefit most from feedback and discussions with fellow CE learners. (pp. 39–40)

In addition to disliking theory, these students have a particular distaste for math and statistics (some call the latter "sadistics") and when the facts that these concrete experiencers do learn are not applicable to their own lives they easily become bored and apathetic. Therefore I begin my course by describing a set of "facts" that students then use to create and revise a social theory.

USING FACTS TO CREATE A PERSPECTIVE

With these potential problems in mind, I have geared my introductory course away from the typical survey course and have several goals which are partially fulfilled by the following exercise. First, I hope that the introductory course is an enjoyable learning experience for students (as well as myself). Getting students to come to class is half the battle and they are more likely to come if they feel comfortable and can laugh a little. Second, students will retain more material if they take an active part in their learning process. Critical thinking is impossible for students who simply copy down the lecture material and regurgitate it on the test. Since "critical thinking is best promoted through structured, purposeful activities" (Rubano and Anderson 1988, p. 34), I incorporate a number of in-class exercises which allow students to interact with each other and foster the thinking process as well as oral communication skills. Third, since many students are concerned with their future careers and liberal arts colleges are not vocational schools, I try to give my students many opportunities to improve their problem-solving skills which will not only give them an edge in the job market but will also help them to solve the ultimate problem of what they are going to do when they graduate.

THE BOMB SHELTER EXERCISE: A TANGLE OF FACTS

Most introductory students have a difficult time thinking about how societies are organized and conceptualizing societies as concrete "things" with "parts" that move and change. Fewer still can immediately grasp the notion that a society, like an individual, has certain needs. Yet, this way of thinking about societies is necessary for students to understand the role institutions play in the ultimate problem of societal organization. To foster this understanding and to sharpen students' critical thinking skills, I have incorporated a modification of the "Who Shall Survive" exercise originally developed to tap group decision making skills. In this exercise I divide my class into several groups of 4–5 students. I read the following scenario and distribute the fact sheet below to each student:

> The much feared nuclear war has become a reality. The entire world has been destroyed, except for 15 people in a remote bomb shelter in Northern Canada. No technological advances remain. It will be months before radiation drops to levels safe enough for plant life to reappear. Unfortunately, only enough food remains to support 7 people. Your task is to decide who of these 15 people shall survive. The decision should be based on insuring skills needed to keep the human race from becoming extinct.
>
> *Dr. Dane:* 39, white, no religious affiliation. Ph.D. in History, college professor, good health, married, one child (Bobby), active and enjoys politics.
>
> *Mrs. Dane:* 38, white, Jewish, A.B. and M.A. in Psychology, counselor in mental health clinic, good health, married, one child (Bobby), active in the community.

Bobby Dane: 10, white, Jewish, mentally retarded with IQ of 70, special education classes for 4 years, good health, enjoys pets.

Mrs. Garcia: 33, Spanish American, Roman Catholic, 9th grade education, cocktail waitress, prostitute, good health, married at 16, divorced at 18, abandoned as a child, in foster home as a youth, attacked by foster father at age 12, ran away from home, returned to reformatory until 16, has one child (Jean).

Jean Garcia: 3 weeks old, Spanish American, good health, nursing for food.

Mrs. Evans: 32, black, Protestant, A.B. and M.A. in Elementary Education, teacher, divorced, 1 child (Mary), good health, cited as an outstanding teacher, enjoys working with children.

Mary Evans: 8, black, Protestant, 3rd grade, good health, excellent student.

John Jacobs: 13, white, Protestant, 8th grade, honor student, very active, broad interests, father was a Baptist minister.

Mr. Newton: 25, black, good health, claims to be an atheist, started last year of medical school but suspended, homosexual activity, seems bitter concerning racial problems, wears new wave clothes.

Mrs. Clark: 28, black, Protestant, college graduate in Engineering Electronics, engineer, married, no children, good health, enjoys outdoor sports and stereo equipment, grew up in the ghetto.

Sister Mary Kathleen: 27, white, Nun, college graduate, English major, grew up in upper middle class neighborhood, good health, father was a businessman.

Mr. Blake: 51, white, Mormon, high school graduate, mechanic, "Mr. Fixit," married, four children (not with), good health, enjoys outdoors and working in his shop.

Miss Harris: 21, Spanish American, Protestant, college senior, nursing major, good health, enjoys sports, likes people.

Fr. Frenz: 37, white, Catholic, college plus seminary, priest, active in civil rights, criticized for liberal views, good health, former college athlete.

Dr. Gonzales: 66, Spanish American, Catholic, medical doctor in general practice, has had 2 heart attacks in past five years but continues to practice.

After reading this scenario I remind my students that each person in their group must be in total agreement of the choices. About 15–20 minutes before the class ends I ask each group to list their choices on the board, then to explain why they chose that particular person. I make a running list of reasons on the blackboard. In my concluding comments I tell my students that they have just uncovered the needs of a society and that social institutions such as the family, the economy, the political system, religion and education have evolved to meet societal needs. I also remind them that the last third of the course is devoted to examining these five institutions in detail.

CULTIVATING COHERENCE IN PERSPECTIVE

It is interesting to see the processes students use in making their choices. The first few minutes are typically spent reading over the list of survivors and making some tentative choices of people to eliminate immediately. The first criterion students use to ensure the survival of the human race is the survivors' ability to procreate. Almost every group "nukes" Mr. Newton who is described as a "homosexual. . . ." Comments such as "He can't do much good here" and "He won't do it" are quite commonplace among groups. The second person usually to be eliminated is 10 year old, mentally retarded Bobby Dane. Yet doing away with Bobby is not as easy as nuking Mr. Newton, for Bobby's parents are also survivors. Dr. Dane is a history professor and Mrs. Dane is a counselor and students begin to wonder how the Danes will react if their son is killed. This dilemma gets students thinking about the fact that societal needs involve more than just the ability of its members to procreate. Life must have quality and there are survivors who have skills which will improve the quality of life in the bomb shelter. Some groups decide to keep one or both of the Danes and claim that Dr. Dane's knowledge of history is needed to prevent a war in the future and that his leadership ability is needed to keep the group moving in the right direction. Mrs. Dane is valued for her counseling background and skills to keep the survivors from killing each other or going crazy. Other groups decide to do away with the entire Dane family, despite their assets and rationalize that Dr. Dane "is a history professor and is boring" or that Mrs. Dane, at 38, "is too old to have kids" or is genetically inferior since she already has one retarded son.

ASSESSING COMPLEX RELATIONSHIPS

At this point the groups usually begin thinking about health and well-being and begin to focus on those survivors with a medical background. Dr. Gonzales seems like a good choice until the groups discover that he is in his 60s and has heart problems. Most groups favor the young nursing student and some groups ask me if they can keep Dr. Gonzales on until he teaches Miss Harris more about medicine and fathers a child. "Can we keep him for awhile—he'll probably have a heart attack while he's 'doing it' with Miss Harris, then we'll be back down to seven." I always respond by saying that only seven people can be supported and an eighth person would cause someone to go hungry.

Now that the groups are thinking about skills beyond procreation, the need for technology becomes a concern. Mr. Blake is usually picked as a survivor because he is nicknamed "Mr. Fixit" and has a background in mechanics. Also high on the list of survivors is Mrs. Clark who has a college degree in Engineering Electronics. An added boon is that Mrs. Clark is 28 and capable of bearing children. Mr. Blake is 51 but in good health and some of the groups match these two up as a couple.

Throughout this exercise age becomes a concern. Students do not want to let old people survive for fear they will die before they can contribute to the survival of the group. Yet, what constitutes "too old" varies even within the same group. Mr. Blake, for example, is not "too old" at age 51 yet Fr. Frenz, a Catholic priest, is deemed to be "too old" to father children at age 37, despite being a former athlete. Perhaps this is due to the celibacy vows Catholic priests must take. As one group stated, "He's too old and since he's never done it before he's too old to learn." Some groups automatically cross off Fr. Frenz and Sr. Kathleen for they feel that, although they may have some skills to offer, they will be a burden because of their refusal to have children. Other groups, grappling with the decision to kill Mrs. Dane the counselor, decide to keep Fr. Frenz for his seminary training (which usually includes counseling skills) and make a special rule which states that he can give up his celibacy vows for the greater good of the survivors. These students usually add that Fr. Frenz will be very happy about this arrangement!

Concerns about age can also be seen in the debate over whether to keep three week old Jean Garcia. Jean is the daughter of Mrs. Garcia who is also one of the 15 survivors. Mrs. Garcia is 33, had a difficult life as a child and is a prostitute. Despite her background most groups see her a valuable member of the shelter for she "knows how to do it" and can keep the men happy. Yet, her daughter is still breast-feeding and will not be able to contribute to the survival of the group for some time. No group has ever chosen Jean as one of the seven survivors, for others are deemed to be more valuable. A few of the groups, however, have tried to sneak Jean in as the eighth person and claim that since she is still breast-feeding, she is not consuming any of the food. This dilemma, along with that of the Danes makes some groups concerned over the problem of keeping families intact. Some groups adopt a "Guppy Breeding" model and count up the number of males and females among the seven survivors. To maximize the number of children born, these groups include more females than males (usually 2 males and 5 females) and assign the surviving males the job of studs. These groups unanimously choose 13 year old John Jacobs as one of the males for this task. Other groups adopt a "family" model and are concerned with pairing up certain individuals. These groups tend to keep 3 males and 4 females.

TOLERANCE: LEAVING ROOM
FOR DIFFERENCES

A small number of groups are concerned with making sure at least one of the seven survivors has a strong religious background. When asked why, these groups state that having someone who can teach morals is important. An even smaller number of groups are concerned with making sure there are some black and hispanic survivors in the group. Usually these groups have at least one minority student participating, yet for them the ultimate goal is a melting pot, where biracial or multiracial babies will be born.

Finally, groups become concerned with the ability of the survivors to teach the future children and begin looking for someone with an education degree. Mrs. Evans is usually chosen for her outstanding teaching abilities and her capacity to procreate. The fact that she has an eight year old daughter who is an excellent student is an added plus. Mary Evans is also picked as a survivor and most groups make some comment about pairing John Jacobs with Mary for future children.

INDUCTIVE THINKING TO SOCIAL THEORY

As one can see, solving the problem of who shall survive to insure the continuation of the human race is no easy task. Most groups grapple with their choices for at least half an hour and yet, the vast majority of groups come up with similar choices and use similar techniques to solve this problem.

In the data generating stage of critical thinking, students must use their working theory to develop concrete alternatives to solve a problem. Many processes can be used to generate solutions yet each solution must be evaluated and this often leads to more ideas or a revision of the working theory. Thinking is very much a process and my students tend to use inductive processes to solve the problem of societal organization.

My students begin this exercise with limited information about what it takes for a society to survive. The introduction to the bomb shelter exercise hints at only one societal need, the replacement of deceased members through procreation. Thus, the first choices my students make involve identifying survivors that have the physical reproductive capacity to bear children. Yet, as I have shown earlier, simply stopping at this point does not produce an adequate solution since more than seven survivors fit these criteria. Now students are faced with making further eliminations and start to make inferences about other societal needs. Their inferences are by no means orderly and their criteria for judging the worth of any one survivor is not spelled out beforehand. Rather most groups waffle back and forth over each survivor developing a set of criteria as they go until the magic number seven is reached. At every decision students must evaluate their working set of criteria and it is precisely here where they begin to develop a set of societal needs.

The concluding part of this exercise reaffirms my students' ideas about societal needs. Since no one group has identified all the societal needs, keeping a running list on the board helps students to see the areas they have overlooked. In my typical introductory class of 35, the seven or eight groups together usually identify at least one need which each of the five institutions (family, economy, politics, education, religion) arise to meet. Later on in the course, when we examine each institution in detail, one of the first questions I ask my students is "What are the functions of this institution? In other words, what does this institution do for society?" As a result of this exercise, my students need only to think back to their decisions on who shall survive to formulate their answers.

REFERENCES

Kolb, David et al. (1979) *Organizational Psychology: An Experiential Approach.* 3rd ed. Prentice Hall, Inc., Englewood Cliffs, NJ.

Rubano, Gregory, and **Philip M. Anderson**. (December 1988). "Reasoning and Writing with Metaphors." *English Journal*, pp. 34–37.

Wolfe, Donald, and **David A. Kolb**. (1979). "Career Development, Personal Growth and Experiential Learning." In Kolb et al. (eds.) *Organizational Psychology: A Book of Reading*. 3rd ed. Prentice Hall, Inc., Englewood Cliffs, NJ, pp. 535–563.

RICHARD JENSETH

Analyzing the Languages of Gender

> Every thinker puts some portion of an
> apparently stable world in peril and no one
> can wholly predict what will emerge in its
> place.
>
> *John Dewey*, Experience and Nature

I would like to describe an extended assignment sequence I developed for my introductory writing courses which invites students to think critically about what I call "the languages of gender"—those various symbolic activities which to some degree shape the way men and women in our culture understand themselves and each other. Before I get to the specifics of this sequence, however, let me say something about the theoretical and pedagogical premises which inform it.

A SOCIAL-EPISTEMIC ORIENTATION TO CRITICAL THINKING

First, this pedagogy assumes that writing is a way of learning as well as a way of communicating what is learned. Though students write in a variety of modes and for a variety of aims and audiences, ungraded exploratory writing, done in class and out, plays an especially important role. Some of this writing is shared, some not. Some is workshopped and revised, most not. Students keep all writing in a course portfolio to be turned in at semester's end. Revisions to drafts show the evolution of a student's thought.

Second, there is the importance of the sequencing activity itself. As I characterize it here, assignment sequencing involves the deliberate arrangement of writing, reading and speaking activities around some intellectual issue or problem, one worthy of sustained analysis from multiple perspectives. Each task assumes (and often refers to) the previous, and anticipates the next, which gives the sequence a cumulative effect. As they weave their way through the sequence, students are asked to reflect upon what they have said before, to see ideas from yet another angle of vision, and to question previous conclusions. In other words, students are invited to learn from their own learning, and from the learning of their classmates.

Finally, let me briefly mention the broader theoretical assumptions which underlie this entire critical activity. To use James Berlin's terms, this sequence begins in a social-epistemic orientation to language and knowledge: language is not a transparent or neutral mirror of the "real world," nor is it simply a convenient way to talk about a reality which exists "out there," independent of our experience. Rather, language is the primary means by which "worlds" are created, by us, in our daily encounters with the flux of experience. Language creates the world, says Berlin "by organizing it, by determining what will be perceived and not perceived, by indicating what has meaning and what is meaningless" (57). If we know the world only indirectly, through our various symbolic representations, it follows that the *way* we represent the world to ourselves to some extent determines the world we can know, which in turn determines who we can be and how we can act in that world. One aim of this course, then, is to help students recognize something of the power language has in and over their lives, and to instill in them what Vincent Leitch calls "a vigilance about language—its productions, slipages, congealings" (24).

AN EPISTEMIC SEQUENCE: WHY DOES "SEXIST" LANGUAGE MATTER (AND WHO SAYS SO)?

Now to the critical pedagogy which attempts to enact some of these theoretical concerns. This sequence began when I brought into class a sampling of "rules" on sexist language from various handbooks and official guidelines (from the National Council of English and Modern Language Association, for example). Typically, these guidelines present two columns of words:

DON'T	The average American loves his coffee.	DO	The average American loves coffee.
NO	fireman	YES	fire-fighter
NO	man and wife	YES	husband and wife

I asked everyone to study the guidelines carefully and then to react to them in a piece of informal writing, done out of class. I wasn't sure exactly where all this would lead us, but I had guessed they would greet these official recommendations with indifference—as something only a dedicated feminist (or liberal English professor) would take seriously. Instead, far from being bored or mildly amused, they were frustrated and angry. "Come on! How does 'chairman' hurt anybody?" insisted one male student. "It's too picky," said a female writer. "If a woman wants to be a fireman, who's stopping her? Who worries about a word?" Many were especially angered by the voice of the guidelines, which they saw as pushy and dismissive. "Personally, I take offense when someone tells me my language is wrong, and that my common everyday non-sexist words offend them," said one male writer. "Who do they think they are?" asked a female writer. "It makes you want to use the wrong word."

Somehow, what had been intended as constructive advice about language and society had become for these readers a showdown over authority: either they would submit to the authority of the text (and teacher) and stop using "wrong" words, or they would not. Rather than ignore or disguise this struggle, we made the showdown itself the first target of our critical reflection. Just what sort of a problem *is* sexist language? Why do some people take what one student sees as this "frivolous fussing" over "fireman" or "mankind" so seriously? Who grants handbooks, or teachers, or feminists authority over such matters? Why had these guidelines made people so angry and resentful?

As it turned out, our discussion and informal writing suggested that beneath their anger at those "pushy" guidelines lay a deeper frustration with "pushy" feminists (and liberal college professors) who always seem to be making demands about something. "When people start becoming offended when I say the word 'mankind' instead of 'humanity,' " offered a male student, "they need to get their life's priorities in order . . . there are things far more sexist and offensive in the world." Our dialogue and exploratory writing allowed us to further probe this anger, to unmask its disguises, to reflect upon its consequences. As we examined the form and the language of the guidelines—"arbitrary roles," "biased phrases," "victim of socialization"—they gradually began to experience how words and structures impose an order on experience, how they inevitably compose a version of reality—in this case a version incommensurate with their own. Inquired one suspicious critic, "Since when is sex arbitrary?"

REVISING THE GUIDELINES

Later, a two part writing assignment sent them back to re-see the handbook guidelines and what they had said about them. In part one, a senior editor of the handbook publisher assigned them to revise the guideline insert as they saw fit, eliminating examples they found unnecessary or too extreme, adding examples they felt more appropriate for today's student. They were also to revise the opening paragraph which explains the importance of the guidelines to students. The second part of the task was a formal report which explained to the senior editor (their boss) why they had made the changes they made.

After everyone had written several early drafts of their revised guidelines, we shared the results in small group workshops and in class discussions. As it turned out, most writers had focused first on changing the didactic "voice" in the opening paragraph. "Less preaching, more advice," one student critic said of her suggested revision. Most had also eliminated the *Yes No, Do Don't* format: "Not so naggy," offered one critic. As for the specifics of the guidelines, many students eliminated all but the most blatant examples of sexist language ("sweet young thing," "call my girl for the details"); most had pretty much ignored more subtle forms of sexual stereotyping. Said one female student, "The word 'man-made' does not suggest to me any sexism . . . the word simply means that [something] is artificial." Another female student offered that "today, when people say businessman or fireman, we know they mean man or woman, even if they don't say it." "Does that mean there is no problem here at all?" I asked. "Is it all a figment of this publisher's imagination?" They agreed not, and so we took time to reformulate our questions: What is sexist about sexist language? What is there about how language works that can help explain why sexist language matters to our lives? How is sexist language like (or unlike) other ways that language affects our lives?

PERCEPTIONS OF GENDER

We decided it might help to set our questions in a broader social and political context, so for the next few weeks we read and discussed articles on sex roles and media ("Television Advertising: The Splitting Image" by Martha Mannes), gender and childhood ("Down with Sexist Upbringing" by Letty Cottin Pogrebin and "Images of Relationships" by Carol Gilligan), and gender and work place discrimination (Pogrebin's "How to Make it in a Man's World" and "Gender, Status, and Feeling" by Arlie Russell Hochschild). We also analyzed persistent images of women in television shows and films: the unflappable Mrs Cleaver, dizzy but lovable Lucy, the tough-skinned (yet vulnerable) professional women on "LA Law" or "Hillstreet Blues." (My students were also quick to notice the persistent images of men on television, from the familiar tough-guy to the silly sitcom father.)

Once we had explored these contradictory or competing images, we went back to our larger questions: What difference do symbols make? Do such images, does language itself, mostly reflect our world as it is, or do they somehow shape that world? Rather than take on such big questions directly, the next several assignments examined the role of sex roles and stereotyping in their own lives. We started with a simple questionnaire:

Because I am a man, I must _____.
If I were a woman, I could _____.
Since I am a woman, I get to _____.
If I were a man, I would _____.

Once they had quickly responded in writing to a dozen such prompts, they wrote an informal essay which summarized and reflected upon what they had said. I gathered the writing and later shared representative responses with the class. In a sense, each writer had composed a kind of gender role "self-portrait," and our far reaching, lively workshops of the portraits allowed us to further probe the origins and the power of such conventions. Why can't men cry? Why are women expected to? Why are men expected to be brave? Why do "aggressive" women make men nervous?

Finally, the next writing assignment asked them to revise their initial responses to the questionnaire on sex-roles, but this time with a slightly different twist:

> Imagine that anthropologists visiting from some other land or time were to find what you have written. Try to help them see what sex roles actually are in 90s America (not what we wish they were like, and not what extremists on either side claim they are like).

The revisions allowed students to reflect critically about what they had said the first time. Many used the time to eliminate frivolous responses ("If I were a woman . . . I couldn't play pro hockey) and to further explore rich ones ("If I were a man . . . I would have to drive around lost for hours, too stubborn to ask for directions.") The task also encouraged critical reflection by insisting that they briefly interpret their responses for that reader from the future. For example, they had to lend some context to a man's response that "Since I am a man . . . I don't have to worry about figuring out day care, or feel guilty about leaving the kids," or a young woman's observation that "If I were a man . . . I could be sexually active without being considered a 'sleaze.' "

Eventually, our focus shifted to the role of language in other forms of discrimination or stereotyping. Prohibitions against less subtle forms of racial bias—words like "nigger" or "coloreds"—have become part of our unconscious cultural make-up. Yet, about a third of my all white students were surprised to hear (after being corrected by classmates) that many blacks find "negro" equally demeaning. Yes, to say "nigger" is to speak not just a word but a world, but how do we explain the sanctions against "negro"? Why do some blacks now prefer "Afro-American," or "person of color" to "black"? And here again, who decides, and why do people comply, or forget to comply, or deliberately refuse? As we shifted back to our own experience, an assignment asked them to collect and analyze all the "labels," good or bad, used to refer to themselves—"freshman," "nerd,"

"Christian," "teenager." Which have the most power for them, or over them? Which are assigned (and by whom?) but not gladly accepted?

CONCLUSION

In the last week of the sequence we returned to the handbook guidelines, not so much to add or delete particular examples as to reconsider the question with which we had begun our work together: What is sexist language—and who says so? I won't pretend we reached anything like a consensus; that was never the point of our critical enterprise. What we had created instead was a series of more powerful, more subtle questions, questions which begin to take account of the very real power that words have in and over our lives. Is the word "fireman" a problem because a handbook or writing teacher says so, or because it makes it harder to know a world in which women are free to fight fires for a living? Are our "assigned" roles at work or at home natural and inevitable, or are they socially constructed, learned, and therefore open to revision? Questions like these must indeed put some portion of our apparently stable world in peril.

WORKS CITED

Berlin, James. "Contemporary Composition: The Major Pedagogical Theories." *The Writing Teacher's Sourcebook.* Ed. Gary Tate and E.P.J. Corbett. New York: Oxford University Press, 1988. 47–59.

Leitch, Vincent. "Deconstruction and Pedagogy." *Writing and Reading Differently: Deconstruction and the Teaching of Composition and Literature.* Ed. Douglas Atkins and Michael Johnson. Lawrence, Kansas: University Press of Kansas, 1985. 16–25.

Elizabeth J. Stroble

Belief and Doubt: Testing Concepts in Religious Studies

> Methodological doubt is only half of what we need. Yes, we need the systematic, disciplined and conscious attempt to criticize everything no matter how compelling it might seem—to find flaws or contradictions we might otherwise miss. But thinking is not trustworthy unless it also includes methodological belief: the equally systematic, disciplined and conscious attempt to believe everything no matter how unlikely or repellent it might seem—to find virtues or strengths we might otherwise miss.[1]

Undergraduates entering religious studies classes at a public university are usually prepared to believe *or* doubt—not both. Their motives for enrolling in such courses are many: to reinforce prior convictions, to denounce disbelieving professors, to examine a particular tradition, to debunk religious faith, to satisfy liberal studies requirements. Few are ready to embrace the contraries in inquiry that Elbow labels the believing game and the doubting game. Without first believing, students are too prone to doubt—to reject anything "other," to hold to preconceptions, and simply to argue against discomfiting tenets without feeling their force. Belief and doubt are necessary to accomplish the important objectives of a course in religious studies, whether it be Introduction to Religion, Women and Religion, Islam or Contemporary Ethics. Students must do more than study "about religion"—recalling religions simply in terms of their leaders and characteristics. Rather, "studying religion includes studying about religions

---

[1] **Peter Elbow,** *Embracing Contraries: Explorations in Learning and Teaching* (New York: Oxford University Press, 1986), 257.

and teaching about how those who see the truth of life in their religion make their case."[2] Empathetic understanding and critical study, sympathy and objectivity, belief and doubt—the foundations for thought in a religious studies curriculum—but how can we urge both in our students? This chapter documents a writing to learn approach to that question.

WRITING TO LEARN IN THE RELIGIOUS STUDIES CURRICULUM

With funding from Northern Arizona University's Office of Professional Development and the Center for Excellence in Education, I have worked with several professors of religious studies to develop writing to learn assignments in the religious studies curriculum, for courses as divergent as Religion and Bioethics, History, of Religion and Politics in America, Phenomenology of Religion, and Religions of the World. After reviewing course syllabi and other sources on the content of the religious studies curriculum, I asked four professors to prioritize a list of 30 goals to identify the "very important" learnings for any undergraduate enrolling in a religion-related course. These six received the highest priority:

1. to acquire the basic terms, concepts, principles, and methods for understanding religion.
2. to comprehend contemporary society through a grasp of symbols, practices, and concepts of religion
3. to comprehend the significance of religious life in human existence
4. to gain an awareness of religious diversity
5. to comprehend the importance of religion in culture
6. to examine one's own values, assumptions, and biases

With these goals in mind, I developed and adapted a number of writing to learn assignments. All focused on using writing as a means of thinking, learning, and discovering. Here I will share the results of three assignments when they were tested in a Religion 311 Judaism class.

Religion 311

During the fall 1990 semester, Dr. Sandra Lubarsky tried several of these assignments in her Rel 311 class at Northern Arizona University. She adapted for her own purposes three of the writing to learn models for an exam question and for out-of-class papers. Her general goals for the class were to "examine in detail the religious tradition of Judaism," exploring

---

[2]**Martin Marty,** "Around Religion, About Religion, Of Religion, and Religion: The Issues in Public School Teaching Today," *Religion and Public Education* 15 (1988): 398.

the history, theology, and practice of Judaism. Seven students in the class agreed to provide me with copies of their exams and papers and to share their reactions to the writing assignments. Words from Daniel, Kim, Carla, Jared, Rosa, Helen, and Jennifer will measure the success of these writing to learn assignments.

WHY WOULDN'T THEY SAY? DISCOVERING INHERENT CONTRADICTIONS

These assignments ask students to explain why a named individual would *not* make an attributed statement. Students must comprehend how a tradition's believer would speak to detect the contradictions inherent in the attribution. In a twist on the believing and doubting games, students must envision a believer's position well enough to reject the false assertion. The writing task demands content mastery, thoughtful consideration of a tradition's tenets, and reasoned rebuttal of the quotation. Because students must know basic terms, concepts, and principles as well as comprehend the significance of a religion in the believers' lives, several of the "very important" objectives are addressed by these writing prompts. For the Judaism class Dr. Lubarsky adapted one of these assignments as a question on the midterm.

> Why wouldn't the following statement be made by a rabbi of the sixth century common era?
>
> "Since the fall of the Temple, we are like fish out of water."

Student reactions to this kind of test question, as opposed to her more straightforward questions (tracing the history of the Jews and the development of their ideas from Abraham to the Diaspora) were positive. Helen explained, "I liked the question because I'm thinking of my own justification and I'm still using the ideas we learned in class, but it's my ideas, so I like that because I can make more of a personal answer." Rosa felt that the question "made you use what you've learned in class and give your own insight on why a rabbi of the sixth century would or wouldn't do something as they would in another time." Students displayed these insights in their answers:

> *Daniel:* The statement would not be made by a rabbi of the sixth century because of the Prophetic message. . . . Most important the Prophetic message also says that they do not need priests but they need rabbis as teachers, they need to perform acts of loving kindness, but most importantly, they do not need a temple to worship because God is everywhere.
>
> *Jared:* One must study Torah and studying with a rabbi is replacing the priest. With the printing of the Mishrah, all people have access to

the discussions and to the scripture. So the Jews are not fish out of water, they are more adapted to the outside world than before.

Jennifer: God had given them all that they needed to worship him. They had the Torah, both written and oral. . . . It was their responsibility to study the Talmud, and to live a good life by following the teachings of the Talmud.

As Carla summarized, "you had to use creativity besides just textbook facts. You had to use textbook facts to get an answer but then you had to use knowledge and creativity to come up with backing for your answer, so I liked that question." By taking the perspective of sixth century Jews, students played the believing game and were able then to doubt the statement attributed to the speaker in the test question.

WRITE A REFERENCE: TAKING AN OBJECTIVE STANCE

While all of the assignments developed address at least one of the six "very important" goals, this kind is designed to help students comprehend society through a grasp of symbols, practices, and concepts of religion. Writing reference material requires not only knowledge but also the ability to highlight important information and to explain complex concepts to a nonconversant audience. Students must suspend disbelief to write a convincing entry; likewise, they must systematically doubt to document the symbols, practices, and concepts in an objective manner. For her Rel 311 class, Sandra gave this assignment as a topic choice for one of three letters that students write to her during the semester. Students could choose this assignment:

> The editor of a new reference book on Judaism has asked you to write the entry on "covenant." As you prepare this entry, draw on your knowledge of covenant gained through your reading of Genesis, Exodus, Amos, Fackenheim, and Buber.

Rosa's entry included these statements:

> The Jewish people, unlike other religions, don't claim to be the "only" people of God. They proclaim to be chosen by God but never say that other people can't be accepted by him. . . . God shows his love of all humanity through covenants given to different people at different times. He shows that just because Abraham was chosen to lead the people to the promised land, this does not establish them as any more deserving of God's love than the other people on earth.

Rosa believes that Dr. Lubarsky's purpose is to "make you think more about what you've learned." Helen added that the letter format is useful "since we have to put it in our own words in the form of a letter I think that it's more of my understanding of it than a paper would be because in a paper you're concerned with the format and everything." What did Helen learn from writing this reference entry? She learned "how Jews interpret their covenant with God." The significant feature of this assignment is the form and the audience. They require the student to understand an alien concept—in this case covenant in Jewish theology—well enough to explain it authoritatively for someone who may know little about it. Professionals who write articles for reference books are hired to bring their expertise and insight to the task without promoting dogmatic opinion. When students successfully adopt the professional voice, they learn an objectivity born of empathy and analysis.

Rosa, a non-Jew, shows an empathetic and analytical perspective on the covenant relationship. The postscript to her paper indicates the success of the writing assignment in leading Rosa to formulate her concept of the covenant for others:

> Dr Lubarsky, I know that this isn't exactly what a reference book would want as an introduction on the covenant but it is what I would like to tell people about what I have learned about the covenant so far in this class.

YOU DECIDE! WEIGHING DIFFICULT CHOICES

This writing assignment places students in decision-making situations. The prompts are based on contemporary issues that help students gain an awareness of religious diversity, to comprehend the importance of religion, and most importantly, to examine their values, assumptions, and biases. Interesting variations can be created by asking students to defend a position they do not hold or writing a response to a previous response from another person's point of view. Students are required to role play, take a position, and defend it. Sandra gave students this choice:

> You are a teacher in the public schools. The parents of a Jewish student request that if you are going to give attention to holidays such as Christmas and Easter, you also pay attention to Jewish holidays. What is your reaction? How would you defend your decision?

Two students wrote these comments in defense of teaching Christian and Jewish traditions.

> *Kim:* I gave this a great deal of thought. I never realized the possible subliminal messages I could instill by only representing one religion. . . .

> At the very least my students are going to learn that when they are unclear about something, they can read and study until they make up their minds.

Carla: I believe teaching the difference between religions is a good idea, but I also believe that many parents do not feel the same way. For this reason I plan on sending a letter to each parent explaining what I will be doing and if they feel strongly against this type of education, an alternate assignment will be given to their children. The purpose of teaching the differences is to "prepare the student for life."

Although neither of these students has taught, the writing prompt allows them to draw on their own public school experiences, place themselves in the role of teacher, and respond to parents' concerns with a new appreciation for religious diversity. No doubt their analysis of the situation is informed by their most recent experience with the academic, rather than apologetic study of religion. This kind of assignment, demanding persuasion instead of description, exposes biases and their bases quickly. It could serve well as a pre-and post-indicator of students' awareness of diverse religious traditions and their recognition of the need for non-sectarian treatment in secular environments.

CONCLUSION: BELIEF AND DOUBT IN RELIGION 311

As I worked with colleagues to develop consensus on religious literacy goals and to create the writing assignments sampled above, I was unsure how they would help professors and students accomplish their goals in a specific class. Sandra Lubarsky hoped her students would, among other objectives, "gain an informed understanding and appreciation of the complex dynamics of one religious tradition: to learn how a religious tradition responds to the demands of continuity and change." For Jewish and non-Jewish students, informed understanding and appreciation may prove demanding cognitive tasks. One topic choice designed by Sandra is particularly illustrative of the multiple perspectives students must assume to reach understanding and appreciation.

In the Jewish tradition, the Pharisees are held in the highest esteem. They are praised for their attention to Oral Torah, for their focus on intentionality (on "the heart" of the believer and not just the actions), for their conception of God as loving, etc. In the Gospel According to Matthew, the Pharisees are presented as "scribes" and a "brood of vipers." (Read Matthew 23.) What are we to make of these opposing descriptions? Why do you think that such different appraisals of the Pharisees exist? Do you think one is clearly right or wrong? Why or why not? If you were a leader in a Christian church, how would you present the Pharisees to your congregants?

A Christian student in the class explains how this assignment caused her to alternately doubt and believe Jewish and Christian teachings as she explains why she chose this topic:

I don't know. The one I chose was about the Pharisees and I don't know a lot about the way the Jews knew the Pharisees or know the Pharisees. All I knew was how we view the Pharisees. It was hard for me because as Christians we view the Pharisees as evil and wicked and Jews do not believe that and it was really hard for me to incorporate that into the paper. And I read it at first and thought I'm not going to do any of these but #1—that's what I'm going to do because that's my major and that's what I'm going to do. [#1 was the You Decide option.] But I read 4 and said I don't agree with this but maybe I should write why I believe and explain why I believe. And I had to read a lot, a lot of Matthew and John and Isaiah. I read a lot of Isaiah because the Jews how they believe that the Pharisees were good people but yet in Isaiah it was he already prophesied that they will become evil and the Jews said, no, no, they're not evil, and one of their prophets was saying so, that they were going to be even if they were not now. They will be. *So I had to kind of make that true to myself* that because what she was saying because they really did do a lot of great things for the Jews and I think that's great but I was kind of going back and forth you know and I was really getting confused on my religion and the Jewish religion and which one was right and I said no, no, I've got to really research it. *It opened my mind.*

Another non-Jew made this comment about the purpose of the letters:

are to look into why they think that way, not so much that we have to take everything that they believe is true but to understand where they came from and how it developed. There's an idea, for instance, Biblical, that's handed down through generations and that we kind of take them as true rather than evaluate them ourselves and look at the source and say is that what I really, really think or just what someone has told me? I had to try to *keep my eyes open to possibilities,* not that it has to be that way but it's a possibility that it didn't happen that way.

She went on to say this about class discussions:

But one thing about the class. I know I have to kind of like when I'm in the class and talking about Jewish-Christian relations I have to kind of I really have to concentrate on *taking myself out of my opinions* and placing myself in a different perspective like *placing myself as a Jew* because a lot of times I feel. I start to get defensive because I think it's really important in this class you have to go in with an open mind and be able to *kind of transform yourself.*

Embracing contraries—the purpose of each of these assignments—takes students beyond their initial motives for enrolling in a religious studies class. When students are asked to de-center, to see Jewish practice and beliefs from the perspective of Jewish history and theology, they must re-examine prior convictions. When students are asked to find incongruencies in religious assertions, they debunk inaccuracies rather than religious belief or unbelief. When students are asked to objectify a foundational concept, they examine a tradition for its internal validity and consistency rather than its consonance with their own beliefs. When students are asked to make informed decisions about issues of religious diversity, they satisfy liberal studies requirements in the best sense: they use knowledge to inform their world view. Embracing the contraries of belief and doubt—simultaneously accepting and questioning Jewish tradition—requires students to adjust preconceptions to accommodate new conceptions while assimilating the new conceptions to fit the newly examined preconceptions. The process causes some disequilibrium, but the result for these students, who were able to transform themselves, open their eyes to possibilities, take themselves out of their opinions, and make it true to themselves, was a greater understanding and appreciation of the Jewish tradition and of themselves.

NOTES

I acknowledge the influence and assistance of the following professors: John Bean, Richard Gelwick, Arne Hassing, Sandra Lubarsky, Stephen Sapp, Robert P. Scharlemann, Paul E. Stroble, Jr., and Warren Vinz. I also thank the students who participated in this study: Philip Cohen, Gayle Gemmill, Becky Hoffman, Liz McNeal, Monica Prerovsky, Bethann Smith, and Greta Swasey.

Louis H. Henry

Clustering, Writing, and Discussing Economic Issues

Sometimes it is difficult to distinguish between analytical and critical thinking. But analytical abilities are a necessary requirement for critical thinking. As a critic you need to be acquainted with the basic principles of what makes something good—be it good art, good literature, or good economic policy. Critical evaluation on any topic demands more than a knee-jerk version of "I don't know much about _____ but I know what I like." If you are going to criticize the economic policy of the Federal Reserve, for example, or the governor of your state, you first need to understand some principles of economic theory. Throw in some political and historical information, add a dash of fallacy-free thinking, and you are likely to come up with a decent analytical view of a particular policy. Thus the first requisite is the acquisition of knowledge, and then the use of that knowledge in concert with an ability to think analytically in general.

Economic theory—the way economists think (logical positivism prevails for the most part)—equips students with one such analytical tool, while, at the same time, it provides the knowledge to judge economic issues. In fact, economic thinking can be used to deal with some subjects seemingly far removed from the realm of the dismal science itself. Students, however, should be able to take this ability and go an extra step, that is, to question, analyze alternatives, interpret and, eventually, make independent judgments.

In my classes I use clustering and writing (a writing-to-learn technique), often coupled with small group discussion and debate, and an "analytical" format in the evaluation of an issue or problem. I have even used the combination of the writing-to-learn technique and the analytical format during an examination. (The students are primarily freshmen and sophomores in a principles of economics class.)

WRITING-TO-LEARN TECHNIQUES

As an avid disciple of the writing-across-the-curriculum (WAC) movement, I have used writing assignments and exercises both in and out of the classroom for about five years. While still using the old standby of transactional writing (term papers, position papers and the like), I have concentrated mostly on writing-to-learn procedures, especially journaling. Students write for themselves rather than for me.

My journal assignments are focused on specified topic or question and are used in class. Students state the material in their own words—questioning, evaluating, discovering, and integrating. For example, at the beginning of the semester I often ask students to journal on "economics." With this exercise I hope to allay some fears and prejudices that often accompany those eager faces before me. Preconceived notions can often sabotage their efforts so I use this journal entry as a takeoff for discussion on how "difficult," "boring," or "sinister" economics is. Later journal assignments are used to focus their thoughts on a particular question raised in class, or on a short news article related to the topic under discussion.

When I first learned of these writing strategies, I was delighted to discover that students' efforts do not necessarily have to be graded, an issue brought up most in faculty WAC workshops. Moreover, this type of writing is self-diagnostic. It is a way of getting in touch with a source of knowledge that is critical for true learning and creating. In this case, such writing comes with the double bonus of helping students learn how to think while making them better writers.

Clustering and Free Writing

The particular journaling technique I use has two parts. Part one is called clustering which is a free-association exercise with a word, idea, or art image. Clustering, then, involves the intuitive, non-linear modes of thinking, a so-called right brain activity. Part two taps the logical mode (left brain dominance), that is, students write a vignette inspired by the clustering. (See Figure 1.) Such in-class journaling, used for a few minutes, is designed to focus attention on a major theme of the day's topic and to provide a mechanism for improved retention.

I select a word, write it on the board, and draw a circle around it. Three steps are involved:

1. Students copy and encircle the word or statement in the upper quarter of a sheet of paper.
2. Without engaging the rational mind (thinking "what 'should' be written, what is expected, or what does the prof want?"), students begin a free association with the encircled word. They use the simple device

FIGURE 1

> It may sound strange that Greenspan makes me think of the bathtub, but that's where I read the article—until I fell asleep and nearly drowned! Greenspan, the chief of the Federal Reserve System, believes that the federal deficit does affect the economy in a bad way. By the government using up so much of the country's resources, it lowers investment which leads to a lower GNP (the "crowding out" effect). Is that what happens? At present we have a national debt that is over $3 trillion and the economy is slipping into a recession but can that be blamed solely on the deficit?

of drawing an arrow from the circle and writing the first word or words that come to mind. Students may also think of a word related to the "second" word and may construct a chain of associated words. I urge them to shoot the cluster words in all directions from the circle in order to avoid being in a linear thinking mode, that is, making lists or constructing logical outlines.

3. At some point, an urge to write occurs. It usually involves one of the connections that was made during the clustering exercise—an important train of thought that emerged. It is not necessary to write about every word or idea that is put on paper. This brief writing exercise may take the form of a few paragraphs or just one; it may come out as a poem, a short story or dramatic scene.

The class usually spends six to ten minutes on the entire exercise. Students do not have to write in the context of the discipline. They simply react to the word, write about its meaning, and perhaps focus their minds in the direction desired by the instructor.

The hypothesis, put simply, is that students will better understand and retain a concept if the right brain mode is also brought into the picture. The cluster word is chosen to perform a dual role: as a key recall word and a key comprehension word.

The dual process of clustering and writing enables students, then, to focus on a topic first by tapping into an emotional or intuitive reaction and then by writing about it, which involves the logical functions of thinking. The exercise often reveals to students opinions of which they had been unaware, insights that are new to them, and facts and ideas long forgotten. Most importantly for present purposes, through such exercises students begin the analytical thinking process. For example, in Figure 1, the cluster word "Greenspan" elicited an interesting response from one student. Clearly the student is moving from a point of apathy to one of interest and inquiry—the *sine qua non* of analytical thinking.

However important free association and free writing are in the process, though, they do not necessarily result in a brilliant piece of analytical thinking. To address this issue, I turned to two additional techniques, namely, small group discussion and a structured "analytical format" for analytical writing.

SMALL GROUP DISCUSSION AND ANALYTICAL WORKSHEET

At first I tried small group discussion centered around a short news article. Groups of four or five students discussed the assigned issue, took a position, and selected a spokesperson. Each group was heard from in turn and debate and discussion ensued. The activity was most lively at times and it was especially delightful to overhear principles students arguing about economic issues and using the jargon—actually verbalizing economics! I once read that the more senses involved, the greater the learning outcome. So here students were listening to economics, writing about it, reading it, and now speaking it. Unfortunately, some of the opinions resulted in some of the best examples of economic quackery I've heard in a long time—and some of the fuzziest thinking on economic and social issues imaginable!

As a result, before small group discussion, I now ask the students to first cluster and write a response to an article or idea and then to spend a few minutes on a simple analytical worksheet—a one page questionnaire with small spaces between each question for their responses. Last semester I used the following five questions:

1. What is the main idea of this assignment?
2. How does the author support the idea? Mention at least three facts.
3. Can you identify any weaknesses in the argument?
4. How would you argue against the main point?
5. Note any instances of bias, propaganda, or fallacious thinking contained in the assignment.

The results in general were fairly good. As a matter of fact, for the goals of analytical thinking, the results were far superior to those attained by the journal assignments and small group discussions without the worksheet's structure. Nonetheless, the journaling and the group discussion remain a vital part of the exercise; they bring in the added elements of free thinking and writing for insight as well as the synergy of group interaction. Connect these with some structure, add a bit of knowledge and voila! straight, clear-thinking undergraduates! In the assignment noted above, for example, after having read Alan Greenspan's article, "Deficits Do Matter," the students clustered "Greenspan," and completed the worksheet and its five questions. They also had read material that took the opposing view. The assignment for this particular question was simply first to cluster and write on "Greenspan" on the reverse side of the worksheet and then to complete the worksheet. One student's clustering efforts have already been noted in Figure 1.

After the students clustered "Greenspan," they completed the worksheet. Admittedly, it was very difficult to "identify any weaknesses in the argument" or to "note instances of bias or propaganda or fallacious thinking" in the work of such a prestigious author as Alan Greenspan. Thus I pointed out that he does have a political point of view and that not all theorists agree with him on many points.

So encouraged, most students made an excellent effort on the "weaknesses" question by noting the other side of the question; for example, as one student wrote:

> Deficit spending can also have an expansionary effect on the economy, an important point during a recession when private investment is lacking and one doubts whether or not there is a crowding out effect.

There were valiant efforts too to critically evaluate the piece by pointing to biases, propaganda and fallacious thinking such as the following three excerpts:

> The appeal to patriarchal pride is propaganda to gain support for his views. It works.

> The comparison to the Japanese saving rate misleads since the Japanese are known for their recent high rate of growth and for savings rates that are culturally based.

> The use of highly negative language and making it seem so personal to us is good writing style for his purposes, but it is still propaganda.

It was a good exercise in that the students were deliberately looking for counterarguments, for biases, for manipulative language, and, after considering these issues, were able to come to a position of agreement or disagreement with Greenspan.

In general, then, to facilitate analytical thinking I rely on exercises that focus on both logical and intuitive modes of learning. Specifically, by coupling a writing-to-learn task with a structured or analytical instrument, and following through with small group discussion and debate, I see considerable improvement in the way students can size up an issue and effectively analyze and critique it.

Chapter 3

Examining Ideas and Relationships: Theory Testing Processes

‌In earlier chapters we described how the mind reorganizes and interprets information flowing in through the senses. In this section, we will look at thinking that occurs independent of the senses, resulting in new ideas or new ways to think about problems. Once ideas are alive in the mind—becoming aspects of prior knowledge—we can move them with great speed and flexibility into novel patterns, proposing relationships and imagining new ways of viewing the world. Writing, painting, design, medical diagnosis and treatment, and most other creative acts begin with movement among ideas in the mind. In its ability to move concepts and visions into new patterns, the mind achieves its insight and creative power.

MOVEMENT IN A HYPOTHETICAL UNIVERSE: WHAT IF?

Once we have developed a set of ideas, we can begin moving those ideas around, asking new questions, testing relationships, thinking hypothetically, imagining alternatives, and projecting different visions of the future. Free of its reliance on sensory data, the human mind can manage its ideas without constraint. Free of external stimulation,

We can juxtapose distinct ideas to create a new one.
We can speed time and view invisible forces working to shape events.
We can create visions of a future that does not yet exist, and then imagine ways to bring that future into being.

The human mind does not depend on information from experience in the physical universe. It can create experience in its own right. "What if?" is the creative question. Thinking hypothetically, we ask questions that can change our universe and our experience of it.

To focus on the power of the mind to create and manage ideas of different kinds, let us take an imaginary journey to the beach. Any of us can imagine a beach at twilight, creating whatever vision we would prefer to behold—sand, sun, and water brought together for our own pleasure. Let us look out over the water. Sunlight streams in over sunset clouds, a dancing chimera of gold on the waves. Our minds can "see" water and sand, no matter where we are actually sitting. Bored with that prospect, any of us can import some background music; for some, a string quartet from behind a dune; for others the Beatles playing Eleanor Rigby. We don't need an orchestra to hear such music. We can imagine walking on this imaginary beach. Some of us might use the golden sunset moment to imagine the tug of the moon that brings the tide up the sand. We can speed and "see" this imagined tide more accurately than we could actually observe creeping tidal motion in the ocean. Moving further toward abstraction, a few of us might connect the idea of tides of the concept of gravity, an invisible physical force shaping the sphere of the earth itself. We can stand on an imagined moon and "see" that earth from a distance. From that hypothetical perspective, a few of us might want to multiply the idea of gravity by a factor of X and imagine all of this—sand, sun, sound, and tide—collapsing into an infinitely dense speck that a few others might then name a "black hole." In fact, no human has seen such thing as a black hole; still, we can all imagine one to think about. Miracles such as black holes take eons to evolve in the physical universe; in the modeled universe of the mind, a few seconds will do. Moving ideas in the mind can generate extraordinary insight and creativity.

LANGUAGE AS METAPHOR

In the strictest sense, the process of thinking is a process of managing metaphors. To the extent that all language is a metaphor for experience, all learning requires metaphoric thinking. Bill Eddy, who teaches Environmental Studies at the University of Vermont and provides Public Radio with commentaries on culture, has traced this sense of the word to its Greek origins:

> The word metaphor, itself, can be traced back to two Greek terms—"meta" meaning across or beyond—and a second term "Pherein" spelled with an initial P-h sound which was the Greek verb "to carry" or "bear," and later showed up in English as "ferry." A ferry boat is one designed to carry or bear passengers. It also showed up in the final syllable of the English word "transfer." A metaphor, then, carries or transfers meaning from one sense experience to another. Thus, it makes possible entirely new ways of seeing and interpreting experience.—something that poets have been especially good at for a long time. It is a peculiarly human capacity of which most of us are completely unconscious. . . . So words might be described as verbal images for non-verbal sense experiences. It is interesting then to consider that the sensory data that come from the world around us have been the same for all humans everywhere. It is the interpretation of those data that has given us such widely differing views of reality—interpretations shaped by the meta-

phors of the particular language inside our minds to create very different worlds outside. (Vermont Public Radio, March 1991)

We use familiar words to examine the unfamiliar. We use what we know as a platform for understanding what we cannot yet understand. We use our mental models to imagine changing the world of physical experience.

What are the representational languages the mind uses to construct its metaphoric world? Literature relies on spoken sounds and written symbols. Physics relies on spacial languages and mathematics. Music, clearly, focuses on patterns in sound and may note them in ink on paper. Chemistry has devised its own notation system, based in algebra. History has relied on written record, but has also turned toward other artifacts of culture. Sociology has borrowed from both literature and mathematics. Computer science has recently provided mediating languages for all the disciplines. The academic disciplines, such as literature, physics, and psychology, seek symmetry and "truth"; the applied sciences and professions, such as journalism, engineering, and counseling, borrow parts of language and method from the disciplines and apply them to problem solving in human experience. In each discipline and applied area, the use of language is guided by "rules," ways we have learned to express relationship.

Ideas, represented in one or more language systems, make up the universe of the mind. Protected from the tumult of experience by the bony fortress of the skull, the human brain is an organ built to play with abstractions. Locked in its protective case, the mind cannot work directly with the physical environment. (It needs muscle and bone for that.) Left to its own devices, instead, it reduces all things to representations. Images, sounds, words, algebraic equations, geometric figures, and rhetorical patterns may have little in common—except that they are tools for the mind to use in modeling experience. Clearly, the more the universe of the mind reflects the actual workings of the universe, the more power the individual can exert over physical experience.

RECONSTRUCTING IDEAS

Most of the academic disciplines have developed a vast structure of concepts that they use to describe relationships in some section of the physical universe. English teachers use words such as theme, tone, motif, and structure to signify connections in a text-based universe. Sociologists may describe how an "identity" is negotiated through "interactions" with "significant others" in the universe of group relationships. In geometry, mathematicians may distinguish between concrete figures with specific constructions and dimensions, and an even more abstract world in which they conspire to merge postulates and theorems into proofs. In some fields, such as art and music for example, dominant concepts remain flexible and adaptable to the individual thinker. In other fields, such as mathematics and chemistry, concepts and their relationships are prescribed more exactly to support reliability and communication.

An expert in any field may have no trouble moving swiftly around an elaborately constructed universe, woven entirely of concepts and their relationships. Novices in those same fields may have to experiment carefully with one idea at a time.

When we asked our undergraduates to describe theory testing processes in their own disciplines, most students recognized the powerful influence our conceptions have on our decisions and actions. One English major developed a metaphor from common experience to explain a process he saw as pervasive in human experience.

> Sometimes thinking shapes our experience. We think of things before they happen in order to alter reality. One puts a saucer under a tea cup because of his past experience drinking tea. What we are able to think about is expanded by relating two or more old concepts to make a new one. (Steve Cobb [English])

Like Steve, other students saw the source of ideas in inductive thinking, but also recognized the power of the mind to reshape ideas or create new ones once a few ideas were in place.

> Theory testing allows us to confirm what we build in inductively. This is a time when the student is a critic of what he/she has accomplished so far. By questioning her/his own work, the student becomes aware not only of what needs to be changed but *how* it might be changed. (Marci Foster [Environmental Studies])

In environmental studies, the network of relationships one assumes active in any setting directs the approach one takes in solving problems.

Remaking ideas can be carried out with almost absolute freedom, an idea that did not escape most art students. Still, as Amy King pointed out, the ostensible freedom of making something new is most productive when governed by self-conscious control.

> Thinking in art is not a linear process. Spontaneity and individuality are both important aspects to the creative process. It is these factors that cause art to seem free. The emphasis on freedom to change your mind, make mistakes and define your own goals masks the rigid steps of the thinking process. This is what makes art human, and what makes it fun, above all. (Amy King)

How can we teach students to refine the ideas they already hold or test the relationships among ideas they are learning? Students such as Sarah recognized the challenge implied when we throw one idea up against another:

> Rereading an author with new knowledge would be a way of enabling students to test their theories and abstract thoughts. Comparing works from different authors, eras and societies would also be a reader's form of theory

testing. Journal entries can encourage the skills of theory testing, making arguments against an author's idea or theme. (Sarah Rutledge [English])

Even in the fluid universe of the mind, connecting ideas and creating new ones is as active a process as a form of inductive thinking, but without the props provided by verifiable fact.

MANAGING THE INTERNAL UNIVERSE

Cognitive psychologists have begun to refer to these mental models as *schemata*, complex networks including broad concepts, causal assumptions, and procedural scripts—as well as a vast repository of specific images, sounds and feelings—all linked in a vast network of connections. In thinking about a subject, we usually activate not just one facet of what our minds may hold, but the whole glowing network of related ideas. Learning to think effectively involves learning to control movement among connected ideas in the modeled universe of the mind.

Some part of the mental models we create are constructed inductively from experience, through processes described in the preceding chapters. It is likely, for example, that most of us construct a schema for the concept of female largely by induction—from extensive contact with females who may vary quite wildly in most characteristics, but who share some attributes. We import other general concepts, however, from the storehouse of assumptions established by our culture. We have probably imported concepts such as "military industrial complex," "global warming," and "deconstructionism" from the general culture or from some individual whose experience allowed him or her to induce them originally. Thankfully, just a few of us take the time to induce and disseminate intricate models for narrow bands of experience. Then, the rest of us can use both our induced abstractions and imported abstractions to better model the world in which we operate. Our models tell us what we can expect from experience—and let us imagine what we may want to change (see Figure 3.1).

CONSTRUCTING IDEA NETWORKS

In early learning, the things we abstract for our minds to manage have direct equivalents in experience. We learn to read by holding books. We learn to count by stacking blocks. We learn science by watching mealworms or tugging ropes through pulleys. In high school and college learning, students struggle increasingly to connect ideas that may not have any direct equivalent in their experience: bell curves and literary themes and power vectors. More perplexing, they have to manipulate these abstractions skillfully in order to create ideas or solve increasingly complex problems. Complex mental models can give the individual extraordinary powers of critical analysis and creative thought.

Within each discipline or applied area, the languages bring order and great power. Across the disciplines, however, the whole edifice of the school or university appears chaotic. All too often, chaos is what students experience in trying to learn. The ordinary school or college curriculum asks students to do something few teachers would dare to do—to cross the boundaries dividing disciplines and applied sciences three to eight times a day. At every border crossing, the governing language and its rules change. In three to ten minutes, we expect a student to leave literature class and begin a mathematics class. In literature, we expect students to use a verbal language to discover connections in text. In mathematics, we expect the same student to use another symbol system to solve specific problems. Literature classes are often conducted under the rules of induction—gather pieces until you can fashion a coherent whole. Mathematics classes are often taught as deductive exercises—select a rule and its procedures that will solve this set of specific instances. We cannot expect students to make these endless crossings without guidance. The teacher in a content area must be both a language instructor and a guide to the rules that govern invention in the established culture of a discipline. If teachers can show students how to construct better models for the world in which they live, the students may learn more efficiently—and gain control over a wider spectrum of human experience.

TEACHING STUDENTS TO MANAGE IDEAS

Seeing learning as managing ideas is not an easy step for any student. Because our world is most tormented by complex problems, rather than simple ones, learning to manage complex ideas is enormously important. At the high school and college levels, students need to move away from the belief that learning is an act of memory, if only because abstract rules, principles, theories, laws, social forces, trends, and other aspects of mental modeling have become essential to successful problem solving.

The teachers who wrote articles for this chapter have all discovered ways to teach students to examine ideas and relationships. Some have sought to teach critical analysis of ideas. Others teach their students to create new ways of thinking. We have grouped their strategies as they respond to three challenges in examining ideas and relationships:

1. Making metaphor: The challenge of seeking out familiar metaphors for unfamiliar ideas
2. Expanding ideas: The challenge of testing important relationships among ideas and assessing their implications
3. Creating new vision: The challenge of fashioning new ideas for use in solving problems (See Figure 3.1.)

FIGURE 3.1   Teaching students to manage ideas

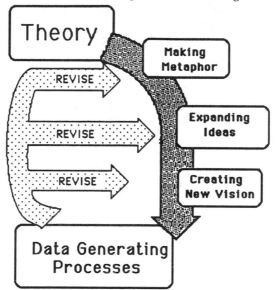

As in previous chapters, we have tried to mix disciplines to show that a particular kind of thinking is not necessarily the province of a specific content area.

Making Metaphor

Thomas W. Rishel recognized how hard it is to teach geometry as if the material were all new. Teaching postulates and theorems as if they descended from the sky simply confirms a student's sense of helplessness at the border crossing between life and mathematics. What if geometry is just a metaphor for common experience? Rishel sends his students outside the classroom to look again at what they already know—the campus of Cornell University. In the familiar they may spot the abstracted patterns that can bring unusual power to the human mind.

In teaching literature, Phillip Anderson and Gregory Rubano saw that their discussions of literature stalled easily because students had little prior knowledge to use in interpreting classical texts, if they read to interpret at all. Why not teach students to use provocative but common metaphors as a doorway to character analysis? If students can recognize the resemblance between a character in Shakespeare and objects from daily life, they can also search the text more efficiently to extend that metaphor.

Charles Garoian uses metaphor to introduce critical analysis in the art museum at Penn State University. To begin critical analysis, his students do not stand back and analyze a work of art from critical distance. First they create a personal work of art or demonstration that reflects their sense of what the artist is trying to show. In front of the class, they first explain their own work, a metaphor for the unfamiliar painting or sculpture. Then, they turn to the artist in question and present a lecture to the rest of the class.

Diana Mayer Demetrulias uses metaphor to expand her students' understanding of statistics. Memorizing formulae and working through problems failed to teach statistical concepts. Metaphor shows students the distinctive elements that make different statistical concepts useful. What if students were asked to see different statistical tests as members of one family? How would different statistical tests respond to calamity? By using familiar ideas as a base, she devised a method for helping students understand difficult concepts—and their relationship.

Expanding Ideas

Camille Blachowicz recognized that the vocabulary of a content area is the key to model making in any content area. Asking students to memorize vast lists of words, however, is counterproductive. The students who most need the words have the least success with that process. Also, a list of memorized words disguises the relationships that give power to ideas. Why not see vocabulary building as testing words against each other? By asking her students to assert a base of relationships first, she empowers them to add new elements, testing new ideas against the structure of relationships they have asserted. New vocabulary becomes part of the mental network they are creating, and the network expands in size and complexity.

Ingrid Daemmrich wanted her sociology students to recognize the pervasive power of rituals in human experience. She could begin teaching by lecturing on the power of rituals in cultures of the world. Instead, she asks her students to examine first their own recent college experience and to develop a hypothesis explaining a familiar ritual. With that hypothesis in view, they then begin examining rituals that are increasingly removed from their personal lives, altering their initial hypothesis as new patterns emerge. In doing so, they gain analytic and predictive power.

Creating New Vision

Herbert Leff, Ann Nevin, Donald Meeker, Jeanine Cogan, and Gary Isenberg began to see that their psychology students were not learning effectively because they did not actively work to reconstruct and apply the ideas of psychology. To make their students aware of the mental processes that make ideas useful, Leff developed the format of an awareness plan, an exercise requiring students to apply difficult ideas to daily problems.

Awareness plans create novel solutions, but they also give specific form to creative thinking processes.

George W. Chilcoat wanted his students to recognize how popular art reflects culture, specifically in nineteenth century America. His students create dime novels to represent American Culture. Recognizing that dime novels reflect popular values in ways that more formal writing may ignore, he asks his students to study both nineteenth-century culture and the conventions of the dime novel. His students look carefully at indicators of cultural value during the nineteenth century, then write their own dime novels reflecting the values they perceive. Their writing itself becomes a vehicle for the ideas they are trying to analyze. Dime novels from different students become the subject of interpretation for the class.

THOMAS W. RISHEL

The Geometric Metaphor: Writing and Mathematics in the Classroom

Conventional wisdom has it that mathematics and writing are about as far apart as academic disciplines can get. Maybe that's true in other areas of mathematics (although I doubt it), but when it comes to my geometry courses, From Space to Geometry and Geometry as Metaphor, neither could exist without the substantial number of writing assignments they contain.

Four years ago I received a grant from the Exxon Educational Foundation to design and teach a geometry course for students without any mathematical background. From that grant came the first of my two courses, From Space to Geometry. My original thought, I must admit, was that course design "shouldn't be hard"; I'd just get together some readings in the history and philosophy of mathematics which would convey the "true spirit" of geometry, and off I'd go!

The process turned out to be much different, however; for, the more I read, the more I understood that the "true spirit" of geometry is contained in its problems, solved and unsolved; and an honest course would have to explore those problems—regardless of the students' backgrounds.

After I had offered the course for two years, word got out that "something weird" was going on in the Math Department. The Director of the John S. Knight Writing Program, having heard about my methods, asked me if I would like to translate my assignments from "writing in math" to "math in writing." In other words, could I redesign my course as a writing course? Never one to profit from past mistakes, I readily agreed. Out of this experience came Geometry as Metaphor. I'll now describe these courses.

COURSE DESCRIPTIONS—PRELIMINARIES

Both courses begin the same way. Under the guise of "finding out about the students' background," I initiate a discussion of what they know about geometry and/or remember from courses taken. In this way I can find out the individual students' levels of attainment so that I can start to tailor the course to those levels. I have the students tell me some of the words and phrases they think of when they hear the word "geometry." From this discussion comes a real mix, which I casually write on the board. Some of the words:

> point, line, plane, angle, solid;
> definition, axiom, proof, theorem;
> surface, straight, "curvy";
> Euclid, Pythagoras;
> "a-squared plus bee-squared equals cee-squared";
> "my teacher, Ms. Jones," "how things look";
> compass, "ruler," "one o' those angle things."

I catalog the words by type, as I have done above. For instance, a tool used by a geometer is obviously not the same thing as a formula, nor is it the name of a geometer.

You may wonder how some of these words actually come up in discussion. I help by asking leading questions: " 'Straight,' as opposed to. . . ? What do you mean, 'Pythagoras'?"

Eventually I ask the students for a definition of geometry. Various suggestions have been made over the years, but the one I always get, sooner or later, is that "geometry is geo-metry, that is, it's earth-measurement." Now my trap has sprung, and I am ready to begin the course. I suggest that we take "earth-measure" as a working definition of geometry.

I give the students an assignment. It's a writing assignment, but such a minimalist one that they don't readily see it as such. I ask them (in writing) to

> Go to the campus Arts Quad. Measure, by any method you want, the height of McGraw Tower, the tallest building on the Quad. Write up your "solution" on one sheet of paper as if it were a lab report. Use any diagrams you think appropriate to explain your methods.

Students have some questions about the assignment. Can we work together? (Yes, but use separate writeups.) Do we have to be neat? (I will grade your assignment, and I must be able to read it.) Can we *really* use any method we want? (I won't bail you out if you are arrested.)

When the project is done we have a discussion. We classify methods of measurement by type: some use Pythagoras; others, similar triangles; estimation is popular, as are physical methods such as dropping stones from the top of the tower. I explain the Pythagorean Theorem, in case someone has forgotten it; and "similar triangles," Because many will have.

We discuss the writeups. I don't force the students to read their prose, but when (inevitably) someone starts to look at his or her paper as a memory aid, I say "Go ahead; read it to us." I am especially interested in the use of diagrams, and their meaning for both the reader and the writer. For instance, I lead the students towards such questions as: to what extent does the "picture" do a better job of explaining the text than the writing? In what way is the *diagram* the real report?

We also consider the "concept" behind the measurement. Do the students "see" the measurement method, then do it; or do they let the method find them? For those who "see" the method first, I ask them how that compares with the diagram they have in their writeup. In other words, I want to know to what extent the picture they have in their heads has been the impetus for the entire process.

But this last is too much for the students to grasp in an hour and fifteen minute discussion, so I turn back to the question of their methods. "Why did you drop a stone? Will you always get the same answer if you use this method?" They are very quick to discuss air resistance, dropping versus throwing the stone, etc. "What about Pythagoras—or similar triangles?" Here they are usually more certain; "Pythagoras" is, after all, "a *theorem*," so it must be true, right? And similar triangles is, well, "similar."

Now I bring out a beachball. "Let's draw a triangle. Let's look for some ninety degree angles. Let's measure some lengths of lines." By the end of the hour and fifteen minutes, the students have seen that the supposedly certain Pythagorean Theorem does not hold on the surface of the beachball, and thus on the surface of the earth.

But they, reasonably, don't believe. "You changed the definition of straight line." "No, I didn't; I never defined straight line." So we spend a day discussing "straight," and what it must have meant to Euclid and Pythagoras; and how we might need to change of definition for the purposes of earth-geometry. We also discuss whether it is actually possible to measure angles on the earth. ("But didn't Euclid do it? So you must be able to.") After another day, we have a new geometry, one which *does* apply to the surface of the earth, and which we call elliptic geometry.

And now we know that geometry is not just "geo-metry," "earth-measurement."

ONWARD TO THE "REAL" COURSE

So the course can really begin. We can talk about, and write about, such topics as:

When you think of the surface of the earth, what image do you have? In general, what do you think a surface is?

How do you define "straight" on the surface of the earth? . . . On other surfaces, such as a doughnut, or a trumpet? How about defining "angle"; and how should one be measured? What does a triangle look like on a trumpet? Can you make a square on such a surface?

What do *straight* and *flat* mean? How can you measure the "curviness" of an object? What does a word like "measure" mean in this context?

Suppose you are a two-dimensional bug, living *in*, as opposed to *on*, the surface of the earth. What do you look like? What can you see? And suppose your two-dimensional universe were a cylinder, say, instead of flat. Is there any way you could ever discover this fact?

Since the earth is not flat, why did Euclid create the geometry that he did? Did he believe that the earth *was* flat (and how could you prove this), or did he have something more difficult, more exotic in mind?

In my writing class, Geometry as Metaphor, from this point we follow a slightly different path from that in the From Space to Geometry class (the mathematics class also has some separate topics which I won't describe here). After we discuss our first paper, we rewrite it as a letter home ("Dear Mom and Dad; You always wondered what you were getting for your twenty thousand dollars. Well, yesterday I measured the height of . . . ."). This gives us the opportunity to discuss, along with mathematics, such topics as the difference between description and narration, audience, and tone.

Later I have the students write an argument paper. For instance:

Some say the earth is round. Prove or disprove. While you are doing so, reflect on the meaning of the word "round."

It is easy for me to pass from this assignment to the one stated differently earlier: What did Euclid know, and when did he know it?

I am sometimes asked how my "math in writing" class differs from the "writing in math" class. I think the easiest way for me to describe the difference is to say that in the mathematics class, I am primarily interested in the mathematics and use the writing to help explain the geometric concepts, whereas in the writing class I concentrate on writing as the topic, with mathematics as the content.

An example from the classroom helps to illustrate this. One day on the way to my writing class I saw that an art instructor had placed a number of geometric forms on the Quad so that his students could sketch them. I asked the instructor if I could send my class out to write about what they saw while his group sketched. After twenty minutes, my group came back to the classroom where we read our papers. Each student seemed to have taken a different viewpoint; one wrote about the geometric forms themselves, another about the students who were sketching and why, a third about himself watching the students sketching, and yet another about why the instructor might have chosen this assignment.

The class then discussed the use of viewpoint, and how it affected the language used in the essay. For instance, we discussed whether the student who wrote about the geometric forms used more passive voice than those who spoke from a more personal viewpoint. We also asked ourselves for whom we were writing, and how this might have affected the language we used.

The above are topics we obviously don't bring up in the math class.

SOME IN-CLASS PROJECTS

The Geometry as Metaphor and From Space to Geometry classes now reconverge with a series of projects which are usable in either. A few weeks into the semester I give an assignment:

> Go to a place you like. Sit there and describe it. Compare it to a place you don't like.
> Now look at the words you have used in describing your places. How may of these words have to do with geometry, in some sense or another? What do you think geometry may have to do with whether you like or dislike these places?

Students return to class to discuss the places they have chosen. As they speak, I write on the board individual words and phrases that they have used that are somehow "geometric." Some of these words are those we automatically think of in such a context, such as:

> large, small, open, closed, planar, square, angular

Another set of words, while still being "geometric," starts to edge toward metaphor:

> regular, even, ordered, balanced, proportional, shapeless

Still other words, describing motion, are geometric in a different sense:

> smooth, flowing, graceful, easy access, no movement

When a sufficient number of words has been collected, I point out how each set had led the writer to another set of words or phrases, supposedly nongeometric, as when "large and open" leads the writer to "a sense of freedom and independence," or "closed in" brings on a "white and gray room with no space," as well as "suffocating" and "confining." We note that some geometric cues can lead to conflicting thoughts, as when "clutter" brings on "confusion," while "clutter that is mine" triggers the phrases "comforting" and "makes me feel at home." "Regularity" can lead to "clarity," but also "monotony." One of the best examples of this came from a class last semester, when one of my football players described how a particular structure was "not lined up properly," and allowed as how that fact "angers me." When I challenged him as to whether it was really anger that he felt, he replied, after a pause, "Yeah. You know. It shouldn't be that way."

Our discussion often takes two or three hours, touching on issues of architecture, design, art, and personal safety. Once we have a vocabulary in place and see that geometric words can be metaphors, we are ready to carry the project further.

My next assignment to students is:

> Go to the local art museum. Choose a work or set of works, in any medium you want. Evaluate the work using the geometric vocabulary that we have previously constructed, along with any other geometric words that you think may apply to the art, such as "dimension" or "perspective."

By now the students have some idea of what such an assignment is about. They happily use and understand phrases such as a "the way the sculpture arranges and modifies the space around it," or "the artist's 'trick' of leading our eye to the darkest, center area of the canvas, where the darkness leads us back out to the edges again." The students can see how the use of light and shadow leads the eye through a canvas to attach itself to a focal point. They happily discuss "vanishing points and lines," and what these have to do with the type of mathematics called projective geometry.

One of my favorite quotes on this topic is from a woman who said "I don't see much geometry in this work. It's just a small octagonal pot with a textured glaze that gives it a feeling of depth."

But this series of assignments is not yet done. My next paper may or may not surprise you, depending on how you've reacted thus far.

In both the math and writing courses I give the students a poem, "The Idea of Order at Key West," by Wallace Stevens (5), the one that starts "She sang beyond the wisdom of the sea." The assignment begins by asking the students to read the poem through thoroughly twice. After the second reading, they are to underline any geometric words they find, especially concentrating on the penultimate stanza:

> Ramon Fernandez, tell me, if you know,
> Why, when the singing ended and we turned
> Toward the town, tell why the glassy lights,
> The lights in the fishing boats at anchor there,
> As the night descended, tilting in the air,
> Mastered the night and portioned out the sea,
> Fixing emblazoned zones and fiery poles,
> Arranging, deepening, enchanting night.

We then draw a picture, based on the geometric words we have chosen, of where the "we" of the poem are during this stanza, and what it is we are seeing—the lights on the fishing boats reflecting in the water are sending "emblazoned" latitude lines through that water toward us. We discuss the fact that this picture looks very much like the one of the earth we drew so often when we were comparing earth geometry to the geometry that makes similar triangles and Pythagoras work. Then we consider what this picture might have to do with the poem's final stanza:

> Oh! Blessed rage for order, pale Ramon,
> The maker's rage to order words of the sea,
> Words of the fragrant portals, dimly-starred,
> And of ourselves and of our origins,
> In ghostlier demarkations, keener sounds.

We discuss the word "order," and where that order may come from, and who the "maker" might be in this stanza. We discuss what all this might have to do with geometry, and whether the "geometry" we talk about is "something out there" or "something inside us." We compare the making of a geometry which fits the earth with the "arranging the night" of the "maker." We ask where the "ghostlier demarkations" may be, and whether we can ever get to them.

And finally, we see that by using geometry as if it were a knife, we can get to the core of a thought, and thus that there is hope that we can map the depths of "ghostlier demarkations" and "keener sounds."

EXPANDING ON THE CONCEPTS— DIGGING DEEPER

Now both classes switch directions again. Having had time to absorb some of the ideas from the "earth-geometry" sections, the students are ready to expand on those concepts.

Among the new ideas the students have had to absorb are those of a *surface*, a two dimensional object which isn't necessarily flat; a *geodesic*, a shortest path which is generally (and usually) not a "straight" line; and *curvature*, a property of geodesics. All of these concepts are basic to a discussion of modern physics and mathematics, where we talk about more than three dimensions, not less; about the curved paths light must take; and about the possible shapes of the universe.

Some of the writing projects I assign the students at this time:

> You are a three dimensional bug who wants to know if she lives in a closed and finite universe. How might you decide? What about a flat universe? An orientable one?

> We have been comparing Euclidean, or plane geometry with elliptic. Write down some facts that are true about plane geometry that are not true about elliptic, and vice versa. Start by comparing "lines" with "geodesics." Then think about triangles; how do they compare in plane and elliptic geometries? Can you say anything about squares in elliptic geometry?

> Look at a map of the earth. Compare latitude lines with longitude. How do they differ, and why do you think they were made to differ that way? What effect does this have when we need to measure distances between points on the surface of the earth? What other ways can you think of to make lines and angles on the earth? Finally, why do maps of the earth that you see in books so often distort the true shapes?

POSSIBILITIES FOR FINAL COURSE PROJECTS

I discuss in class some mathematical topics which might give the students ideas for their final projects.

We consider higher dimensions. In particular, we compare four spatial dimensions with Einstein's model of spacetime, which has three spatial dimensions and one of time. We discuss superstring theory, which requires that the universe be constructed of more than four dimensions. We consider the possible shapes that physicists offer for such a universe, and ask ourselves (*a la* the three dimensional bug problem) how we might determine whether such an unseen universe exists.

After looking at films of the hypercube in the fourth dimension, we derive formulas for vertices, edges, faces, and hyperfaces of some high dimensional hypercubes. In so doing, we learn that we can reason quite precisely about objects that we cannot see and cannot draw.

I explain to the students the theorem that classifies all possible compact surfaces. I then inform them that the analogous theorem for compact three-dimensional objects has not yet been found. Since we claim to live in a three-spatial-dimensional universe, we have ample opportunity to discuss the meaning of this fact.

We move on to hyperbolic geometry, one in which curvature is negative. We construct various models of two dimensional hyperbolic geometry, starting with lampshades and trumpets, and working toward the more mathematical Poincaré half-plane and disk models. Using the Poincaré disk model, we do hands-on compass constructions of lines and triangles. When we measure the sums of the angles of our triangles, we always get a number less that 180 degrees. We try to find other "facts" that we were taught from Euclidean geometry that turn out to be untrue in hyperbolic. I have the students write up some of the new discoveries they make as well as any questions and conjectures they have about this latest material.

I point out to the students that the current thinking of mathematical physicists is that the universe is hyperbolic. We discuss the by-now natural question of how these physicists might verify their assumption. I mention Gauss's early attempt to find the geometry of the universe by measuring the angles of a triangle from some European mountaintops.

A PRIMER ON PROJECTS

By this time students have begun thinking about their final projects. At about week ten of the semester I have the students write to me two short paragraphs:

"I am thinking of doing my final project on . . . ."
"I may need the following kinds of help. . . ."

During the next week I replace one class with half-hour meetings with individual students. This meeting helps settle their topic; it gives me a chance to help them with ideas and references; and, most importantly, it gives each student a chance to talk with an "expert" about mathematics without appearing foolish. At the same time I have the opportunity to reject or amend any ill-formed topics; and I can learn something about the students' topics so that I may actually become an expert, if necessary, at a later date.

For the next week and a half I talk in class about some topics of my own choosing. I often discuss taxicab geometry, a deceptively simple type of metric geometry where the distance between objects is measured in "city blocks," but which leads to some extremely disquieting pictures for the geometrically uninitiated. For instance, a "circle" in taxicab geometry actually looks like a square; and the set of all points equidistant from a pair of points is a "barbell" shaped figure (Krause, 2). This topic lets students know that the pictures they draw actually depend upon the type of distance they choose. For many this is a slightly disconcerting fact.

SOME FINAL PROJECTS

Students both write up and lecture on their final projects. Some choose artistic or design-related topics. Some examples of these, with selected quotes from the students'* papers, follow.

In a paper entitled "The Use of Geometry in Cubist Painting," the student author says that "Cezanne's maxim 'you must see in nature the cylinder, the sphere, the cone,' led Braque and Picasso to geometrize nature."

The writer of "The Geometry of M. C. Escher's Work" claims that "[w]hat gives Escher a reputation as being more 'mathematical' than 'artistic' is both his uncanny ability to represent modern topological concepts in his work, and also his classic, objective style. His work is not intimate or emotional; it maintains a scientist's distance from the beholder."

"The objective in ['The Use of Space in the Guggenheim Museum and its Effect on the Works and the Viewers'] is to further my knowledge of the ways in which mathematics is inherent in all art, including, obviously, the means by which artwork is displayed. . . . I will . . . [go] into substantial depth concerning the setup of the artwork, explaining how it is designed to suit the structure of the museum itself, and will also explore the following topics concerning specific pieces: perspective of both artist and viewer, lighting, dimension, and the artist's attempt to overcome its limitations, and also the spacing of works in the design of this particular museum."

One student did an exhaustive analysis of the Cornell Performing

Arts Center; another of Philip Johnson's "glass house" in New Canaan, Connecticut.

In "Geometry of a Camera Lens and Perspective Distortion as Determined by Analysis of Parallel Lines", the author "enlarged some . . . photographs and drew in the 'straight' lines to demonstrate the curved convergence of parallel lines as seen by the elliptic geometry of a spherical lens."

In "The Effects of Balance on the Effectiveness of the Printed Page", the student author says "There are many elements of geometry which are very important to creating an effective advertisement." Among these she includes shape, balance, equilibrium and stress. "Stress is caused by a lack of balance," she notes, and tells us that "It is the most effective of all visual means in creating a . . . response to a message."

I have had a couple of papers on optical illusions, in one of which the author designed such an illusion for the reader. Last year there was a paper on the Porteus Maze Test, an early test designed "as a psychological measure that would give a fairer index of the social sufficiency of mentally retarded children than the Binet Scale."

Some students write papers on aspects of relativity theory; others on what I might call "alternate universes." Two students, unbeknownst to one another, chose such topics last semester. One called his project "Torusland: An Explanation of a Shooter's Life." He began, "Imagine a raisin bagel. Now imagine that the bagel feels infinitely smooth; the raisins that you see on the surface exist, but they are completely flat. You now have an image of the world that I hope to present as Torusland." After describing in some detail a game called "shooting," the author explains the various paths a beam of light could take through his torus-universe, and then describes why the game of shooting would not exist in Flatland and Sphereland. "In Flatland if you were to shoot a burst of light in one direction it would never come back. . . . In Sphereland, however, if people shot a burst of light it would take exactly the same amount of time to come back in any direction."

The second "alternate world" student chose to fashion a "torus-earth." He discussed gravitational attraction; how rockets would fly; where the icecaps would form; what would happen to rivers; how distances would be measured; and other odd physical phenomena which would occur in such a world.

Yet another student taught hyperbolic geometry to her high school students, and wrote an analysis of the methodology and experience.

Last semester a student interviewed some people to see whether "[g]eometric shapes and patterns have an effect on the way a person feels." After a great deal of empirical data concerning two, three and four (!) dimensional forms, and the words they conjure up ("happy, confused, strong, unstable"), he concluded "It is quite obvious that geometric shapes create emotional responses in people. . . . On the whole, two dimensions were considered boring and created the lowest emotional response. . . . It is clear that people enjoy three dimensional objects much more than any others. I feel this is because we are three dimensional and we therefore relate to and enjoy this dimension the best."

Two students in the past three years have been able to prove a mathematically difficult theorem which is a corollary to the classification theorem for compact surfaces. This theorem states that a surface called the Klein bottle, which is not an orientable surface and cannot be "built" in three dimensional space without cutting through itself, is topologically the same as the connected sum of two copies of another unbuildable surface called real projective space. I mention this fact for two reasons: parts of the course contain some mathematically highly sophisticated topics, which at least some of the students understand very well; and, while all students complete a final project, some projects are more "literary" than others.

Another student from my earliest class wrote a more mathematical final project outlining a proof of a well-known theorem sometimes called "the mountaineers' theorem," because it has to do with the number of pits, peaks and passes that can exist on the surface of the earth.

My last sample is from a student who analyzed another of Wallace Stevens' poems, "Study of Two Pears." I think her excerpt beautifully captures the spirit of the course. While reading what she says, consider how far her feeling is from that taken by so many geometry students who say about the subject, "everything has been discovered anyway, so why bother studying it."

"In the first stanza, when [Stevens] says, 'pears are not viols,' he emphasizes the fact that they are fully three-dimensional objects rather than objects which in comparison could be seen as closer to two-dimensional (namely, stringed instruments)." Later she observes,

> The essence of this theme is also in [Stevens'] last stanza: "The shadows of the pears are blobs on the green cloth. The pears are not seen as the observer wills." We can all see the pears but the image we each hold is not any more the real thing just because we . . . "will" it to be. Likewise, geometry provides us with a way to communicate but it does not insure accuracy, nor does it guarantee that what I see, or what you see, or what I tell you to see is what is actually there.

CONCLUSION

Geometry is not an easy discipline to teach. While writing this manuscript I have been thinking of all the topics I have left out. (How about the day we examined the loaded language in the *New York Times Magazine* description of a scientist? . . . or our discussion of where logic stops and linguistics takes over? . . . or the day we played tic-tac-toe on a cylinder to see if there is a winning strategy? What about the discussion of the library at Alexandria? Don't forget the Euler characteristic, and regular polyhedra.)

Some years ago, while I was designing these courses, but before I had ever taught them, a kindergarten teacher told me a story. In one of her classes she had a student who was severely spatially disoriented. When he was asked to sit back in his chair, he would refuse to do so because he didn't know if there was anything there. He was afraid he would fall over into "outerspace," or worse! Anything that he could not see did not exist for him.

Sometimes when I am in front of my class and a student asks a question, one I have never thought of, one I *could* never have thought of, I feel a bit like that little boy—as if I am going to tilt over into some undiscovered "outerspace," never to come back. But there is one difference between me and that little boy: I don't mind the feeling!

My class has been a great voyage of discovery for me, and, I hope, for my students. I thank them for going with me on such a mathemagical journey.

WORKS CITED

1. **Cole, K. C.** "A Theory of Everything." *New York Times Magazine*, October 18, 1987: 20–28.
2. **Krause, Eugene F.** *Taxicab Geometry*. New York: Dover, 1986.
3. **Rishel, Thomas.** "Writing in the Math Classroom; Math in the Writing Class: Or, How I Spent My Summer Vacation." *MAA Math Notes Number 16— Using Writing to Teach Mathematics*. Ed. Andrew Sterrett. Washington, DC: Mathematical Association of America, 1990: ??–??.
4. ———. "The Idea of Order at Geometry Class." Paper presented at the Conference on College Composition and Communication, Chicago, March, 1990.
5. **Stevens, Wallace.** *The Collected Poems*. New York: Vintage, 1985.

ADDITIONAL WORKS USED IN THE COURSES

Abbott, Edwin A. *Flatland*. New York: Dover, 1952.

Armstrong, M. A. *Basic Topology*. Maidenhead, England: McGraw-Hill, 1987.

Bachelard, Gaston. *The Poetics of Space*. Tr. M. Jolas. Boston: Beacon Press, 1969.

Banham, Reyner. *Design by Choice*. London: Academy Editions, 1981.

Barr, Stephen. *Experiments in Topology*. New York: Dover, 1964.

Blackett, Donald W. *Elementary Topology*. London: Academic Press, 1982.

Brown, Richard G. *Transformational Geometry*. Palo Alto, CA: Dale Seymour Press, 1973.

Burger, Dionys. *Sphereland*. New York: Barnes and Noble, 1983.

Ching, Francis D.K. *Architecture: Form, Space and Order*. New York: Van Nostrand Reinhold, 1979.

Coxeter, H. S. M., M. Emmer, R. Penrose, and M. L. Teuber, eds. *M. C. Escher, Art and Science*. New York: North Holland, 1986.

Davis, Phillip, and Reuben Hersch. *The Mathematical Experience*. Boston: Birkhauser, 1981.

Do Carmo, Manfredo P. *The Differential Geometry of Curves and Surfaces.* Englewood Cliffs, NJ: Prentice Hall, 1976.

Forster, E. M. *Alexandria: A History and a Guide.* New York: Oxford University Press, 1986.

Francis, George K. *A Topological Picturebook.* New York: Springer-Verlag, 1987.

Greenberg, Marvin Jay. *Euclidean and Non-Euclidean Geometry,* 2nd ed. Reading, MA: Addison-Wesley, 1980.

Greenbie, Barrie. *Space and Spirit in Modern Japan.* New Haven: Yale University Press, 1988.

Gregory, Bruce. *Inventing Reality.* New York: Wiley, 1988.

Grey, Jeremy. *Ideas of Space.* Oxford: Clarendon Press, 1979.

Griffiths, H. B. *Surfaces.* London: Cambridge University Press, 1976.

Heath, Thomas L. *Euclid's Elements.* New York: Dover, 1956.

————. *Mathematics in Aristotle.* Oxford: Oxford University Press, 1936.

Huntley, H. E.. *The Divine Proportion.* New York: Dover, 1970.

Ivins, William M. *Art and Geometry: A Study in Space Intuitions.* New York: Dover, 1964.

Kaku, Michio, and Jennifer Trainer. *Beyond Einstein: The Cosmic Quest for the Theory of the Universe.* New York: Bantam, 1987.

Kandinsky, Wassily. *Point and Line to Plane.* New York: Dover, 1979.

Kippenhahn, Rudolph. *Light from the Depths of Time.* New York: Springer-Verlag, 1987.

Krause Eugene F. *Taxicab Geometry.* New York: Dover, 1986.

Lawlor, Robert. *Sacred Geometry.* New York: Thames and Hudson, 1989.

LeCorbusier. *The Modular 1 & 2.* Tr. P. DeFrancia and A. Bostock. Boston: Harvard University Press, 1986.

Leshan, Lawrence, and Henry Margenau. *Einstein's Space and Van Gogh's Sky: Physical Reality and Beyond.* New York: Macmillan Publishing, 1982.

Lord, E. A., and C. B. Wilson. *The Mathematical Description of Shape and Form.* Chichester, UK: Ellis Horwood Limited, 1986.

Martin, George E. *The Foundations of Geometry and the Non-Euclidean Plane.* New York: Springer-Verlag, 1975.

Massey, William S. *Algebraic Topology: An Introduction.* New York: Harcourt, Brace and World, 1967.

Millman, Richard S., and George D. Parker. *Geometry: A Metric Approach with Models.* New York: Springer-Verlag, 1981.

Misner, Charles W., Kip S. Thorne, and John Archibald Wheeler. *Gravitation.* San Francisco: W. H. Freeman, 1973.

Paramon, J. M. *Perspective.* Los Angeles: HPBooks, 1982.

Pedoe, Dan. *Geometry and the Visual Arts.* New York: Dover, 1976.

Peterson, Ivars. *The Mathematical Tourists: Snapshots of Modern Mathematics.* New York: W. H. Freeman and Company, 1988.

Petit, Jean-Pierre. *The Black Hole.* Tr. Ian Stewart. Los Altos, CA: William Kaufmann, Inc., 1985.

————. *Here's Looking at Euclid.* Tr. Ian Stewart. Los Altos, CA: William Kaufmann, Inc., .

Polya, George. *Mathematics and Plausible Reasoning.* Princeton, NJ: Princeton University Press, 1954.

Rees, Elmer G. *Notes on Geometry.* New York: Springer-Verlag, 1983.

Rosenfeld, B. A. *A History of Non-Euclidean Geometry.* New York: Springer-Verlag, 1988.

Rucker, Rudy. *Geometry, Relativity and the Fourth Dimension.* New York: Dover, 1977.

Schattschneider, Doris, and Wallace Walker. *M.C. Escher Kaleidocycles*. Corte Madiera: Pomegranate Artbooks, 1987.

Stevens, Wallace. *The Collected Poems*. New York: Vintage, 1985.

Tafuri, M. and F. Dal Co. *Modern Architecture 1 & 2*. Tr. R. E. Wolf. New York: Electra/Rizzoli, 1976.

Trudeau, Richard J. *The Non-Euclidean Revolution*. Boston: Birkhauser, 1987.

Van der Waerden, B. L. *Science Awakening I*, 4th ed. Leyden, The Netherlands: Noordhoof, 1975.

Weeks, Jeffrey R. *The Shape of Space*. New York: Dekker, 1985.

Wenninger, Magnus J. *Polyhedron Models*. Cambridge: Cambridge University Press, 1971.

My thanks to students Robert Kurzban, Eliza Barfus, Cynthia Cheney, Deborah Lippert, Antony Kalm, John McNiff, and Robert Houck for consenting to be quoted for this paper.

GREGORY RUBANO AND PHILIP M. ANDERSON

Metaphorical Portraits
of Literary Characters

Current views of thinking acknowledge varieties of intelligence and recognize that cognition takes place in diverse forms. Variously expressed as "frames of mind," "multiple intelligence," or "modes of knowing," these perspectives broaden the definitions of teaching thinking (Eisner; Gardner). Multiple concepts of cognition promote new ways of perceiving traditional disciplines and justify the cognitive value of a wide range of educational activities.

While different modes of knowing may apply to any academic discipline, one mode of thinking may be more appropriate than another. In the arts, the preferred mode of knowing is aesthetic rationality, i.e., "the aesthetic function of form as a source of experience and understanding. . . ." (Eisner 26). Aesthetic rationality is not limited to the arts, though it is a preferred mode of knowing in the arts.

One key psycholinguistic form for representing aesthetic understanding is the metaphor. Though frequently treated in literary studies as merely a figure of speech, metaphor is a form of representing experience, a form of representation that lies at the heart of literary cognition. To think metaphorically is to read in a literary way and to respond in an aesthetic form.

The following exercises demonstrate both the development of metaphorical fluency and the application of metaphorical thinking to literary character analysis. The fluency exercises are a necessary antecedent to the analysis and essay writing. Students are presented with analogies from which to choose for developing extended metaphors. They may also develop their own analogies. But, for literary analysis activities, and to initiate this type of activity, the teacher normally provides the initial analogies for student response.

DEVELOPING METAPHORICAL FLUENCY

The basic goal of introductory instruction in metaphorical thinking is for students to produce metaphors they can use within the process of exploration, though not as a final representation of their understanding. Students are introduced to the expedience of metaphorical thinking for generating possibilities and new perspectives. The teacher must make a purposeful effort to increase the students' fluency and confidence in this regard.

Often this means beginning by presenting the students with examples of metaphors and analogies that are to be applied to non-literary contexts. As the following examples reveal, the greater the students' familiarity with the metaphor and its components, the better the chance they can approach it and modify it to their liking. Most essential is the idea that through additions to a core metaphor students can transform the focus and the meaning of the metaphor.

Initially, the teacher's role is to encourage multiple interpretations and to suggest re-interpretations and additional directions that emerge when the metaphor is examined and extended. The directions to the first exercise force them to do so but the teacher's "playfulness" during the classroom review of the students' productions makes the point clearer. In effect, the teacher is modeling both a frame of inquiry and an attitude of mind.

INITIAL EXERCISE

Directions: Each of the analogies lettered "A" was written to suggest a dominant trait or characteristic of adolescents. "B" and "C" are additions to the first analogy.

1. Write down what you think analogy "A" suggests about teenagers.
2. Read analogy "B." How has the analogy been changed? How has that change affected your interpretation?
3. Read analogy "C." How has the analogy now been changed? How has that change affected your interpretation?

Analogy #1: A teenager is . . .

A. A car on a highway entry ramp.
B. A car on an entry ramp about to enter a congested highway.
C. A car entering a congested highway only to leave on the first exit.

Teacher Guidance: After the students have discussed various possibilities, the teacher can evoke more by asking some of the following questions. Students may add their own questions as well. All discussion is quickly paced, with the constant reminder to students that they are the ones producing meanings, changing them at their discretion. Parts of the metaphor may be added or deleted without first knowing the significance of that change or articulating it.

Some possible follow-up questions to ask include:

Is this a one-way highway?

How do you merge?

Where can the exit lead to?

Is the idea never to exit the highway?

What streets lead to the highway?

How is highway driving different than around town?

Any Jersey barriers in the scene?

What rest areas could be used before exiting?

How does this apply to other age groups?

The exercise is fun, sometimes whimsical: (Are all teenagers driving the same vehicles? Do you know anyone who is driving backwards on the entry ramp?). Sometimes serious: (Which exits are toll exits and how heavy is that toll?). Sometimes provoking: (Is the high speed lane to be avoided? Can you sometimes be forced to pass by a tailgating car behind you? In what way are all teenagers' driving habits the same?). We are always delighted at the students' inventiveness. One student laughed and then explained by depicting parents as a car that pulls up along side, travelling at the same speed as you, so that you can't merge into the speed lane.

Reflection: After discussion, the students are asked to pick any analogy (the student will determine the scope of the analogy) and discuss some aspect of their own lives in light of it. These personal responses are private journal entries.

Analogy #2

A. A person walking down a dark, lonely lane.
B. A person walking down a dark, lonely lane who is stopped by a watchman.
C. A person walking down a dark, lonely lane who is stopped by a watchman and then proceeds to walk past the farthest light on the lane.

Teacher Guidance: Are there any lights along the lane? Does this lane lead to another? What does it look like? Does it have a watchman as well? How is the return trip different?

Reflection: Same as above.

Analogy #3

A. An electron moving around the nucleus.
B. An electron accelerating as it moves around the nucleus.
C. Make your own next addition.

Teacher Guidance: What keeps the electron within the orbit? Why is it accelerating? Will it spin off the nucleus? Can electrons lose speed and fall into the nucleus?

At this point, it is important to allow students to discern the flexibility of the metaphors. First, they are asked to use any of the metaphors discussed as a way to further explore and understand any other subject or relationship. Again, they are encouraged to modify the originals in any way they see fit. Playing with the metaphoric possibilities, not forcing a fit, is the emphasis.

Teacher Guidance: Prompts may be needed (other possible topics): different stages of life; personalities with whom they are familiar; abstractions such as "friendship," "patriotism," "morality"; social collectives such as the homeless, the elderly, aspiring athletes, et. al. Reading the newspaper will provide personal interest stories, current events, etc., which can be conceived through metaphor.

These stages of metaphor production are especially important for two reasons. As mentioned previously, they are means for stimulating easeful production. Yet fluency per se is not the goal. In fact, the fluency exhibited is constrained within the cognitive structure of the exploration. Making students apply one metaphorical template to different contexts produces an interaction that gives new meaning to both the metaphor and the represented experience or information.

When the ingredients used to represent are themselves part of the reconceptualization process, fluency becomes part of the design of metaphorical thinking and the metaphor assumes its role as a means to discover meaning. To do so, the metaphor must go beyond what Max Black calls its "substitutional" function, that is, the use of metaphor to stand in the place of some literal equivalent. Instead, it must take on the distinctive capacity to "create the similarity rather than . . . to formulate some similarity antecedently existing" (Black, 37).

METAPHORICAL PORTRAITS
AND CHARACTER ANALYSIS

Having established these cognitive functions, the teacher can turn to literary texts and use metaphors and analogies to help students engage in the pre-writing stage of character sketches. We find it best to begin by returning to the familiar analogy of the car on the highway. Having recorded the initial comparisons developed by the students, we now reintroduce them. Of course, the only difference is that we focus upon the literary character, in this case, Macbeth or Lady Macbeth.

The teacher should model the metaphor examination process so that it is anchored in discussion specific to the character and the work under consideration. Specific textual support now comes into play, though the questions are duplicates or hybrids of the original ones:

- What highway is Macbeth entering? Is it a one-way highway? How does Macbeth manage to merge? This question often leads to discussion of the the irreversibility of Macbeth's decision and the role of Lady Macbeth. Also, the discarded moral and societal prohibitions against the act come into play.
- Does Macbeth travel in a different vehicle? Is the fuel different? Often discussion of the differences between Macbeth, Lady Macbeth, and Banquo becomes the focus. Also, Macbeth as "everyman" discussions, complemented by society/conscience restraints.
- Do Macbeth / Lady Macbeth have rest areas? Are these characters wearing safety belts? The role of Macbeth's fevered sleepless mind and pestered senses is thus introduced, as are the differences between the two characters.
- How are the witches tailgating cars? The method of the witches is fitted to the nature of the man. Who tailgates Lady Macbeth? The Lady Macbeth as her own worst enemy concept; the irrepressible conscience's operation.
- Is it possible for Macbeth to travel in the high speed lane without being reckless? What does he experience as he drives in this lane? The psychological progressions of Macbeth; the sense of immunity from natural environment about him.

The discussion emphases cited are not carved in stone, especially since different interpretation of what a highway represents are always possible and should be encouraged. This is not to say that all necessarily goes smoothly in initial discussion. The most frequently encountered problem is that students try to reduce the metaphor to plot representation. Accordingly, Macbeth collides with three other cars and is driven off the highway of life in the final accident (i.e., the killing of Duncan and Banquo; the death of Macbeth at Macduff's hands). Persistent reminders that such minimal use of the analogy is not desired eventually impels students to loftier visions.

The character sketch itself now begins to emerge. Although students could be asked to use the highway analogy, we prefer to give them an assignment sheet which introduces additional metaphorical possibilities.

Macbeth Metaphor Essay

Directions: Choose one of the following metaphors and write a two-page character analysis essay about Macbeth or Lady Macbeth.

1) Macbeth/Lady Macbeth is a cat in a tree.
2) Macbeth/Lady Macbeth is a jet fighter pilot.
3) Macbeth/Lady Macbeth is an atomic particle.

Use the following format:

1. The introduction should extend the initial metaphor to further define the focus of your analysis (e.g., "a car on a highway" extended to "a car entering a congested highway only to leave on the first exit").
2. The body of the paper should explore the appropriateness of the metaphor through at least three specific references to the text (e.g., specific comments by the characters about themselves, statements made by others about them, or actions of the characters).
3. The conclusion should return to the original metaphor, showing the significance of the character's traits to a possible meaning of the play (e.g., "Perhaps Shakespeare is suggesting that there is no turning back from certain decisions. Certain highway exits have no re-entry point.").

However, we do return to the highway analogy one more time—as a means of modeling for students a way to return to the analogy to help write a conclusions which presents a possible theme of the work being read. In fact, this component of the metaphorical approach addresses a traditional problem in the conclusions of character portraits: the failure to generalize to theme. To formalize these connections, three possible approaches may be taken. Since each produces a conclusion evolved from the chosen metaphor, each promotes coherence of thought.

Dissimilarity: The writer focuses on how the metaphor breaks down.

Example: The driver of a car can use a map to direct her path. Macbeth discovers that the paths he travels upon are uncharted. What tempts him and us may then, according to Shakespeare, brings us to new worlds, some impossible to traverse.

Prediction: The writer makes a prediction that evolves from the metaphor.

Example: What Shakespeare may then want us to consider is that if we travel in speed lanes of immorality we may find the engine overheats quickly. The suffering is immense.

Resolution: The writer makes a declarative statement that resolves the situation presented in the metaphor.

Example: What emerges from *Macbeth* is the realization that there are no ways to protect oneself from the consequences of immoral acts. There are no safety belts that are effective in high speed travel.

In this particular assignment most of the students chose the "cat" metaphor. "Macbeth is a cat" is an apt choice because it requires little "extension" of the metaphor until the conclusion method forces such activity. It may also be the one that best captures the relentless instinctive drive and ferocity of Macbeth, as well as the helplessness of this distraught figure. A few of the student examples seem to suggest such an advantage. However, each student has introduced a personal twist in tone and implication.

Student Examples: Cat Analogy

Student A:

Introduction: Macbeth is a frisky kitten let loose for the first time. Seeing a chipmunk he dashes up the rugged bark without a second thought. But before he realizes it, he is so high in the tree that he is too fearful to crawl down. Macbeth's ambition blinded him from seeing all consequences.

Conclusion: All of these qualities suggest a driving impatience which ultimately leads to his doom. Perhaps if he had been content to watch the chipmunk from a window, it would have come to him. There is no fireman capable of rescuing this cat from the tree.

Student B

Introduction: His claws grind their way into the wooden branches. The poor feline stands alone at the top desperately searching for a way to be restored to a level where he will again be amid others. Such is Macbeth.

Conclusion: A question Shakespeare presents is, "Is it human nature to become so excited about the future that we jump thoughtlessly into our dreams?" The cat led himself into the situation where he now must remain until the fire rescuers bring him down to the plush green grass. If you want to climb a tree, you must be able to jump out of the tree to get back down to the ground.

Student C:

Introduction: In his tragedy *Macbeth*, Shakespeare accommodates many emotions which are ultimately relative to each other. The character of most powerful emotion and action is Macbeth himself. When analyzing Macbeth's ambitious yet frightened character, one sees a kitten climbing a tall oak tree.

Conclusion: Shakespeare may have been saying that one cannot change the future or return in time. The kitten has it easy because if he has enough courage he can climb back down. Macbeth, however, cannot climb down the ferocious tree he had climbed.

Another student brought the following insight to her conclusion:

> Macbeth went too far before looking back. The cat, when not frightened, should look down before climbing to the top. If he does, he will be able to see what he had left behind on the ground below.

Composed within the context of other choices, the following additional metaphors provided fertile ground for examination as well:

- The distraught King is a skier who, after clumsily boarding the chair lift, encounters no trouble in getting off until he reaches the summit.
- Macbeth is a cartoon character who slips on and then rolls down the mountain slope. Gradually, he is nothing more than a snowball with eyes.
- Macbeth is a parachutist who in the excitement of free fall forgets to pull the ripcord. The ground thus came up harder and faster.
- Macbeth is a parachutist who leaves his parachute behind in the plane.
- Macbeth is a parachutist who thinks the ripcord is on automatic.

What may be most striking about the metaphorical portraits is the quality of poetic expression. One young woman's highly metaphorical introduction reveals how far students can advance from the disengaged voice and shallowness which characterize traditional character sketches.

> The open meadow and rich soil nurtured the lone oak. The nobility of its magnitude and bulk and the splendor of its sway in the autumn gales. The stealthy kitten encircled the tree's base. In a second a streak of white shot up the roots of the tree as the cat's claws carried it to a solid arm. Although the sunlight was more intense on the kitten's coat than when she had sat on the ground, she desired more heat. She dragged her body up the tree's trunk until it became narrower and began to sway ever so slightly. The cat climbed to the top in a passion for the sun.

The student did not abandon this use of poetic and highly symbolic language to carry forth meanings which a more pedestrian approach and language could not support or generate. Her final few paragraphs are infused with splendid imagery.

> It was only a moment before the sun travelled behind a cloud. The cat then became aware that its glossy white fur had been soiled by the climb. The tender arm at the peak of the tree below the cat's paws snapped and fell with the kitten to the ground. . . . When the cat's

weight proved too much and her greed no longer supported her feverish drive, the cat fell below the ground from which she had begun.

She was not the only student to continue to use the metaphor throughout the piece. Here is the entire character sketch one student offered of Lady Macbeth.

Impetuously, a first time parachutist denies her fear of heights, her phobia of airplane travel and ventures forth against her nature. As the plane leaves the ground, she forces herself to ignore the flutterings in her stomach and the thundering roar of the engine vibrating throughout her body. She closes her eyes and pretends the powerful wind entering through the open door of the plane is just the familiar ocean gusts of the beach.

The fearful parachutist, Lady Macbeth, attempts to deny her intrinsic reservations and calls upon the forces of darkness to harden her feminine inclinations toward morality: "and fill me from crown to toe, top full of direst cruelty . . . Stop up the access and passage to remorse, that no compunctious visitings of nature shake my fell purpose." Lady Macbeth needs to expedite the murder of Duncan for she senses that time will only languish her determination.

In order to accomplish the lurid deed, she dissembles her fears with artificial courage: "That which hath made them drunk, hath made me bold." Yet, the truth of her nature begins to show as she cannot kill the king because he resembles her father.

The airplane levels at the intended point, and the parachutist realizes there is no turning back. No longer enthralled, her evanescent courage forces her to analyze her actions. Yet, still clutching her inner strength, she is determined to persevere. As she arises to assume the stance in preparation for the long plunge toward earth, her heart throbs in her ears and her knees jolt in thrusts of paranoia. Approaching the edge of the plane, she strains to stand still but she knows that she is too petrified to move her hand and pull the ripcord.

At first Lady Macbeth is able to moderately fetter her escaping remorse and protract her appearance of stability in order to function. Her inner turmoil is revealed as she sighs, "Tis safer to be that which we destroy than by destruction dwell in doubtful joy." Soon she bemoans her nefarious acts and becomes consumed by her inability to purify herself. Yet, while she dwells in an unreal world, she laments the permanence of the blood spots on her hands and she demonstrates an unusual desire to be strong as she inveighs Macbeth for his fear.

Through Lady Macbeth's character development, Shakespeare explores the conflict of ambition versus conscience. Can a person successfully deny an emotional commitment to their actions in order to obtain a desired goal? Like the parachutist who has to come to terms with her anxieties, a person has to face the reality of her actions and consequently fall prey to her morality. The person who pushes off her nature is plunging to her death.

There may be some diction errors in this essay, and some of the interpretations are debatable, but it represents a consistent "argument" as well as a wonderful piece of creative writing. Far from being used austerely as some rhetorical device, the metaphor has been incorporated into this student's thinking and composing process.

The metaphorical process outlined here and some of the exact teacher guidance questions can be brought to any character examination. In addition, character examination need not have its culmination in an essay. A post-reading analysis of Willy Loman, of Hester Prynne, or of Jay Gatsby can be initiated by having the students select one of the analogies from the exercise sheet just reviewed. (At some early point, however, the class should create new ones and engage in the same process of part substitution, deletion, and suppression.)

Peer groups can also be established in which the members' inquiries nurture re-vision. Each group can be given the same metaphor and asked to discuss its implications. For example, each member of the group can be asked how Jay Gatsby, by the end of the novel, is the electron accelerating about the nucleus. After discussion, the group can commit to one representation, which may include appropriate deletions, additions or substitutions.

These representations are then given to another group who must give their interpretation of what that metaphor suggests. This activity provides a particularly effective review session. A variation which serves such a function is to require students to apply the same analogy to character pairs: Nick/Gatsby; Willy/Biff Loman; Hester/Dimmesdale, e.g.

In any case, the metaphorical model of cognition (as representative of one form of aesthetic rationality) serves important linguistic and cognitive needs of the students. Equally important, the model allows students to approach the literary arts in an appropriate frame of mind. If the literary arts are to teach thinking, then aesthetic rationality is the means as well as the goal.

WORKS CITED

Black, Max. *Models and Metaphors*. Ithaca, NY: Cornell University Press, 1962.

Eisner, Elliot. "Aesthetic Modes of Knowing." *Learning and Teaching the Ways of Knowing*. Ed. Elliot Eisner. 84th Yearbook of the National Society for the Study of Education, Part II. Chicago: University of Chicago Press, 1985. 23–36.

Gardner, Howard. *Frames of Mind*. New York: Basic Books, 1983.

CHARLES R. GAROIAN

Using Cross-Disciplinary Metaphor
to Understand Art

A course in art history can play an invaluable role in the general curriculum of a high school or college. It can provide students with an opportunity to learn about the artistic achievements of past civilizations, the works of the old masters, whose visual expressions of the human condition parallel the great works in literature, music, science and mathematics. More importantly, the study of art history enables students to develop a broader world view as they acquire this a significant link to the history of ideas, and to use art historical concepts as a resource for creative thinking.

The study of art history cultivates critical thinking skills whereby students learn to describe, analyze, and interpret history through the visual language of art. Complementing visual literacy, students also develop research skills in reading, writing, and the criticism of art. Accordingly, a course in a high school or college presents opportunities for students to develop visual and verbal thinking skills concurrently. Through works of art, they can enter into a discourse with history. They can use historical concepts to produce new metaphors.

If the production of metaphors assumes creative thinking, the teaching of art history can be used as a resource for creative thinking. In accordance with this purpose, I'll describe a teaching strategy for the adaptation of art history as a creative thinking tool.

CROSS-DISCIPLINARY STRATEGIES

Contrasting ideas in art history with those in other disciplines are extremely useful to creative thinking. Under such circumstances, students first learn the historical value of works of art. They learn that art reflects the social, political, economic and aesthetic milieu of each historical era. Thus, art works represent the ideas and feelings about the human condition in the past.

Next, students learn that ideas and images in works of art can be contrasted in ironic ways with those in other disciplines. For example, although the concept of "nature" may be expressed differently in art, science and literature, the painter does so visually, the scientist mathematically, and the writer through the use of verbal images. Their obvious linguistic differences notwithstanding, all three disciplines are dealing with the perception of the same phenomena. The appropriation and ironic juxtaposition of cross-disciplinary concepts, enables students to learn how to produce new ways of thinking about familiar concepts like nature.

The displacement of concepts from their familiar historical contexts to strange new ones results in contradictions that are essential to the creative process.[1] The outcome of these creative contradictions is the production of new metaphors and the revitalization of old ones. The following exercise teaches students how to produce creative contradictions through the ironic juxtaposition of art historical concepts with those in other disciplines. The purpose of this exercise is to create cross-disciplinary metaphors.

1. In the context of an art history lesson, ask students to research, write, and prepare a slide-illustrated lecture on one of the following topics:
   a. the art of a culture or civilization (examples: Egyptian, Roman, Italian Renaissance, French Baroque).
   b. a stylistic period in art history (examples: Romanticism, Impressionism, Cubism, Dadaism).
   c. the oeuvre of one specific artist (examples: the works of Giotto, Leonardo da Vinci, Jacques Louis David, Pablo Picasso).
   d. a single work of art by a single artist (examples: Gianlorenzo Bernini's *David*, Theodore Gericault's *The Raft of the "Medusa,"* Marcel Duchamp's *The Bride Stripped Bare by Her Bachelors, Even*).
2. While doing research on their respective topics, have students find parallels between concepts in art history and those they are studying in other classes. Comparisons can be made, for example, between the function of fertility rites and symbols found in ancient art, and today's attitudes toward sexuality and birth control studied in biology, health, and social science classes. Based in Euclidian principles, the linear perspective in Renaissance art works can be compared with concepts learned in mathematics classes like geometry.
3. Ask students to use the two found concepts together in the production, direction, and performance of a cross-disciplinary activity that will result in a metaphorical link between the two concepts.
4. Provide students with a rationale for the activity based on the creative thinking strategies discussed herein. Explain the function of metaphor in art and the purpose for making metaphoric connections with concepts in history. Inform them that metaphors are often abstract and esoteric due to their strange juxtaposition of ideas.

5. Ask students to organize materials, objects, or equipment that are necessary for the performance of their respective activities. Then have them rehearse their performances and their slide-illustrated lectures prior to presenting in class.
6. After each lecture and performance, ask the presenting student to describe, analyze and interpret their metaphors. Encourage a discussion that will include all students in the class.

Through exercises like those above, art history can serve as a resource for creative thinking, especially when appropriated art historical images and ideas are ironically juxtaposed with those in other academic disciplines. By contrasting theories of modern art and science, for example, students can learn to draw parallels between ways that today's artists and scientists view the world.

CUBISM AND NUCLEAR PHYSICS

Originating from the impulse of a common experience in the late nineteenth and early twentieth centuries, Cubism and Nuclear Physics illustrate such cross-disciplinary parallels. As concepts, they represent a paradigm shift in artistic and scientific thinking. As disciplines, they have greatly affected the conditions of human life and our planet.

From a conceptual perspective, both Cubism and Nuclear Physics have separate principles, theories and assumptions. Most students are introduced to these perspectives because they are endemic to the understanding of contemporary art and science. Yet, most students and perhaps most teachers have little or no idea of their commonalties.

With Impressionism and Cubism which followed, artists like Claude Monet, Paul Cezanne, and Pablo Picasso began to question the traditional assumptions of art and, in particular, the academic view of pictorial space. Accordingly, the figure-ground relationships in their paintings are in flux, background and foreground are broken up and undergoing a metamorphosis, merging into a unified field. These artists changed our modes of perception from the illusionistic window-view of the world inherited from the Renaissance to abstraction, a view reflective of the conditions of modern life.

With scientific zeal, these artists went beyond the traditional assumptions of art history to explore new materials and new forms. By paring away the representational images of traditional art, they revealed permutations of line, shape, texture, color, space: the expressive structure of art. Through there investigations into the nature of visual form, they laid the groundwork for a new language, a new world view, based on abstraction.

As students compare the developments in modern art history with those in science, they will find striking parallels. For example, with Albert Einstein's Principle of Relativity (1905) and Werner Heisenberg's Principles of Uncertainty (1927), physicists began to question the absolutist theories established by Sir Isaac Newton two hundred years earlier. The theories of these modern physicists revealed an understanding of the physical world which was, heretofore, imperceptible through the human senses.[2] The experience of subatomic structures found in nuclear physics, for example, is not possible through concrete-sensory perception. Consisting of microscopic phenomena, they can only be "seen" in the minds-eye as abstract concepts or with the aid of special technologies. Furthermore, their exploration and understanding is only possible through the abstract language of mathematics.

There are many other parallels that can be drawn between Cubism and Nuclear Physics. Their abstract, yet conceptual, characteristics represent the complex and contradictory questions that artists and scientists have been dealing with since the early part of this century. As students become aware of the parallels that are generated from the ironic juxtaposition of contrasting academic disciplines, they learn to use concepts from school to create metaphors that raise questions about their own lives and the world in which they live.

STUDENT EXAMPLES OF CROSS-DISCIPLINARY THINKING

The following two examples of student work illustrate cross-disciplinary strategies where a topic from art history, and another from across the school curriculum, were brought together to create a metaphor.

Sisyphus on a Treadmill: Leslie was preparing to lecture about the relationship between European existential literature and modern art in the art history class. She brought together concepts she had learned in art history and in English. The specific works that she juxtaposed were the writings of Franz Kafka and Albert Camus with the sculptures of Alberto Giacometti. The art history classroom was prepared with two slide projectors and a lectern from which she would speak.

For the performance of her activity, Leslie decided to use a treadmill as a visually and conceptually appropriate metaphor expressing the hopelessness and futility in existentialism. She telephoned Lydia's Health Spa, a local health club, and asked permission to borrow their treadmill exerciser for a classroom activity. Much to her surprise, her request was granted.

The treadmill weighed 300 lbs. It was heavy and awkward to carry. To assist her, Leslie found ten husky students. Together they loaded the treadmill into a borrowed van and delivered it to the art history classroom prior to her lecture.

During the entire fifty minutes of her presentation, Leslie walked the treadmill at a medium pace, never stopping (Figure 1). Slides of

FIGURE 1   Leslie lecturing from a treadmill

Giacometti's sculptures were projected on large screens to her right and left side (Figure 2). As she walked, she addressed "the plight of human beings in the modern world. Without God, they are left to contemplate their own destinies. The hopelessness in Kafka's *The Trial*, the futility in Camus's *Myth of Sisyphus*, and the gaunt and alienated human figures that comprise Giacometti's sculptures all represent the hollow characteristic of modern existence." These concepts, combined with the image of Leslie "going nowhere" and the monotonous sound of the treadmill's rollers, provided a powerful metaphor connecting the literature and sculpture of these modern masters.

Entropy and Art: In discussing the action paintings of Jackson Pollock, Brad set up a visual and conceptual metaphor juxtaposing the artist's process of painting, his imagery, and the process of particle movement and decay in nuclear physics. He titled his activity: "Entropy and Art."

For his activity, Brad brought to the art history class materials and equipment from the high school physics laboratory. They included: dry ice, a metal plate, a slide projector, a straight pin, alcohol, and a bottle cork. He also prepared lecture notes and slides illustrating Pollock's art work.

With the materials and equipment he appropriated from the physics lab, he constructed a cloud chamber in the art history classroom. This device is used by physicists to track the movement of subatomic particles being released from microscopic amounts of radioactive material as an illustration of the entropic process in nature.

Brad placed an isotope of radium on the head of pin (Figure 3). Imbedded in the bottle cork, the pin was suspended in the cloud chamber below a small piece of alcohol-soaked cloth. He then fastened and sealed the cloud chamber onto the metal plate, and completed the construction by placing it on the block of dry ice (Figure 4).

For his final step, Brad projected the intensified light of a slide projector through the chamber. The alcohol condensed and formed a cloud layer upon the cold metal plate. As subatomic particles dispersed from the isotope and passed through the cloud, they created additional condensation through their paths, thus making their movement visible. Figure 5 shows particle activity in a cloud chamber.

After Brad performed his activity, he went on to lecture about Pollock's work, action painting, and how the artist's process of painting metaphorically illustrates entropy in art and nature (Figure 6). According to Brad, "both the dispersal of paint from Pollock's body onto the canvas and the spread of ideas from art into society, function as metaphors of the dissipation and degradation of energy found in nature."

FIGURE 2   A Giacometti figure

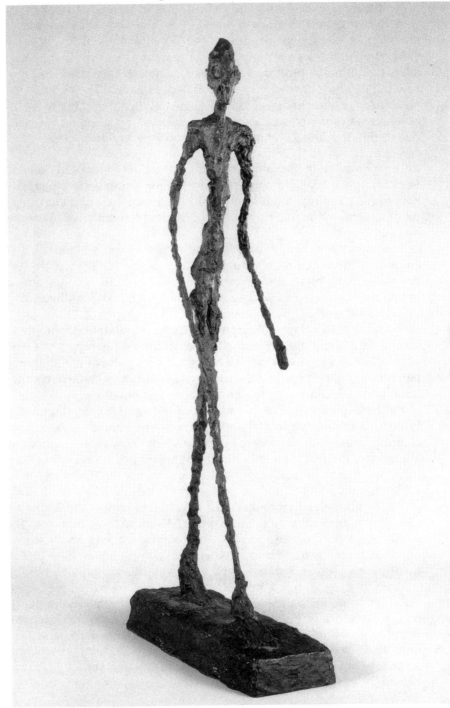

FIGURE 3   Brad placing radium on a pin

FIGURE 4 Brad assembling his cloud chamber

FIGURE 5   Particle activity in a cloud chamber

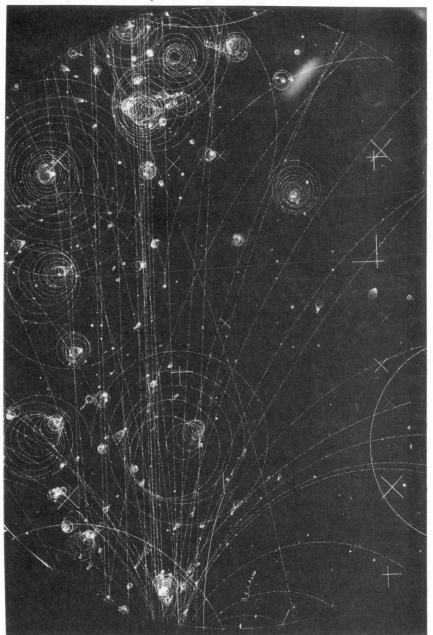

FIGURE 6 Pollack's work as process and product

Through their performances and lectures, these two students explored the historical assumptions that separate art, science, and literature. By appropriating concepts from across the curriculum, and from life, they learned to create a "collage" of images and ideas whose ironic connections shed new light on old metaphors as well as resulting in new ones. Thus, the cross-disciplinary teaching exemplified herein relies on art history as a significant resource for creative thinking. Together with other subjects in the school curriculum, art history contributes to a student's comprehensive understanding of past ideas. More importantly, it enables them to participate in history by creating new ways of knowing.

BIBLIOGRAPHY

1. **Rothenberg, Albert.** *The Emerging Goddess: The Creative Process in Art, Science, and Other Fields.* Chicago: The University of Chicago Press, 1979.
2. **Bronowski, J.** *The Ascent of Man.* Boston: Little, Brown and Company, 1973.

DIANA MAYER DEMETRULIAS

Thinking About Statistics

For some of us, the legacy of statisticians such as Scheffe, Fisher, and Pearson is evident in the richness and brilliance of statistics. Yet a typical and incredulous student once said to me: "Do you mean that Pearson r and Spearman *rho* are actually named after real people? Do you mean they voluntarily spent time and a professional career finding genuine pleasure in the development of statistics? How lunatic!"

This student's sudden insight even though full of scorn and shock illustrates the problem. Because statistics uses a mathematical basis for talking about important human problems, students often view statistics as a body of knowledge with indisputable rules, arcane formulae, and tedious calculations. As a result, a teacher of statistics typically faces a classroom of students who display boredom, apprehension, or loathing.

Consider the passion of the following poem written by a graduate student, Kurt Engel:

Statistics

Statistics is not a 4-letter word
        But it should be.
Most certainly to be pulverized, purged. Banned.
Computers add a lethal dimension when students engage in THE battle:
T
   t

        r   F   Beta? Discriminant functions? Covariance?
Multiple regression?
It is not possible to win the skirmish when the prancing parameters,
   the murderously-blended multivariate analyses and the canonical
   correlations collectively march.
The brain is taken through terrain rough and unchanneled.
Once the first bite of the textbook is timidly nibbled,
the war escalates into a full-scale attack.
The horror has no end.

However, the mathematical symmetry and order of statistical thought as defined in the poem are only surface characteristics. They are the remnants left by the imaginative, persevering statisticians of the past. To move students from a preoccupation with arcane methods of others to the creation of their ideas, the teacher must design a course that moves students beyond computations of known statistics, beyond mastery of numbers and numeracy, and beyond fear resulting from slavery to absolute rules. The "beyond" is a concentration on statistical *thought*, a process that employs creative and critical thinking skills. It is the magic of statistical thought that we must transmit to our students.

IN THE BEGINNING . . .

For introductory statistics, research, and measurement classes at the high school or college level, it is necessary to address the students' feelings of tension and torment. I adopt a playful tone in class and assignments. I structure group work, class discussions, and application exercises so that they are exploratory rather than competitive and convergent. I reward creativity, risk-taking, and imagination. I model a tolerance for ambiguity. These elements of classroom climate are not the same thing as having fun or using humor. The atmosphere is more similar to a child's delight in exploring something new, yet to do so requires hard work, perseverance, practice, repetition.

The following questions are examples of types of introductory questions that a teacher may employ as a means to foster creative thought about statistical terms and concepts. These examples are intentionally simplistic in design. As students gain in their sophistication with statistical thought and exhibit less inhibition to creative responses, the questions asked of them should increase in complexity.

- *Suppose* the measures of central tendency were applying for a new job at the local video store. Prepare a short resume of their credentials (strong points, skills, job experiences, etc.).
- *Suppose* that parametric and nonparametric tests were involved in a group therapy session. They are discussing their problems in being understood by teachers, students, and parents. Write a script of this therapy session.
- *Suppose* that you are the proud parent of five different correlation indices. Describe your various children to a new neighbor.
- *If* you were an analysis of covariance, would you prefer to tiptoe through the tulips or walk on thin ice? Please explain.
- *Consider* each of the statistical tests of significance. *Suppose* that these statistical tests were candidates for the following offices or positions in a school election: President, Treasurer, Homecoming Queen, School

mascot, Cheerleading Captain, "Most likely to Succeed," "Most Humorous," and "Most Talented." Cast your vote for the office or position in the school election that you believe is the most appropriate for each statistical test. If you believe that some other office or position is more appropriate than those I have specified, please write your own! Let your imagination run w-i-l-d!

- *How* would a hog on thin ice describe a multiple regression analysis?
- *How* would a curvilinear relationship look to a person of the same shape?
- *Your* parents named you "Scheffe test." What kind of person are you?
- *I know* only about monster movies. Explain reliability and validity to me.
- *If you were to pick* a statistical concept that is *most like you* in behavior, temperament, or appearance, which would you choose *Why*?
- Please select one of the responses below and explain your answer.
     The *most likely person* to use statistics would be one who:
     a. wears a mink coat and swimming fins to a demolition derby
     b. pets strange dogs
     c. reads and outlines the Yellow Pages instead of walking
     d. orders pistachio yogurt and a chili dog for breakfast
     e. none of the above; it's a person who . . .

Several intellectual skills result from students' responses to these types of questions: imaginative thinking, taking multiple perspectives, employing unusual mental angles to shift viewpoint, flexibility of thought and perspective, rethinking established patterns of thought, and associative thinking.

RESEARCH IN THE POPULAR PRESS

Consider this methodology: End a class session with a picture and short article from a news magazine. It is important to choose a topic of great interest and possible amusement to high school or college students (sports, food, sex are usually the ones I choose). An example is an anthropological research study of the relationship between weight and sexual appetite which was reported in *Time*. Ask students to read the article and bring to class their questions (not answers) in response to the following directions:

This article is typical of the manner in which popular magazines report the findings of research studies. Although interesting conclusions are stated, the reporting of the research is incomplete and should lead to a cautious and reluctant acceptance of the conclusions. As an enlightened scholar, indicate the types of questions you would ask the researcher in order to elicit more specific information about the study, its design, sampling techniques, data collection, statistical analyses, and conclusions.

For example, the *Time* article states that endomorphic women are more responsive to erotic stimulation and have greater sexual appetites than their thin sisters by a factor of almost two to one. In an attempt to understand the researcher's conclusion, students will ask initially questions of clarification:

- How are fat and thin defined? How was the weight of the women measured to assure truth and reliability (Most people lie about their weight!)?
- Were there various elements included in the definition of erotic stimulation and, if so, how would this affect the responses when the data were analyzed?
- What in the heck do you mean by endomorphic, erotic stimulation, and sexual appetites?
- How were the data on sexual appetites collected and from what sample? Self-report via a telephone or written survey? Unobtrusive observation (ho-ho—where do we sign up as a research assistant?!)?
- "Almost two to one." Huh? How many and what's "almost?"

After questions of clarification, the discussion becomes more sophisticated and gives students practice in drawing inferences, making judgments, identifying and applying criteria, and suggesting alternative hypotheses for an observed phenomenon.

The result is a richness of insight and a variety of responses far beyond that which occurs when students are asked to answer questions generated by the teacher. When students present their questions during class discussion, they engage in a process of critical inquiry and scrutiny—the hallmark of a profession of teachers/scholars. As an extension of this exercise, I also ask students to add to the conclusions of the researchers by giving their own alternative explanations. In addition, they are asked to write hypotheses that might guide the research studies if they were replicated. As a final part of the lesson, they are asked to work in triads as a collaborative research team and to generate hypotheses and a research design which extends the research of the area under discussion.

Another use of the popular press is to ask students to read a research report in a popular magazine and on the basis of the information contained in the article to respond to a question. For example, a research study on the effect of pop quizzes on student retention was conducted and a summary appeared in a popular magazine and in a professional journal. Students were asked to suppose that one of their colleagues in the schools asked them for advice about giving pop quizzes. The students were asked to give advice on the basis of information contained in the popular magazine. After they had written their responses, they were asked to read the research report in the professional journal. Then a discussion was held which included the following questions:

- If you had read only the secondary source (popular magazine) and not the primary source (professional journal), would you have drawn different conclusions and given different advice to your colleague?
- What limitations/delimitations exist in the design of the study that were not reported in the secondary source and may lead the reader to unwarranted generalizations?
- What are the advantages/disadvantages of synthesizing research studies into short articles for popular consumption?
- The results of this research study have statistical significance. Do they have practical significance to teachers?
- What areas for additional research about pop quizzes would you recommend?

These strategies engage the student as active learners who are given practice in reading and understanding research. But more importantly, it contributes to students' understanding of the importance of critical inquiry when reading research.

GAGS AND GIGGLES

Since most thinking about statistics and research design is evidenced in prose and symbols, the opportunity to express one's knowledge and wit may be achieved through the visual. The use of cartoons as a medium of expression allows for the inventive juxtaposition of language and the visual and for associative thinking.

The technique is simple. Select cartoons or comic strips from the newspaper, blot out the words, and duplicate them. Ask students to illustrate their knowledge of a statistical and research terminology or concepts by writing captions for the cartoons. The students are asked to do so in such a way that it is clear that they understand the meaning of the statistical terms, that the dialogue make sense for the situation depicted in the cartoon drawing, and that the cartoon is f-u-n-n-y or imaginative.

The example as provided in Figure 1 was written by Pam Hurd Servie and illustrated by Richard A. Levering. It illustrates her understanding of the importance of interpreting IQ test scores and national norms within the context of a well-defined comparison group.

The students have fun with this assignment and take pleasure in reading those submitted by classmates. They also report the difficulty they experience in the juxtaposition of three elements: selecting a statistical or research concept that matches the visual components of the cartoon and that is funny.

GENERATING HYPOTHESES

This activity is rich with possibilities for the development of the students' skills for making inferences, speculative thinking, making predictions, elaborative thinking, sensing multiple explanations, dialectical reasoning and creative inquiry. In this assignment, students are encouraged to discuss and defend their ideas and to defer judgment of others ideas. This latter request has been demonstrated to foster perceptual openness so that a large number of quality ideas may be generated.

The materials that serve as the content for this instructional strategy may be drawn from a variety of fields. Because one of my course goals is the expansion of students' sensitivity to gender and racial equity, I often use research studies related to this topic.

In the example that follows, the students are asked to find a study about biracial children and their schooling. This topic has a sufficient number of research studies to allow for a variance in findings, yet the collection is not so large as to make comparisons and contrasts overwhelming. This strategy is also used to introduce the concept of meta-analysis and the role that statistical analyses play in the conclusions drawn from multiple research studies.

As a result of their collection of research findings, students discover that the studies of biracial children and their schooling appear to provide equivocal findings. An equal number of the studies report that there is and there is not a differential performance, behavior, values, and attitudes between biracial children and children of single racial minority groups.

Through various small group and whole class discussions, students work together and struggle with the following types of questions:

- What hypotheses can you suggest that would explain these equivocal findings?
- What are your multiple hypotheses for understanding the variables that may affect the schooling of biracial children?
- What are the competing hypotheses that should be considered before you plan additional research on this topic?
- What are the possible courses of action a researcher might employ to define and measure the construct?
- Two of the studies of biracial children report the same findings, yet disagree on their conclusions. What are the central controversies embedded in their conclusions? What are the assumptions about race that may have led to opposing conclusions? To what extent may statistical treatment of data or methodological decisions have contributed to the debate? What critical reasoning did the researchers use for their arguments? With which of these two researchers do you agree? Why?

FIGURE 1   Student cartoon illustrating statistical comparison

It is suggested that these questions and others like them might best be attacked by groups of students working together. By doing so we are not only achieving the goals related to cooperative learning, but we are building a sense of the community of scholars. Within our profession, our individual research studies rarely have significance in themselves. Rather each study is part of a collection in which intellectual thought and support for our professional work occurs through the interaction of scholars.

SUMMARY

Several educators, writing in the late 1960s during a period of disenchantment with public education, suggested a system of teacher education that had intellectual creativity at its core. This type of program would nurture creative future teachers who show a preference for divergent, rather than convergent thought. In this regard, teachers would view themselves as teachers and learners in pursuit of questions—not answers. More recently, this view of the educated person is heard again. It is suggested that the nurturance of intellectual creativity in higher education has been an unexamined assumption, a presumed outcome of liberal and professional education, but one that is not apparent in the pedagogy of the classroom. The challenge to the teaching profession is to assure a compatibility between our words and actions in the classroom.

Statistics may be one arena in which this challenge is the most difficult. However, it is my hope that we may communicate to our students that statistical thinking, as an extension of scientific and mathematic thinking, is a creative endeavor.

CAMILLE L. Z. BLACHOWICZ

Teaching Terminology to Test Ideas

It has been estimated that students' vocabularies grow by over two thousand words a year once they enter the "reading to learn" phase that extends from the upper elementary grades through university (Nagy & Anderson, 1984). A cursory examination of one college freshman's vocabulary study list for a recent week confirms that many of these words are technical and highly subject specific:

Earth science—biome, biosphere, tectonic plate
Literature—synecdoche, metonymy, attributes
Criminal justice—recidivist, appeals, litigation, adjudication
Mathematics—catenary, arc, equilibrium

Dealing with content-specific terminology most often conjures up visions of lengthy study lists, "How to Increase Your Word Power," and the omnipresent, and dreaded, vocabulary notebook. Thousands of students, and their instructors before them, are familiar with the drill of compiling a list of new terms, consulting a dictionary or glossary for meanings, constructing sentences with the new terms, and cramming for weekly quizzes. Also familiar are the coping strategies developed by this approach: focusing on the first or the shortest definition, fudging sentences so innocuous as to be meaningless, and the hysterical definitions that sometime result ("acute angle"—"a very good looking heavenly person").

Content teachers who realize that mastery of subject-related terminology is critical to a student's understanding of a new area of study often resort to the "notebook approach" more by default than by design. Happily for practitioners, models of problem solving and reading comprehension offer alternative, hypothesis-testing models of vocabulary instruction. Because these models suggest a cognitive, rather than associative, approach to the learning of new terminology, they are consistent with the types of learning that go on in content classes.

These models stem from the belief that comprehension is basically problem solving; it requires that the reader be active, bring knowledge to the act of comprehending, make hypotheses and set purposes for reading, and gather information and make inferences before coming to a resolution. This theoretical perspective is supported by research evidence which suggests that good readers do, indeed, engage in these types of behaviors. They use what they know, self-question and hypothesize, integrate information across the text and with their prior knowledge and monitor these processes and their own learning.

Research also amply documents the strong and significant relationship between vocabulary knowledge and reading comprehension and the fact that the learning of new terminology is best achieved when it is embedded in rich, conceptual learning. This article will outline five steps for structuring hypothesis testing instruction for new content terminology with examples from secondary and university classrooms including on example from a social studies classroom where all the steps were combined for one lesson.

FIVE STEPS IN HYPOTHESIS TESTING INSTRUCTION

Drawing on these current models of comprehension and word learning, there are some basic guidelines teachers can use to structure more active, predictive classroom vocabulary instruction:

1. Activate Prior Knowledge. Being by activating whatever the students already know. Asking, "What do I know about these terms?" should be the student's first strategic act. This will also build the habit of making self-assessment the first step in learning. For example, in a history class undertaking the study of World War II, the teacher might start by having the students brainstorm all the terms that they associate with that war (see Figure 1). Brainstorming not only exposes a group to a large number of terms, it also has a "pump priming"effect; the first words suggested activate other responses that might not have been generated at first. Sometimes students propose terms that *don't* fit, generating problems to be resolved in reading or research.

Following brainstorming, a classifying activity can also help students organize their terms and generate categories in which to place new terminology as it arises in the reading. Then, as students read, they can add to their list, create new categories and try and find information about proposed terms about which they have questions or disagreements. In the case of the examples generated by students displayed in Figure 1, students were to watch to see if Gen. Westmoreland was associated with World War II, who "Churchman" might be (Churchill) and if stealth bombers were used in World War II.

FIGURE 1 Brainstorm and classification on World War II

```
┌─────────────────────────────────────────────────────────────────────────┐
│ Brainstorm Terms                                                          │
│                                                                           │
│            grenade        France      panzer           London            │
│            bomber         Italy       stealth bomber   Tojo              │
│            Eisenhower     V-2         Rommell                            │
│            Iwo Jima                   Westmoreland                        │
│            South Pacific              Churchman                           │
│                                                                           │
│ Classification   with more terms added as categories appeared             │
│                                                                           │
└─────────────────────────────────────────────────────────────────────────┘
```

Generals	World Leaders	Locations/Battles	Armaments	?
Patton	Hitler	Battle of Bulge	tank	Westmoreland
Montgomery	Tojo	Pearl Harbor	panzer	Churchman
Eisenhower	Roosevelt	Normandy	grenade	stealth
Rommell	Mussolini	Iwo Jima	V-2	bomber
		France		
		Italy		
		Germany		
		South Pacific		
		London		

As we read, add other terms to list and look for "?" column.

2. Make Preliminary Hypotheses. Next, have students make preliminary hypotheses, predictive connections between terms or between terms
and the topic and structure of the selection; this emphasizes that new
vocabulary words are not isolated elements but parts of rich semantic
networks. Both the process of attaching meaning to a word and the meaning itself are important, so students must be active in generating tentative
meanings to be tested in reading. Whenever possible, these hypothesized
meanings should lead to predictions about the content and/or the structure
of the selection to be read, saving time for the teacher and emphasizing
that vocabulary learning should be text-based. The second strategic step,
then, is, "What do I see in previewing the selection that can give me a clue
to what these terms might mean? What's my best guess?"

For example, from a health class on nutrition, students had brainstormed all the nutrition-related terms they knew and classified them as
related to "Vitamins—Foods—Prevention—Medical treatment—Problems." The teacher then proposed five new terms that she knew would

occur in the selection and asked students to generate possible connections to the categories or terms they already had generated (see Figure 2).

In this step, discussion is critical. In this case, students were uncertain about "bulimia" and "rachitis" and had a limited knowledge of the "World Health Organization." Hearing others' ideas provides confirming *and* conflicting information that generates questions to be resolved in reading.

3. Use Contextual Cues. Have the students read the text so that terms can be encountered in their "natural" environment. It is not necessary for students to have the full meaning of the target words before reading as they will use context, when appropriate, to resolve questions raised by the first two steps. For example, in a sociology class, students made some predictions about the terms *exogamy* and *endogamy*, connecting both to marriage but uncertain as to more specific characteristics of the words' meanings. As they read the chapter on tribal marriage customs, the teacher asked them to pick up specific clues to support or refute their initial ideas and note the text pages that helped them flesh out the meaning (see Figure 3). This is an example of the type of data gathering that can go on after initial predictions about a terms meaning. Besides reading, experimentation, observation, demonstrations, media, interviews and other sources of information can flesh out the defining characteristics of specific terminology.

4. Test And Refine Hypotheses. Use discussion to test early hypotheses about the terms by refining and reformulating meaning after reading using initial cues and the cues from the reading selection. The strategic step here has the student say, "I can use what I read to confirm or clarify my preliminary ideas about what these terms mean." This metacognitive self-evaluation often sends the students back into the text or to and outside reference for more information. Unlike a "cold" attempt to use a dictionary,

FIGURE 2   Possible connections among categories for brainstormed terms and new health terms

---

Categories:

Vitamins—Foods—Prevention—Medical treatment—Problems

New Terms:

pantheatic acid ___could be a vitamin_____
bulimia _____?_____
intravenous feeding ___medical treatment_____
World Health Organization ___could help with health improvement_____
rachitis _____sounds like problem or treatment_____

FIGURE 3   Record of clues picked up during reading as to the meanings
of the new terms

---

endogamy

prediction before reading: *something to do with marriage like monogamy*

clues in reading: *p 13 – endogamous tribe becomes inbred*
*p 16 – person from endogamous tribe was shunned when he
married outside tribe*

conclusion after reading: *endogamy – marrying inside of tribe*

exogamy *something to do with marriage (like monogamy) ex: implies divorce?*

prediction before reading: *p 17 – contrasted with endogamy*
p 17 – stronger bloodiness, fewer birth defects

clues in reading: *endogamy – marrying outside of tribe*

conclusion after reading:

---

however, the students are coming with a hypothesis that needs reframing,
more detail or finer tuning. In a class studying the wildlife of Africa, the
term "springbok" was encountered. Students could tell that this was the
term for some sort of deerlike animal, but wanted more elaborated information. They consulted a dictionary for more attributes of the term: it is found
in South Africa; it is a gazelle; it is very agile; it gets its name from its habit
of springing suddenly in the air.

   5. Claim Ownership.   Have the students use the terms in writing and
additional reading. Students should develop the strategic notion, "To make
a word 'mine,' I must read it and use it."

A CLASSROOM EXAMPLE

Observing the implementation of all five hypothesis generating and testing steps in one lesson reveals the kind of thinking that goes on as students examine content terminology. Take the example of a ninth grade basic social studies class getting ready to read a chapter with this vocabulary:

tepee	dascha
villa	turllo
apartment	mandan
geodesic dome	lean-to
highrise	yurt

The teacher and class went through the following steps:

1. Activate Prior Knowledge. Here the teacher gave each student a "Knowledge Rating Sheet" (see Figure 4) so that each could estimate his or her level of knowledge about the terms. Students were asked to rate the terms as very familiar (I could give a definition or use in an illustrative sentence), somewhat familiar (I have seen or heard this word before), or unfamiliar (Don't know).

The teacher encouraged the students to talk to each other about the terms as they work and to share any knowledge or ideas they might have. As the students worked, the teacher circulated to get a sense of the knowledge base of the students before going further.

2. Making Preliminary Hypotheses. After giving the students adequate time for self-rating, the teacher led a discussion about what was known

FIGURE 4 Knowledge rating sheet

Rate Your Knowledge

How well do you know each of these terms? Check your knowledge level for each.

TERM	3 Can define/use it	2 Heard it	1 Don't know
tepee			
villa			
apartment			
highrise			
geodesic dome			
dascha			
trullo			
mandan			
yurt			
lean-to			

FIGURE 5 Transparency of class predictions about topic

Topic = Dwellings, Homes, Houses				
	Where?	Used Now?	Look Like?	Who?
tepee				
villa				
apartment				
highrise				
geodesic dome				
dascha				
trullo				
mandan				
yurt				
lean-to				

about each term and used an overhead transparency to make notes. For this group of students who lived in a suburb of a large city, "tepee," "apartment," and "highrise" were well established terms; "trullo," "dascha," and "yurt" were relatively unknown.

The teacher then asked some questions to get the students to use the vocabulary to start thinking about the chapter and to generate larger hypotheses about the terms. These predictions would then form the purposes for reading.

> T(eacher): OK, you know something about several of these terms, but let's see if we can use all the terms to get some ideas and questions about the chapter we're going to read. Looking at these terms, what do you think the topic of the chapter is?
>
> S(tudent): Houses
>
> S(tudent): Homes where people live
>
> T: OK. Do you think that all these houses are in the United States?
>
> S: No.
>
> T: Why not?
>
> S: Well, there are some here that sound kind of foreign.
>
> S: Like dascha, and villa
>
> S: And trullo
>
> S: Mandan
>
> S: I think "mandan" is from here because it was something with the Indians we studied.

S: There's a mandan house in the museum, you know, that big earth lodge.

T: Well, this is interesting. It seems like we think some of these are not in the United States but let's put a question mark next to mandan to try and figure that out. (Places red question mark next to mandan) Do you think that all of these are dwellings that people live in now?

S: No. People don't live in tepees anymore.

S: I don't know about that. When we went to Mount Rushmore, I saw tepees.

S: Yea. But that was probably just tourist stuff.

T: Hmm. Interesting. What about the other terms?

S: (Many suggestions with conclusion that class is not sure)

T: Before we read, let's try to think like a textbook author. If you were going to write this chapter about dwellings, what would you tell about each one?

S: Who lives in them.

S: What they look like.

S: Where they are.

S: When they were lived in.

T: OK. We've got some good ideas about what these terms might be and some questions to answer about each one. Let's read the chapter and come back and talk about them.

3. Use Contextual Cues.   The students now read their chapter so that terms can be encountered in their "natural" environment. Though they do not know the specifics about each word, they have a topic to help them organize their reading and several questions to answer about each word. The teacher also gives each a personal record sheet, like the transparency used earlier, to take notes about each type of dwelling as they find it.

4. Test and Refine Hypotheses.   After reading, the teacher uses the transparency version of their record sheet to record student findings about the terms. She follows up on some of the questions from the pre-reading discussion. Students reflect on their earlier hypotheses to find that the dwellings are not, indeed, all located in the United States. However, they are all in current use as dwellings, a fact that is the surprising one of this selection.

When students still lack information to refine their hypothesized meanings, the teacher sends them back to the text to reread. In the case of "mandan," another reference book was brought in to clarify the location of these Plains Indian dwellings.

5. Claim Ownership. By this point the students had heard the targeted terms several times, had used them in discussion, had read them and talked about them. The teacher assigned some writing tasks to involve yet another modality so that the meanings of the terms and their appropriate usage became well established.

A FINAL WORD

Using a hypothesis generating and testing approach to introducing and developing vocabulary proves productive on many levels. First, it develops a strategic approach to vocabulary that is consistent with general problem solving models of learning. Secondly, it uses vocabulary to engage students in a reading selection and saves classroom time for the teacher by having one activity to "double duty" for both vocabulary introduction and reading preparation. Lastly, it injects a note of problem solving and fun into word study that provides motivating for secondary learners.

REFERENCES

Barr, R., Kamil, M., Mosenthal, P., and Pearson, P. D. (Eds.) (1991). *Handbook of Reading Research: Vol. II.* White Plains, NY: Longman.

Beck, I., Perfetti, C., and McKeown, M.. (1982). "Effects of long-term vocabulary instruction on lexical access and reading comprehension." *Journal of Educational Psychology* 74, 506–21.

Blachowicz, C. L. Z. (1985). "Vocabulary development and reading: From research to instruction." *The Reading Teacher* 38, 876–81.

Blachowicz, C. L. Z. (1986). "Making connection: Alternatives to the vocabulary notebook." *Journal of Reading* 29, 643–49.

Johnson, D., & Pearson, P. D. (1984). *Teaching reading vocabulary.* New York: Holt, Rinehart and Winston.

Mezynski, Karen. (1983). "Issues concerning the acquisition of knowledge: Effects of vocabulary training on reading comprehension." *Review of Educational Research* 53, 253–79.

Nagy, W., & Anderson, R. C. (1984). "How many words are there in printed school English?" *Reading Research Quarterly* 19, 304–30.

Pearson, P. D., Kamil, M., Barr, R., and Mosenthal, P. (Eds.) (1984). *Handbook of Reading Research: Vol. 1.* White Plains, NY: Longman.

INGRID G. DAEMMRICH

Evaluating Initiation Theories
in the Composition Course

Composition theorists have characterized the experience of the first-term college student as an initiation into the strange lands of academic thinking and discourse. Increasingly, teachers of first-year writing courses have assumed the role of initiators of neophytes into the academic processes of formulating hypotheses, collecting data, and evaluating critically theories of professional researchers in order to reach conclusions that either support or question their findings. But where does the writing instructor begin when faced with a group of students whose attitude toward critical thinking echoes Mr. Gradgrind's in Dickens's *Hard Times*: "You can only form the minds of reasoning animals upon Facts; nothing else will ever be of any service to them"?

Having had to prove their mastery of certain "facts" in order to be granted entry into college, the newcomers grow impatient, confused, and occasionally even hostile when told that the "real work" in academic disciplines takes place in that nebulous realm beyond fixed sets of data which Knoblauch and Brannon have identified as the "patterns of relationships endlessly evolving through accretion, disintegration and reconstruction" (C. H. Knoblauch and Lil Brannon, "Writing as Learning Through the Curriculum," *College English* 45 [1983]: 467). I propose that an excellent way for the writing teacher to begin the initiation process into these complex and fluid patterns exhibited by academic thinking and discourse is to undertake a critical evaluation of the initiation process itself.

In order to give students what Toby Fulwiler has called "a stake in his or her topic" ("Freshman Writing: It's the Best Course in the University to Teach," *The Chronicle of Higher Education* 31 [1986]: 104), I have expanded the concept of initiation from the compositional theorists' emphasis on becoming acquainted with new discourses to the entire experience of being a first-term college student. This redefinition has allowed me to design a writing assignment that tests the following hypothesis: given the nearly universal requirement of a college degree for any meaningful occupation and the lack of any other commonly observed formal initiation rite in our culture, the first term at college or university becomes for our young people the rite of passage called initiation in other cultures. In their first term, college students undergo some or all of the experiences recorded by anthropologists observing the rituals marking the passage from adolescence to adulthood in native Asian, African, North and South American societies as well as by cultural historians and mythologists studying the texts and artifacts of ancient Greece and the Middle East. According to Arnold van Gennep, one of the earliest initiation researchers, there are commonly three steps in the initiation rite: (1) separation and isolation from home, family, and familiar surroundings; (2) marginality or liminality, that is, a period of belonging to neither the old structure nor the new; and (3) aggregation or incorporation into adult society. The rite is presided over by elders who provide indoctrination into the belief system and practices of the tribe and often includes physical ordeals, including mutilation. Later researchers reported or analyzed other characteristics: that the elders are usually not the parents; indeed, that initiation often entails acquiring knowledge in an unfamiliar, non-domestic context with other young people outside the direct family; that in the rite, the "old" adolescent dies and a "new" adult emerges; that initiation is a symbolic, fearsome journey into the unknown realm of death, hell, the grave, the womb, or water as the origin of life leading to a "resurrection" of a new being; and that it represents a "liminal" state of non-being, an interstructural situation that emphasizes the process of transformation from one fixed state to another.

Procedure

Because the data testing the validity of my hypothesis were the students' first-term experiences as recorded in their personal journals, I devoted the entire term (10 weeks of 1989) to the experiment. On the first day of class, students were given the following assignment entitled "Journal-Keeping": "Each student will keep a journal in order to document present thoughts, feelings, and events as they occur. Always date each entry. This journal should be brought to class periodically for writing, group, and class discussions." Starting with the second class meeting, I devoted approximately fifteen minutes every other class meeting to actual journal-writing. Though I continually encouraged adding entries to the journal outside class, devoting class time to data-gathering emphasizes its importance as well as the need for continual additions. At no time did I hint at the purpose, other than to repeat the widely-held assertion that researcher-writers in all disciplines keep journals in order to collect data and that in order to be useful, this data must be accurate, detailed, and dated. In order to encourage openness and honesty and to discourage attention to stylistics and mechanics, I periodically assured students that their journals were absolute private property; no one would ever read any part unless invited to by the writer. In contrast to professional log-keeping, which is often open to scrutiny by others in the field for purposes of verification, the control of the raw data remained totally in the hands of the writers.

Only after having amassed nine weeks of documented experiences, thoughts, and feelings in their journals were students introduced to my hypothesis: that their recorded data replicate the experience of initiation in other cultures. After a brief presentation of the role of initiation rites in non-Western societies, I distributed the following statements by six social scientists concerning the meaning of this rite of passage for both the individual initiates and their society:

> Initiation rites, with very minor exceptions, are characterized by the fact that they come at or around puberty. . . . the rites seem to emphasize the end of a span of life in which the distinction [between male and female] is not fully established, and to herald a new life period that should be free of ambivalence about the adult sex role. (Bruno Bettelheim. *Symbolic Wounds: Puberty Rites and the Envious Male.* New York: Collier Books, 1962: 20)

> An initiation ceremony, with its attendant physical pain and isolation from parents, demonstrates to the youngster that his nuclear family is no longer his sole protector, refuge, and security. . . . The trauma that is experienced during an initiation ceremony . . . is a shared one, an experience suffered in common with a group of peers and agemates. . . . The experiences of mutilation and isolation with a group [113] not only serve to cushion the shock but also produce an exceptionally strong bond among initiates. . . . These are the people who remain inseparable friends for the rest of their lives. . . . (Yehudi A. Cohen. *The Transition from Childhood to Adolescence.* Chicago: Aldine Publishing Co., 1964: 110, 112–113)

> In philosophical terms, initiation is equivalent to a basic change in existential condition; the novice emerges from his ordeal endowed with a totally different being from that which he possessed before his initiation; he has become another. . . . To gain the right to be admitted among adults, the adolescent has to pass through a series of initiatory ordeals; it is by virtue of these rites and of the revelations that they entail, that he will be recognized as a responsible member of the society. (Mircea Eliade, *Rites and Symbols of Initiation: The Mysteries of Birth and Rebirth.* Trans. Williard R. Trask. New York: Harper & Row, 1975: x)

> Rituals of puberty often mark the shift from few or no demands placed on the youngster to a heavier involvement in labor. (Martha Nemes Fried and Morton H. Fried. *Transitions.* New York and London: Norton, 1980: 272)

> Initiation rituals . . . pose the central riddle or riddles of a society, and as such they initiate or begin the process of spiritual growth for individuals in particular cultures. . . . [T]hese symbols function as riddles that engage the people in a quest to orient themselves within a cosmos of meaning. (Thomas V. Peterson. "Initiation Rite as Riddle." *Journal of Ritual Studies* 1 (1987): 79)

> For the initiate, it is a question of divesting himself of his earlier condition, of dying in order to be born as another being. . . . After the preparations, which all indicate a solemn departure, the initiate is invited to experience the

journey into the realm of death, of the beyond, hell or heaven, hell and heaven sometimes. (Simone Vierne. *Rite, Roman, Initiation*. Grenoble: Presse Universitaire de Grenoble, 1973: 19 [my translation])

These statements were preceded by the following directions:

Below are the statements of six social scientists on the nature and function of initiation both for the individual initiates and for their society. First, read through your personal journal. Then, study the statements below. Which one do your experiences support or contradict most convincingly? Copy that statement as a "warm-up." Next, write a proposition that clearly states whether your experiences as a first-term university student support or contradict that statement. Then, write two distinct paragraphs (= 2 pp.) explanation. Use specific examples from your journal (with dates, quotes, summaries, or paraphrases) to bring to life for us outsiders just how your experiences support or contradict the chosen statement. As any honest "scientist," scrupulously avoid reshaping the data in your journal in order to fit the statement. But don't be afraid to interpret broadly the statement in order to make it useful as an explanation for your experiences."

The students then processed this paper as any other through the stages of group discussion, drafting and redrafting, and two peer- and instructor-readings before adding it to the other papers in their final portfolio.

Results

Of the 35 members of the class, considerably more than half (20) chose to submit the "journal-initiation" paper in their final portfolio. Of these, eighteen validated the hypothesis, while the remaining two refuted it. Of the selected statements by social scientists, Cohen's was evaluated as being the most applicable: thirteen students found that his assertions on separation from home, family, and familiar surroundings and bonding with age-mates undergoing the same liminal experience characterized their first term at the university, while two students found that their experiences contradicted Cohen's statement on bonding between initiates. Vierne's and Eliade's emphasis on the death of the "old" adolescent and emerging of a "new" adult were corroborated by the experiences of two students respectively. Fried and Fried's characterization of initiation as the assumption of responsibility was confirmed by one student. The statements by Bettelheim and Peterson received no response. Bettelheim, in particular, might be more applicable to high school or even pre-high school students reaching puberty, when sexual awareness plays a major social role.

In their critical evaluations of the researchers' statements, the students were able to cite compelling documentation from their journals. Thus, the students drawing parallels between their experiences and Cohen's characterization of initiation as a painful separation from family, old friends, and familiar surroundings based their papers on vivid (if not always stylistically elegant) metaphors and details from their journals to characterize their emotional trauma:

> *Katerina* (9/29/89): I miss my own bedroom and my bed. I miss my parents. . . . I even miss my brothers and sisters and all the noise they make . . . My attitude towards everything seems injured. I want to go home.

> *Joi* (10/10/89): I really miss home now, and the funny thing is I didn't think I would.

> *Marcia* (11/7/89): Right now all I can think of is home. I can't help thinking what my little sister is doing now. How is my dog Salty? How is mommy? I have only been here a short while and home is only a phone call away, but I still miss everyone. I miss seeing their faces.

Other students cited examples from their journal capturing the frightening feelings of loneliness and vulnerability that the unfamiliar territory of initiation can arouse:

> *Jennifer* (Journal 9/14/89): I don't even know where to sign up for a tutor. What's going to happen to me?

> *Konnie* (10/12/89): . . . it is sometimes frightening heading down unfamiliar roads . . . How will I find myself back when I'm lost?

Nearly all students pointed out, however, that unlike initiates in other cultures, their pain was psychological, not physical. Some students affirmed the positive aspect of separation. Drew, for example, supported his view that the pain of separation from parents results in a desirable independence with a citation from his journal (10/5/89): "Up until now, we the generation [*sic*] have been told what was appropriate to do, the time it must be done, and most often not, given an explanation as to why. . . . The guided tour is over; from here on out what one does is his/her own choice." The positive value of gaining independence from parent-mentors was vividly seconded by Jennifer's strong disapproval of her mother's interference in her quest for a tutor in her journal entry of 9/19/89: "Instead of letting me fight for myself, my mom stormed into the room and told the secretary that she would not stand for anything less than a tutor for me."

Students drew equally eloquent parallels between their experiences as documented in their journals and Cohen's statement on the bonding between initiates separated from the protection of the familiar undergoing the ordeal together. They noted that even though they came from diverse backgrounds and environments, unlike initiates in more homogeneous societies, the shared experience of being isolated from families and friends led to a similar substitution of new supportive friends for the ones left behind:

> *Juliette* (11/12/89): Stacey, similar to my family, acted as a security blanket, a protector, and a place to seek refuge.

> *Mike (11/21/89):* . . . almost everyone on our floor is friends with everyone else.

Some students also recognized that data recorded in their journals supported Cohen's statement that agemates undergoing the same trauma would gain a strong sense of bonding:

> *Marcia* (10/15/89): She [her roommate] confided in me by telling me how nervous she was about college, how much she too missed her family and how scared she was as to taking the initiative of making new friends. Without even recognizing it, I too began confiding in her as to my fears about college. I was surprised in finding out that we basically shared the same doubts and fears about this "new adventure." I must admit that I feel more relieved by knowing that someone as close as my roommate shares my feelings.

Two students who had joined athletic teams discovered a particularly strong bonding as a result of training and working together toward the common goal of victory over competitors. As Drew stated in his paper, his joining the swimming team "opened the opportunity to have fifty instant friends when I arrived at school" and thus "cushioned" the pain of separation from family and old friends.

David M. cited his journal entry of 11/21/89 to describe how being part of the team countered isolation from the familiar:

> While celebrating [the ice hockey team's 12-1 defeat of another university team], . . . the captain, a senior, spoke up to me and asked, "Yo, you wanna go out with me and a couple other guys after you get cleaned up?" . . . Just being asked to go out with a couple of upperclassmen made me feel so great. It was like they really accepted me and the feeling of isolation was no longer present.

The considerable redundancy of data presented by students in support of the parallel between Cohen's definition of initiation and their own experience extends also to the affirmative evaluations of Eliade and Vierne. One of the two students who compared Eliade's characterization of initiation as a series of ordeals with her first-term experience centered her evaluation on pain, just as those writers who had chosen Cohen's definition of initiation had done in describing the separation from home and loved ones:

> *Laurie* (10/12/89): I am so tired, words cannot even explain just how tired I am. I was up till three in the morning in an attempt to figure out my computer. I spent an hour writing an English paper, then lost it somehow. I do not know what I did to lose it but I spent most of my night trying to figure it out.

In addition, both students found that evidence in their journals corroborated Eliade's contention that at the end of the rite of passage from adolescence to adulthood, a totally new person emerges. As Laurie concluded, "the rebirth I experienced in initiation can be directly related to the Eliade statement."

Similarly, both Melody and Mark documented with citations from their journal the relevance of Vierne's description of initiation as a journey through death, hell, and resurrection. Describing her struggle against a tendency to postpone assignments, Melody quoted her journal entry of November 18, 1989: "Today, I keep thinking about my death. . . . The reason why I feel this is because my life seems to be going nowhere fast. I cannot get a grip on things." Discussing the possibility of failing Calculus, Mark quoted his journal entry of November 20, 1989: "I believe that the 'Mark' of [high school] must die in order for the real Mark to live once again." Even Steve, the one student who found that Fried and Fried's definition of initiation as the shift to "a heavier involvement in labor" matched his documented experiences, agreed with the others that the first term of college reshapes the student: "I learned to do homework without being told to. I also learned to study for a subject without there being a test on the material the next day" (10/15/89); "It's amazing, but I never thought I would be cleaning my own room without being told to do so. But . . . the slightest crumb would attract many bugs. So, . . . I'm constantly cleaning my room" (10/20/89).

In contrast to the replication of evidence cited by those students supporting my hypothesis, the two students who contradicted it quoted sharply differing reasons from their journals. In keeping with their finding that their experiences reinforced a sort of rugged individualism, each took an individual point of view. Brian contended that the diversity of backgrounds and financial situations among college students resulted in differing levels of maturity and responsibility that hindered the type of bonding described by Cohen during the initiation rite. He supported this critical view by citing the October 18, 1989 entry from his journal: "I'm planning to help Jim today after school like I promised I would. I still can't get over his inability to perform tasks which I take on every day. Maybe tomorrow I'll teach him how to cook an edible meal, unlike the food in the cafeteria." Entitling his essay "Friends Are Hard to Find," David T. found that "[n]ot only has rudeness and immaturity level reached a high that I can't stand [sic], but irresponsibility [in] relationships is outrageous"

(10/12/89). He cited further support for contrasting his experiences with Cohen's statement on the bonding of initiates from his journal entry of November 15: "The people on this campus try to outdo each other in every way possible. Whether with fashions, academics, or athletics, competition never ceases. . . ." In opposition to Drew's and David M.'s view that being on a team encourages bonding, this student found that competitiveness among athletes obstructed the building of team spirit.

Discussion

In the process of using the accumulated data in their journals to take a critical stance toward the initiation theories formulated by six social scientists, the twenty students who submitted a final paper on their findings demonstrated that they had acquired several important skills in writing and critical thinking. By keeping journals over an entire term, they, as well as all their classmates, practiced writing as data-collecting. My presentation in the ninth week of a number of single statements taken out of their original contexts and aligned with each other to form a new context challenged my students to interact with academic discourse in its most distilled form. Together with discovering that texts can be manipulated in this fashion, they learned to match the texts of their journals with those of the theorists. Supported by the text that they had originally created simply to retain their experiences, they gained the confidence to judge authoritatively and convincingly whether or not these statements describe their recorded experiences. Class evaluations of this exercise reveal an appreciation for this opportunity to integrate personal experience with academic discourse. As one anonymous evaluator wrote: "I learned more about the person I wrote about." Another carried the notion of initiation as bonding between agemates over into the class evaluation: ". . . it dealt with a fresh personal experience shared by other members of the class." Faculty evaluation was just as positive: in a university-wide contest of freshman writers, Marcia's essay was judged to be among the five best transactional essays of her class. Both judgments are eloquent testimony to the students' successful shift away from a simple acceptance and repetition of Mr. Gradgrind's "nothing but Facts" stance toward a sophisticated use of their own collected data to test theories that summarize and analyze experiences belonging to totally different cultures.

In making this transition, eighteen of the twenty students who submitted the "journal-initiation" paper in their final portfolios exhibited a willingness to assume control over the process of their initiation into the academic community's ways of testing and evaluating data. By choosing to complete this exercise, they put into practice Knoblauch and Brannon's definition of learning as "the process of the individual mind making meaning from the materials of its experience" (467). The procedure of comparing their journal entries with the theories of professional social scientists provided them with the early initiation into the "strange lands" of academic thinking and discourse that compositional theorists have characterized as belonging to the experience of first-term college students. Still, the exercise is no more than a first step in the lengthy process of moving from uncritical reliance on facts supplied by the "experts" to questioning theories. As two of the twenty papers illustrated, not every novice is ready to make even this first step. Ignoring the theoretical framework, these writers focused exclusively on the data of their recorded personal experiences.

Interestingly, among those students who ventured into the "strange land" of appraising relationships between data, a number exercised their critical stance to question the accuracy of my hypothesis. While eighteen out of twenty students affirmed the validity of my hypothesis, several writers also pointed out that it was only partially true. In our mobile culture, they argued, the experience of initiation is a repetitive one, as individuals move from college into jobs and from one job to another:

> *Drew*: At the end of this initiation, I will go forward into a new lifestyle and begin a different type of initiation, thus continuing in a chain of events throughout my life.

> *Laurie*: The ordeals one must undergo will occur throughout the life of the adult . . . And so, life, even after rebirth, is a constant learning and growing time.

> *Marcia*: The experiences of the initiation ceremony have endowed us with the strength, courage, and vigilance to face the other transitions we will face during our lives. Whether the transition be relocating, becoming a parent, or experiencing other environments, we, the "survivors of the college battle," will be better prepared to face the "curve balls" life will throw our way.

What better initiation into the academic and professional environment can we give our students than the confidence that they have gained by critically evaluating the process of their initiation itself?

Herbert L. Leff, Ann Nevin, Donald W. Meeker, Jeanine Cogan, and, Gary Isenberg

Turning Psychology Inside Out

THE GOAL: THINKING WITH PSYCHOLOGY

All too often education seems to stress the mere *acquisition* of knowledge as an end in itself, without real concern for helping students develop skill in creatively *applying* what they learn. Our quest was to devise an educational process that would enable students to use any academic content to enhance their creativity and enrich their lives. This quest led us on a multi-year development project in an introductory psychology course. After considerable experimentation we emerged with a promising new educational paradigm for turning the "inside" content of psychology—or any other subject—"outward" to apply to just about any type of goal calling for creative thinking.

The essence of this educational paradigm (discussed in full in Leff and Nevin, 1991) is for students to use the "specialist roles" or *ways of thinking* inherent in a particular discipline to enhance special "awareness plans" (procedures for perceiving and thinking) that apply to various life-enriching goals. Here's a brief example to show what we're talking about:

> Let's say you're a student who has just learned about Freud's theories and techniques (such as id, ego, superego, free association, and the like). Let's also say that you are sick in bed with the flu. Furthermore, imagine that you have learned various constructive "awareness plans" such as "regarding even problematic situations as potential opportunities." Now, the question our paradigm would lead you to pose is how to use Freud's ideas to help think of potential opportunities the flu provides. (You might want to take a moment to mull over some possible answers before reading further. . . .)
>
> Here are a few "Freudian" opportunities that might come to mind: gaining easy access to your subconscious through "fever dreams"; following superego directives to catch up on reading or other work you can do in bed; using free association (a process likely to be aided

by resting in a prone position) to generate new ideas that would appeal to your id but not upset your superego too much. If all goes well, you'll feel excited about your creative use of psychology to generate new "opportunity" ideas, and you'll actually follow up on some of these.

THE PROCESS: LEARNING FOR CREATIVE APPLICATION

Our approach engages students in five major steps:

1. Reading over a text chapter to get an overview of the main ideas.
2. Making a "role map" that diagrams the main psychological ideas (concepts and principles), methods, interests, and questions covered in the chapter—the intent being to graphically represent the "thought patterns" of a psychologist specializing in the topics of the chapter. (See Figure 1 for an example of a simple role map. We found that making such diagrams is useful for many students, but the key point here is simply for students to become familiar with the knowledge and ways of thinking characteristic of the subject at hand.)
3. Listing the type of advice such psychologists would give for "enhancing" or making the best use of a few special awareness plans (perspectives or ways of thinking and perceiving, which in this program are oriented toward life-enriching purposes described below)—thus creating "role-enhanced awareness plans" suitable for application to the student's goals or problems. Our program thus far has relied on the book *Playful Perception* (Leff, 1984) to supply model awareness plans.
4. Actually using one or more of these psychologically role-enhanced awareness plans for a personally meaningful problem, goal, or situation.
5. Reflecting on what was learned from each of the prior steps and generating ideas for further development and application of the psychologically enhanced awareness plans tried out.

Students complete weekly reports or "journals" detailing their use of this process. They also attend a weekly discussion group in which they share and build on each other's ideas, results, and problems. These discussion groups are led by advanced students enrolled in a special seminar on facilitating this approach to using psychology to enhance creative thinking.

Before proceeding to some excerpts from student journals, we should note that *Playful Perception*—the students' resource book for awareness plans—presents sample thinking procedures that can be used directly or that can serve as models readers can use to develop their own new ways of thinking. The awareness plans in the book are organized around the following general purposes:

FIGURE 1 Overview "Role Map" for Social Psychology

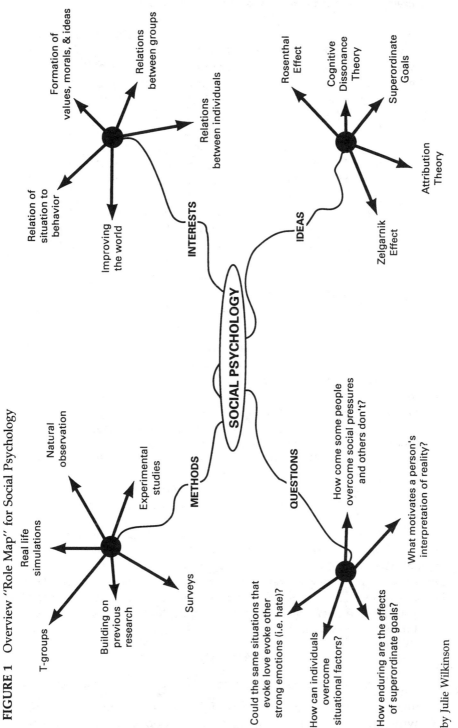

SOCIAL PSYCHOLOGY

INTERESTS

- Formation of values, morals, & ideas
- Relations between groups
- Relations between individuals
- Relation of situation to behavior
- Improving the world

IDEAS

- Rosenthal Effect
- Cognitive Dissonance Theory
- Superordinate Goals
- Attribution Theory
- Zelgarnik Effect

METHODS

- Natural observation
- Real life simulations
- Experimental studies
- T-groups
- Building on previous research
- Surveys

QUESTIONS

- How come some people overcome social pressures and others don't?
- What motivates a person's interpretation of reality?
- Could the same situations that evoke love evoke other strong emotions (i.e. hate)?
- How can individuals overcome situational factors?
- How enduring are the effects of superordinate goals?

by Julie Wilkinson

195

Fun and flexibility   (Sample plan: "Dreaming up alternative meanings for the things and events around you"—such as thinking of your life as a soap opera or your job as a new event at the Olympics.)

Appreciation   (Sample plan: "Finding special or unique value in everything you notice"—such as thinking of all the research time and expertise involved in generating the knowledge presented in a textbook.)

Interest and open-mindedness   (Sample plan: "Looking at the world through different value systems"—such as thinking of what would be important or valuable in a park to a money-hungry land developer versus a lovelorn poet.)

Creative innovation   (Sample plan: "Inventing games that inspire your thinking"—such as a version of 'Can You Top This?' to help a small group jar their creativity when working on a problem.)

Constructive coping   (Sample plan: "Thinking of every moment as an opportunity"—used in our flu example above.)

Synergistic thinking   (Sample plan: "Looking for points in other people's ideas to build on"—even including such cognitive tactics as building on a *reversal* of an idea you don't like.)

A central theme in our "inside out" paradigm is that any subject matter can apply to just about any area of life if the ideas and thought patterns of the subject area are used to enhance awareness plans that themselves can apply to any life issues. We have found that awareness plans serving the above purposes do indeed seem to apply to an extremely broad range of life concerns, including stress management, self-esteem enhancement, creative problem solving, self-motivation, relationship improvement, study skill enhancement, entertainment, and others.

THE OUTCOME: USING PSYCHOLOGY
FOR EFFECTIVE THINKING

Let us now turn to some examples of student applications of psychology as mediated by such awareness plans. The first of these examples is from the journal of a discussion-group facilitator for our program in the introductory psychology course; all the other examples are excerpts from journals of students in the introductory course itself. Each example illustrates a creative breakthrough in the application of an awareness plan combined with psychology content.

EXERCISE I

Kristen Wolanske, Group Facilitator for Introductory Psychology

[In this first example, Kristen Wolanske shows how she used the role of a developmental psychologist to give herself advice for using the awareness plan of thinking up effective actions. Her specific goal, to which she applies the "role-enhanced" awareness plan, is to generate ideas for improving use of time during an average day. She addresses this advice both to herself and anyone else listening in on her journal. . . .]

Role: Developmental psychologist

Awareness Plan: Thinking up actions which would lead to improvements

Goal: Effective use of time

Role-Enhanced Awareness Plan: A developmental psychologist might think of different times of [the] day in terms of stages and coordinate particular times with actions which are best performed during this time in an attempt to improve efficiency in time use.

As an expert I advise you to see each day in terms of life stages. The early morning might be seen as the development of a child. At this time you are acquiring attitudes and emotional feelings towards the day . . . The early morning is like the first year of life and can influence how the rest of the day goes. Perhaps this is a good time to share some love with a friend, i.e. hug to feel good and secure, or play. This stage in the day is often rushed over or forgotten but probably would be advantageous to experience.

Following this might be your adolescent stage at which time, changes in your body play an important role . . . During this time of day it might be advantageous to perform one's daily hygienic practices [and] pamper yourself a little. It also might be good to meditate or exercise or just spend some time with yourself in order [to] integrate your mind and body. This time can also be similar to adolescence in that it is the time to "try on" styles, actions and attitudes. We probably [should] get dressed and establish how we . . . want to look and act that day during this stage.

When you leave adolescence you are breaking away from being a child and now are an adult. This probably extends for the longest part of your day. At the very beginning of this stage it might be a good time to organize the rest of the day by planning out what you have to accomplish (goals). During this stage Schlossberg believes that there are eight psychological issues which can be affected by the events that occur:

belonging . . . mattering . . . autonomy . . . competence . . . renewal . . . identity . . . intimacy . . . commitment.

[Accomplishing your goals] may not be easy and problems may arise but being in touch with the above psychological issues may help direct when you are most effective at performing various tasks. Your schedule which you set early in the adult stage is not concrete and can be followed loosely.

Beware of midlife crisis sometime in the late afternoon when you might feel out of energy or off center. That's ok, use this time for writing (i.e. journals), thinking about how your day went, sort out problems, develop new and exciting project ideas, and perhaps even update your schedule for the rest of the night. Don't get down on yourself at this time but use it to fuel up (mind and body) i.e., have some dinner. Note: not everyday will have a midlife crisis.

After [this stage] there is another stage of high productivity during which you can accomplish many things. . . .

As the night wears on and you enter old age, "Gerontologists have found that many of the problems of 'old age' would occur to most people deprived of loved ones, close friends, meaningful activities, intellectual stimulation, and control over what happens to them" (Rodin, 1988 as cited in Wade & Tavris, 1989, p. 511). At this time of day you might like to visit with friends, family, loved ones, entertain, continue working on projects which you enjoy . . . Most of all try not to leave things that you have to do for this time but do what you want to do.

Following this stage is death when you fall asleep and enter into circadian rhythm, the sleep phase of your sleep/wake cycle.

By examining your day as describe [d] you will be better able to match time with activity and improve your time usage.

EXERCISE II

Gwen Parker, Introductory Psychology Student

[In this example, Gwen Parker uses the role of a certain type of social psychologist to enhance a "constructive-coping" awareness plan. Her general goal here is to enjoy life more, but her specific application involves freeing herself to speak up in class. . . .]

Role: The "Deindividuation and Dehumanization Specialist"

Awareness Plan: To recognize the value of each moment

Goal: To experience life more joyfully

Role-Enhanced Awareness Plan: I've found myself falling into the trap of living only for the future and conforming to expectations of others . . . since I've come to college. I am constantly "sowing" both emotional and academic "seeds" but the "harvest" is never "reaped." The Deindividuation and Dehumanization Specialist states the underlying need of any problematic situation is to individuate the situation and humanize those involved.

Actual Application: I decided to try this [strategy] in [a class] in which there was a definite pressure from both without and within me to sacrifice the moment for the sake of future. . . . Normally, this class is somewhat anxiety-provoking; there are constant referrals to the upcoming term paper and comments about how ". . . students never do their readings" from the professor. . . . Professors wonder why students don't participate more? It's because we're forming for social acceptance and academic "safety" ("better silent than sorry") . . . The [professor of this class] tries to frighten us into participating with threats of grades and we sink further into our fear of future ramifications for doing "wrong" now, and thus we clam up.

I individuated the situation by noticing the professor is *now* asking for questions . . . *now* looking around with a look that says that he expects silence . . . no one else is speaking *now* because they're probably just as intimidated as I am . . . my . . . book is *now* sitting on my lap open to a passage about the contradiction between Puritanism and the work ethic (which is so blatant *now*) . . . and *now* exists a wide open line of communication . . .—a line which has and will not exist at any other time . . . seize this unique, differentiating quality and—

"Yes," I said, "it seems as though the various ideologies we discussed last week ignore these passages very pointedly. . . ." ("Humanizing myself" had once again occurred . . . by individuating the situation I naturally had to recognize and use my faculties of perception, thought, self-awareness, *action*, etc.)

Reflections: [I used this technique at least three other times.] It altered my thoughts and actions in group situations in which I tried it. It gave me conscious control over being "role-conforming." I think many people *try* to value each moment but often without an effective strategy for doing so. This strategy was a way of personifying situations and thus drawing almost "human" relationships between myself and the surroundings. It allowed for progress beyond the mind-blocking stage of merely saying "OK, I'm living for the moment—I'm seizing the day!"

EXERCISE III

Deanna Couture, Introductory Psychology Student

[Here Deanna Couture takes on the role of a type of cognitive psychologist to enhance an appreciation-oriented awareness plan. But her goal is not so much to increase her appreciation of her living room as it is to help herself generate creative ideas for improving the room. . . .]

Role: Memory Specialist

Awareness Plan: To view everything as a work of art in a gallery

Goal: To re-decorate my living room.

Role-Enhanced Awareness Plan: A visitor [to my living room] will have encoded within the first second the information, probably in a visual image. I want to create an impact during that first second so the viewer won't dismiss information but be curious enough to want to retain it longer and investigate further. . . . I will use the idea of the 3 boxes or systems which are not literal but mental processes happening at different stages by allowing my visitor to view only a section of the room at a time, leading the eye and interest to a point, exposing little by little to build suspense and not flood the senses with too much information. . . . A sensory specialist would say to think about pattern recognition for effect. I will group art objects or chunk them in groups of 7 pieces plus or minus two so as to keep the images in the viewer's short-term memory longer. To use deep processing, I'll feature memorable events.

Actual Application: I've been doing some framing and hanging and used this strategy to hang groups of pictures together all relating to nature. My two entrances pique a visitor's interest by not showing the whole expanse at once but directing the eye from object to painting. Because of this exercise, I have decided to have an art appreciation and art history theme.

Reflections: I find that in normal conversation I am applying some of the information from the psychology book. For instance, I was in a conversation the other day where we were laughing about possible alternative meanings of a sentence. I could see how a psycholinguist would explain syntax and surface and deep structuring. I notice people using deductive reasoning and coming up with their own unique syllogism, arriving at conclusions due to their premises. . . . Taking the material and finding a practical application is another level of learning and presents more of a challenge than simply sorting out and organizing the material.

Using the strategy of the memory specialist was probably the first time I really understood how my mind was open to new ideas. I believe it was so because the way I tried to solve the problem was not to use the same old mental site. I got rid of old assumptions and strategies. For instance, I had been trying to solve my problem based on color arrangements and period styles. I overrode these old hang-ups. I was encoding in a way other than functional fixedness. The memory specialist role created a divergent pattern of thinking.

EXERCISE IV

Anonymous Introductory Psychology Student

[This final example is drawn from an unpublished research study by Gary Isenberg (1990) in which he asked a group of students in our course to devote at least some of their awareness-plan applications to enhancing their self-esteem. This student in Isenberg's study chose an awareness plan with a "constructive coping" theme and used a special type of developmental psychologist role to enhance and apply the plan. . . .]

Role: Expert on Erikson and stage theories

Awareness Plan: Seeing everything as having potential to teach you something about yourself.

Goal: Improve self-esteem

Role-Enhanced Awareness Plan: A stage theory expert would advise that stages are natural for people's growth. They start at childhood and run until death. If I used the knowledge about stages I could see things that appear to affect my life (e.g., confusion, frustration, disappointment) as necessary for growth. In this way lack of self-empowerment could be thought of as a natural, unavoidable occurrence and not the effect of incompetence or inferiority. By looking at this I am able to learn that problems with self-esteem are not always destructive, but part of a larger plan for growth.

Actual Application: This [role-enhanced awareness plan] gave me a new way of looking at things around me that I feel cause frustration and the lowering of self-esteem. I used it to look at my life and the problems that occur in it, not as monumental disappointments, but as natural stages that are part of everyone's aging process. In evaluating stage theory, [the text] said that during the college years we see the greatest gains in self-understanding and the resolution of identity conflicts. This [could be seen] as the reason behind my self-esteem confusion.

Reflections: In searching for identity and self-understanding it is necessary to go through stages of self doubt. This makes my problems seem to have some purpose aside from making me miserable. It makes even the most terrible experiences seem like a learning tool in developmental growth.

CONCLUSION

Education can be a much more joyful and creative experience for students, and for teachers, when students are given opportunities to find new and helpful ways to use subject matter. When students are encouraged to think creatively about the subject matter and about their lives, they gain new perspectives and powerful learning skills to find joy in learning and joy in life—as well as to accurately acquire and use the complex concepts of their courses. Moreover, students who learn to use specialist roles to enhance their use of consciously selected awareness plans gain self-empowering skills of perspective taking, understanding and control of their own thought processes, and a wide array of tools for problem solving. Indeed, if education is "turned inside out" in the way we are advocating, students learn that *everything* learned can be a valuable resource for boosting the creativity and effectiveness of their thinking.

REFERENCES

1. **Leff, H. L., and Nevin, A.** (1991). *Turning education inside out*. Book manuscript.
2. **Leff, H L.** (1984). *Playful perception*, Burlington, VT: Waterfront Books.
3. **Isenberg, G.** (1990). The effects of a metacognitive educational model on college students' self-esteem, locus of control, orientation and academic performance. Unpublished undergraduate paper submitted to Psychology Department, University of Vermont, Burlington, VT.

GEORGE W. CHILCOAT

Writing Dime Novels
to Understand Popular Culture

The purpose of this chapter is to discuss and describe an activity known as the dime novel as an alternative to the usual term/research paper in order to help secondary school students develop an understanding of the slave experience in the United States. It can also help students apply methods of historical research in understanding selected historical concepts and themes and in gaining a much needed perspective on the human drama that characterizes history, in general, and slavery and racism, in particular. This article describes (1) the use of the dime novel studying slavery in the secondary history classroom; (2) the historical background of the dime novel; (3) procedure of the technique for classroom use; and (4) debriefing of the activity.

THE USE OF THE DIME NOVEL
IN THE CLASSROOM

Dime novels have always been a mirror of early American society. Although produced mostly for mass entertainment from 1840 to 1910, this form of popular culture dealt with social problems, engaged in moral reform, and made attempts to generally understand society and human nature.

As a teaching method, the dime novel can be used as a means for historical research studying a given historical event or time. The dime novel activity can encourage students to rely on their own application of the historical method and to draw and test their own conclusions separate from those already formulated by teachers, historians, and textbooks. The activity emphasizes the use of original documents and sources as historical content in order to provide information and material for student use. The use of the dime novel can stimulate students to demonstrate imagination and creativity in such skills as posing significant questions, locating appropriate data, subjecting that information to critical analysis, synthesizing these diverse materials, and expressing the results in articulate convincing, oral or written presentation.

The dime novel provides students with the opportunity to offer insights and to state viewpoints about select historical events, themes, and concepts that took place during the eighteenth- and nineteenth-century American agricultural-plantation society. This activity can take students from a narrow me-here-now experience to a broader them-there-then experience by allowing students to demonstrate the spiritual, cultural, social, political, and economic difficulties suffered by the slaves.

It also provides the opportunity for students to develop skills, attitudes, and knowledge to communicate effectively in writing. This activity supports three forms of writing:

1. Expressive Writing—Students use their imagination to develop or convey feelings, insights, or ideas.
2. Argumentative Writing—Students use arguments or emotional narrative to direct or to persuade others.
3. Informative Writing—Students record specific information or convey factual knowledge.

The following list is designed to illustrate a historical approach directed toward the examination of a set of concepts and themes that highlighted the *slave experience*. This list also provides information to help teachers and students to be aware of any one or combination of concepts and themes in which to emphasize and use in creating and writing their dime novel. This list is by no means exhaustive.

Themes and Concepts Dealing with Slavery

caste system	household servants	dehumanization
master class	public conscience	racism
driver	slave-plantation system	slave mongering
bondsmen	chattel slavery	class structure
overseer	African culture	big house
field hands	Ante-Bellum South	miscegenation
gang system	inalienable rights	Middle Passage
task system	legendary genteel planter	auction block
urban masters	anti-slavery societies	social cohesion
insurrections	corporal punishment	praise meeting
slave codes	plantation paternalism	maroon camp
free men	Underground Railroad	Jim Crow
civil rights	planter aristocracy	refugees
manumission	three-fifth rule	abolitionists
emancipation	segregation	slave trading
cotton kingdom	patroller system	slave raiders

HISTORICAL BACKGROUND

The dime novel was a form of American subliterature that gained popularity from 1840 to 1910.[1] Dime novels (a misnomer, as most cost only a nickel at the time) were written to entertain the proletarian reading public with fast-paced action, high adventure, melodramatic dialogue, engaging double-title, eyecatching cover illustrations, and ethically uplifting stories that emphasized the triumph of good over evil. Historically, topics of the dime novel covered events from the pioneering of the West in the nineteenth century to the urbanization of the cities at the turn of the twentieth century. Although making no pretensions to be a historical novel, many of the early stories dealt with real people and actual events in order to sell their product to the public. These early dime novels, patriotic and nationalistic in character, gave a picturesque view of the hardships and struggles of early western life. The story line followed a simple formula: frontier setting, moral hero, rugged individualism, crafty villain, helpless heroine, bold-spirited struggle, and a happy ending.

The dime novel continued to be popular during the late nineteenth century as American society experienced tremendous industrial and urban growth. W. H. Bishop, writing for the *Atlantic Monthly* in 1879, and discussing the social impact of the dime novel, wrote: "It is an enormous field of mental activity, the greatest literary movement, in bulk, of the age and worthy of very serious consideration for itself. Disdained as it may be by the highly cultivated for its character, the phenomenon cannot be overlooked."[2]

The basic theme of the dime novel (keeping with its original simple formula) responded to this growth by underlining financial achievement

---

[1]Historical and literary background came from: Thomas D. Clark, "Virgins, Villains, and Varmints," *American Heritage*, 1(Spring 1950): 42–72; Merle Curti, "Dime Novels and the American Tradition," The *Yale Review*, 26 (June 1937): 761–778; Phillip Durham, "Dime Novels: An American Heritage," *Western Humanities Review*, 9 (Winter 1954–55): 33–43; Charles M. Harvey, "The Dime Novel in American Life," *Atlantic Monthly*, 100 (July 1907): 39–43; Stewart H. Holbrook, "Frank Merriwell at Yale Again and Again and Again," *American Heritage*, 12 (June 1961): 25–27, 78–81; Daryl E. Jones, "Blood 'N Thunder: Virgins, Villains, and Violence in the Dime Novel Western," *Journal of Popular Culture*, 4 (Fall 1970): 506–517; Mary Noel, "Dime Novels," *American Heritage*, 7 (February 1956): 50–55, 112–113; William A. Settle, Jr., "Literature as History: The Dime Novel as an Historian's Tool," in *Literature and History* (University of Tulsa Monograph Series, No.9), ed. by I. E. Cadenhead, Jr., Tulsa: University of Tulsa Press, 1970, pp. 9–20; and Michael K. Simmons, "The Dime Novel and the American Mind," *Mankind*, 2 (October 1969): 58–63.

[2]W. H. Bishop, "Story Paper Literature," *Atlantic Monthly*, 54 (September 1879): 383–393.

and social acceptability in the big city. The three most popular stories that followed this theme were: (1) the city detective, who was able to thwart crime at every turn; (2) the poor boy or girl, who worked hard, practiced clean living and thrift, and with a little luck and a helping hand, was able to achieve monetary success; and (3) the adventurer, who with an unlimited source of money, was able to participate in exciting and hair-raising undertakings.

On occasion, the dime novel constituted a significant social and political statement regarding various moral issues that effected American society. One such dime novel, *Maum Guinea And Her Plantation "Children," or Holiday Week On a Louisiana Estate*, was a slave romance that attacked the morality of slavery and the double standards of slave owners.[3] Published in 1861, this dime novel made a significant social statement by presenting vivid illustrations of pathetic pictures in slave life and of the causal indifference to outright wickedness of white slave holders. For example, the following moving narrative is a story told by a slave woman, Sophy:

> Dey done gone and butchered our people widout judge or jury—hundreds was shot, which was a mussiful death, quick over. But shooting was too good for any but de innocent—dem dey suspected as having had any ting to do wid de insurrection, dey hanged, end whipped, and burned—yes, burned— oh Lord!
>
> . . . I'll tell you how t'was. You see dey come, great lot o' white folks one day, and dey took me, and dey tell me my husband was arested, and in Jersamen jail, and dey say if I 'fess w'edder he was guilty or not, and tell all I know 'bout Nat Turner, dey wouldn't punish me, dey'd let me be in peace— but if I didn't tell every work I knowed, dey would whip me till I couldn' stand. I tol' em I shouldn' say notin' agin my own husband, and I didn't know notin' 'bout Nat Turner . . . Dey stripped me stark naked, tied me up, and whipped me 'till I was 'most dead; but I wouldn' fess. I fainted away, and dey throw pickle on me, and left me and next day dey come back and tie me up ag'in and whip me on my raw back, and den dey turn me around and whip me todder side, till I was raw all around. I kin show you de scars, dey're on my breast, dey're on my back.[4]

With the coming of World War I, the rise of postal rates, and the advent of the pulp magazine boom in the 1920s, the popularity of the dime novel finally faded out.

PROCEDURE

The procedure involves: (1) a brief introduction of the activity; (2) the setting of due dates and the length of time for the activity; (3) the choosing

[3]Michael K. Simmons, "Maum Guinea: or, A Dime Novelist Looks at Abolition," *Journal of Popular Culture*, 10 (Summer 1976): 81–87.

[4]Metta V. Victor, *Maum Guinea and her Plantation "Children," or Holiday Week on a Louisiana Estate; a Slave Romance*, New York: Beadle and Adams, 1861:96.

of a topic or concept; (4) an explanation on the collection of data for writing the dime novel; and (5) the review of the guidelines for writing the story itself.

The introduction of the activity provides for a brief overview of what the students will be doing. The introduction might include information such as a description of what the students will be writing; the page length of the assignment; a brief history and nature of the dime novel, and the purpose of the activity in order to study various historical events and personalities revolving around slavery.

The time for this activity as explained here lasts approximately four weeks. The first two weeks are for the research of the topic and the last two weeks for designing and writing the story. The time can vary according to the abilities of the students and to the desires of the teacher who may want a shorter or longer timed activity.

The teacher can assign a given historical topic or concept to each student or allow the students to either select a topic from a list provided by the teacher or choose a topic of their own interest. Many of these topics are included above.

The following are steps each student needs in locating, collecting, and organizing their information in order to write their dime novel:

1. Determine the event and its inclusive dates.
2. Go to the school, public, and/or college/university libraries.
3. Locate (a) original sources, i.e., newspapers, *The Congressional Record*, diaries, (b) secondary sources, i.e., textbooks, readings, historical books.[5]
4. Collect the needed information such as eye-witness accounts, stories, speeches, etc. As each student collects his/her information, he/she should be answering these types of question—When did the event begin? When did it end? What actually happened? Who did what? Why did it happen? When did it take place? Where did it take place?

[5]W. L. Andrews (1988), *Six Women's Slave Narratives*, New York: Oxford University Press; J. F. Bayliss (Ed.) (1900), *Black Slave Narratives*, London: Collier Books; J. W. Blassingame (Ed.) (1977), *Slave testimony: Two centuries of letters, speeches, interviews, and autobiographies*, Baton Rouge: Louisiana State University; A. Bontemps (Ed.) (1969), *Great slave narratives*, Boston: Beacon Press; G. Bourne (1972), *Picture of slavery*, Detroit: Negro History Press; S. Feldstein (1971), *Once a slave: The slave's view of slavery*, New York: William Morrow; H. W. Jacobs (1987), *Incidents in the life of a slave girl*, Cambridge: Harvard University Press; R. M. Miller and J. D. Smith (Eds.) (1988), *Dictionary of Afro-American Slavery*, New York: Greenwood Press; G. P. Rawick (Ed.) (1972; 1977; 1979), *The American slave: A composite autobiography*, Westport, CT: Greenwood Publishing; S. M. Stern (1976), *The black response to enslavement*, Washington, DC: University Press of America; A. Weinstein and F. O. Gatell (Eds.) (1988), *American Negro slavery*, New York: Oxford University Press.

What kinds of effects did the event have on individuals, society as a whole, and/or government.

5. Organize and outline the information into a meaningful story. Again, students ought to answer the above questions during this organizational time.
6. Apply the information in writing and designing the dime novel story.

The teacher reviews the guidelines in writing a dime novel with the class as a whole during classtime.

HOW TO WRITE A DIME NOVEL

There are three basic parts to the writing of the dime novel: (1) the characterization, (2) the plot outline, and (3) the title cover. The first two parts deal with the writing of the dime novel. The third part emphasizes the needed visual lure for selling the document to the reading public (in this case the teacher).

Characterization

Regardless of the historical theme, development of the characters is the same. Stereotyped, they are of two basic personalities, the hero/heroine[6] and the villain/siren. The qualities of the hero and the heroine read like a Sunday School lesson. They are self-made, well educated, clean living, adventurous, brave, courageous, gentle, modest, unassuming, brilliant, prodigious with any type of machine, animal or weapon, wealthy, or working towards that end, and exceedingly attractive to the opposite sex. Love is purely romantic, a matter of blushing cheeks and palpitating hearts. They always thwart the evil intentions of the villain/siren.

---

[6]Thomas D. Clark (1950) described the dime novel hero as one who "stood more than six feet tall, had coal black hair, black eyes (if not black, then cold grey ones), his limbs were hard and sinewy, he walked with a free and easy, but compact grace, his hearing was superb, he could smell to perfection, sense his way about in the dark, keep his hands off the women, loved god, knew geographical situations by instinct, could see the north star while lying flat on his back in a tangled canebrake, use a knife with dexterity and swim the Mississippi River with as much facility as the average heavy-footed settler could jump a spring branch."

Clark describes heroines as ". . . luscious maidens . . . paragons of beauty and virtue. As attractive as these women were said to be they seem never to have inspired lechery in the hearts of any but the most craven outcasts. They were said to have been so beautiful that they surpassed the daintiness of females in America during the post-Civil War years. Novelists warned their readers that the frontier girls were more attractive than those of the modern period because they did not wear cosmetics and endeavor to bolster flattened figures with false stuffing."

The villain[7] and the siren are lusty cads and uncouth ruffians filled with fiendish and crafty imaginations to thwart the hero and to defraud the heroine through the use of dirty tricks. They exploit the common man, make a mockery of the democratic process, and manipulate the law for personal gain. He or she is usually a victim of social injustice, mental disturbance, or some confused motive. The dastardly villain and unscrupulous siren are felons of every type: spies, con men, arsonists, swindlers, renegades, misers, bushwackers, business competitors, crooked government agents, old line aristocrats, bullies, kidnappers, bank robbers, and crafty plutocrats (bankers, land speculators, capitalists, politicians, lawyers, and sheriffs).

In addition to the hero/heroine and the villain/siren, other characters can be added to carry out the story. These might be friends or "chums" of the hero/heroine, "cronies" of the villain/siren (they never have friends), or mere bystanders that aid in the development, progression, and flow of the story.

Plot

The plot consists of a simple story line or a sequential chain of events, emphasis on the local setting, and plenty of action and dialogue. The story line involves the action taken between the hero/heroine and the villain/siren on a situation that the hero/heroine wants to make right and the villain/siren wants to make wrong (or better yet, to attain his/her own ends). The purpose of the story ought to be introduced at the earliest possible moment, bringing together the principal characters to engage the interest of the reader. A situation is created which calls upon the hero/heroine to accomplish some feat or to choose some course of action. The situation should bring out the conflict and/or the difficulty to be overcome.

After presenting the purpose the dime novel should present a series of situations which involve a conflict between the protagonists and the antagonists and the resolution of the conflict. The ending of the story should bring the series of situations to a climatic end. The reader should have a sense of satisfaction in regard to the happy outcome of the story.

[7]The villains according to Clark (1950) are ". . . renegade white men who trafficked with the Indians, counterfeited money, speculated in land and waylaid travelers . . . It was not unusual for them to be pockmarked, or slashed across the face with hideous knife scars. Their beards and hair were long, scraggy and greasy. Their raiment was worn and filthy, and their language vile and profane. Curiously the novelists had all of their villains speaking in the backwoods vernacular in contrast to the heroes who spoke in a stilted Victorian mode. These scoundrels lusted after women with viciousness, and they spent most of their time trying to win the fair maidens by any means at hand. Their favorite devices were spreading malicious gossip, murdering and kidnapping."

Emphasis on local setting provides the necessary realism to establish the plausibility of the story.

The dime novel is written in third person narrative with plenty of action and dialogue. Action words are used to portray fast, emotional events such as the shooting of a gun (She fired the gun. Bang! Bang! Bang! Bang! Bang! Five times without hesitation). The dialogue is very descriptive so as to provide vivid pictures in the minds of the readers. Add to all of this the historical background and situation, and the dime novel is ready to be written.

A possible narrative sequence might include:

Initial Situation

Characters:	Introduction and description
Place:	Location and setting
Time:	Day/night/week/month/year
Problem:	The beginning of the conflict involving the characters with a problem to solve or a goal to achieve; setting the stage for the remaining action in the story

Ordeal/Events

Event 1:	Things that happen that tell how characters go from ordeal to the resolution. The villain unable to defeat the hero, must turn to dirty tricks.
Event 2:	The hero/heroine's internal reaction, including thoughts, feelings, and goals.
Event 3:	Hero/heroine's attempt(s) to achieve goals and resolve problems.

Resolution

How the characters end the story by solving their last problem and achieving their goal, usually describing feelings and thoughts. The hero/heroine always thwarts the evil machinations of the villain.

Title Page

The title page is used to arouse the reader's interest. It also provides a visual opportunity to describe what actions are written in the dime novel. The title is written in two parts: a primary title written in large, bold type followed by a secondary title, known as a subtitle, beginning with the word "or" written in small type somewhere below the primary title, e.g., *Samuel Saves the Day*, or, *The Peril of Peter Pringle; Eric the Endearing*, or, *Dastardly Dirk's Downfall; Joshua Goodwin and the Greedy Landowner*, or, *the Return Visit to Spencer County*.

The drawing encompasses most of the title page. It portrays an exciting, action scene found in the dime novel. It is in vivid color. The front page should follow this example:

Made-up Publication Name
PRIMARY TITLE
or Subtitle
drawing
Author's Name

During the first two/three weeks the teacher sets up individual student conferences. The student conference reveals problems students might be having, allows the teacher to give further guidelines and clarification in writing as well as in historic content, and eases student frustration. The conferences are held both during class and after school (depending on the time spent on the assignment) and last between ten to fifteen minutes. The student brings a rough outline (the plot, the setting, and the cast of characters), three to four sample pages of writing, and a rough drawing for the title page. These provide the teacher with the opportunity to check on the student's understanding of the assignment and any procedural and substantive problems.

The two major problems that usually occur are the unwillingness to draw the front-page visual and the inability to write in third-person narrative. To handle the first problem we tell students that the drawing is worth a substantial amount of the overall grade. The other problem is more directional and procedural. Some students think they are to write a diary and then proceed in a journalistic or autobiographical narrative. A reminder and some examples of third person narrative from dime novels are all that are necessary to put the students back on the right track.

EVALUATION OF THE DIME NOVEL

Evaluating the written portion of the dime novel is based on the following criteria:

1. The originality of the dime novel.
2. The historicity of the dime novel.
3. The sufficiency and acceptability of the enclosed information within the dime novel.
4. The adequate written expression and readability of the dime novel.
5. The neatness and orderliness of the dime novel.
6. The thorough completeness of the dime novel.

7. The correct form of the title page.
8. The correct use of the format.
9. The evidence of sufficient and acceptable research data for the dime novel.
10. The punctuality of the assignment.
11. The completion of the following questionnaire:
    A. Cite ten significant facts learned from your dime novel.
    B. What three conclusions can be developed concerning this topic on the basis of the facts cited?
    C. What in your dime novel would lead you to accept these conclusions?
    D. Why might your conclusions be wrong?
    E. What facts, events, objects, or values might lead one to reject the conclusions cited above?
    F. What factors would cause the conclusions to change?
    G. What assumptions were made in your dime novel? Were they realistic?
    H. Are the conclusions consistent with the readings and other class activities?
    I. How might these conclusions be applied to other times and places? Other topics?
    J. How do these conclusions relate to you? To us?

DEBRIEFING ACTIVITY

The debriefing activity is used to evaluate the learning, the application, and transfer of the concept or topic. The activity gives students the opportunity to dramatize the past and allow their characters to provide them with viewpoints that make the past believable to the present. The teacher uses a large group discussion where students talk about their dime novels. Students begin with a brief synopsis of their dime novels. Then they focus on conclusions that can be drawn from dime novels about concepts or themes under consideration. Students read passages from literature assignments to support their positions and conclusions. Depending on the controversial nature of the concepts or themes, the teacher may challenge conclusions by providing additional facts that challenge the students' conclusions. The teacher may ask students to do additional reading and thinking about the concepts or themes.

The final phase of the activity revolves around a discussion of how students can apply their conclusions about various concepts and themes to modern society and how they are related to the students and their everyday experiences. In this final phase, learners are able to see, perhaps for the first time, how American history in general, and slavery in particular, relates to their lives.

Chapter 4

え〜 *Applying Plans to Problems: Data Generating Processes*

In any culture, it is remarkable just how many procedures young people learn on their way to becoming adults. In the Western world, shaping sound into sentences, tying shoes, getting dressed, and opening doors are usually well implanted long before children set off for school. Writing, reading, adding, subtracting and making way through a daily schedule come with focused effort. Elaborate procedures, such as those required for researching a paper, engaging in a debate, conducting an experiment, or planning a video production are learned only with extensive practice under careful guidance. Those are the procedures which mark competence in the subject areas.

DEVELOPING SCRIPTS
AND FLEXIBLE PROCEDURES

Procedural knowledge is simply knowing how to do something. Because so much of our time is consumed with doing things, most of us have reduced knowledge of how to do daily tasks to automatic "scripts." By the time we are in high school or college, we have developed a vast repertory of scripted knowledge: how to say hello in the morning, how to dial a telephone, or how to drive a car, even under extremely hazardous conditions. These scripts allow us to respond automatically to predictable events, leaving our conscious minds available for struggling with the unforeseen. When problems are familiar, scripted procedures are wonderfully efficient. When problems are novel, scripted knowledge can lead us astray, if only by suggesting that a simple routine will produce easy answers. Problem solving in the content areas requires turning off the "autopilot" on our procedures so we can revise them appropriately to fit the problem we face.

Cooking provides a good example of an elaborate procedure in which simpler subroutines are also visible. We'll try a simple dinner for four: salsa and dip for the Fritos, broiled chicken, boiled asparagus, and tossed salad, with pie for dessert. Any of us could follow simple procedures for preparing any of these separately—except perhaps for the pie crust. The problem is having them ready simultaneously at 7:00. The experienced cook sees the chicken holding the time line for the rest of the dinner. During the last ten minutes, the asparagus can boil and both will be hot. Salad? Start it with the chicken so it doesn't wilt. The pie? Once prepared, it's ten minutes at 450 degrees, then 35 minutes at 350 degrees. Unfortunately, the pie is in direct competition with the chicken for oven space. The pie crust and filling are in direct competition with the salad for hands-on time with the cook. The salsa fits nowhere on this increasingly complex time line to dinner. To solve this problem, the experienced cook must consult an internal model for steps in all cooking. The experienced cook has modeled the problem of dinner by 7:00 so all the embedded scripts can be made to fit a flexible plan. That plan seeks the best result, but accepts tradeoffs that will compromise the ideal dinner at 7:00: the store-bought salsa, the cold pie, the chicken browned at the cost of flabby asparagus spears.

In academic work, the ability to follow scripts does not necessarily add up to the ability to plan or solve problems. Writing a research paper, for example, is often taught as a series of scripted procedures in a set sequence. Identify a topic, generate a focusing question, search the bibliographic files, collect supporting information on 3-by-5 cards, write an outline, write a draft, and type. Most students can follow the steps in these routines. As English teachers recognize, those steps do not produce a thoughtful research paper.

Papers of high quality result from the influence of planned inquiry on the scripted procedures. "I want to find out whether Exxon fulfilled its social responsibilities after the Valdez oil spill." Such questions include not one topic, but three or more. One of them, social responsibility, would not show up in a routine bibliographic search. A planned attack on the Valdez oil spill would have to begin with a full definition of social responsibility including useful criteria for corporations. Research would have to include precedents for holding corporations responsible, not a topic stated in the original question. Throughout the research process on Valdez and its aftermath, thoughtful students would find themselves refining the original question, making notes on organization, and drafting paragraphs in an unplanned sequence, just to check their progress or shift the direction of their attack. Even typing, particularly in the computer age, is hardly a mindless routine. Transporting blocks of text, checking sentence construction, reviewing the flow of argument, and setting the format can lead to comprehensive last minute changes.

Success in solving problems depends on more than dexterity with routines or scripts; it depends on retreating regularly to critical distance—to check assumptions, identify anomalies, refer to background knowledge, redirect the action, raise new questions, represent the problem from a fresh perspective—to replan when necessary. Experts in a subject have enough background knowledge and experience to leave the scripted track whenever necessary. Novices, who have a great deal more trouble seeing themselves at a distance, quickly grow frustrated when the routines do not pay off in easy solutions.

LEARNING TO SOLVE PROBLEMS

Novices in any area tend to be impulsive when they face a novel problem. "Do something." they say. "Do anything. Do it harder." To reduce the tension of not knowing exactly how, they plug available numbers into some formula they have memorized, start writing with feverish abandon, or splash some primary colors on a canvas. Sometimes the rush toward resolution produces ecstasy. More often, it produces disappointment.

Because the result of problem solving is often public, thinking through steps worries students more than any other kind of intellectual work. They want to appear competent to themselves and others. They know that what they produce will be used to measure their competence. Their limited experience in problem solving often leads them to hope that there is some "right answer" out there that competent procedures will quickly disclose. This right answer will let them off the hook, whether or not they really know how to solve the problem. By the time they reach high school, students are addicted to right answers—just as the supply of right answers has started to dry up. They yearn for simple procedures, like the steps of dialing the phone or tying a shoe, that will unravel the intractible problems they now face—pollution, racial bias, and public corruption, for example. Who can blame students for flailing when the stakes seem so high and the path seems so cloudy?

Learning to solve problems that really make a difference involves considerable discomfort:

- Learning to tolerate the uncertainty of being "in process"
- Stating and restating the problem until it is clear
- Trying an approach based on intuition rather than surety, then trying again with greater knowledge
- Recognizing the value of products along the way that are only proximate to the desired goal
- Stepping back to view particular steps in relation to the whole

Successful problem solvers are able to turn their attention from the alluring goal to the more mundane iterations of laborious steps on an unknown path. Learning to create and solve problems means learning to take control of procedures with a clear guiding purpose in view.

At the end of the semester, we asked college students finishing our course on thinking across the disciplines to talk about problem solving and data generating processes in their own disciplines. Most of the students recognized that procedural learning is a mechanism for converting the abstract models in the mind into concrete form. Some students, particularly in mathematics and the technologies, recognized their own disciplines as a flexible system of procedures and methods.

Let's say a student is challenged by a word problem on the area of a rectangle. The student decides to create a flow chart for this type of problem. The student's creation looks like:

Problem ——— Draw ——— Write ——— Solve the ——— Use length-
           a   equation   equations   width to find
         picture   for area   area

After building this chart, the student tests it by trying problems dealing with perimeter and length and width. After generating many solutions to many different problems, he may reflect that the flow chart procedure helped and worked. (Christine Lovullo [Mathematics])

Some students also recognized the extent to which choice directs procedural thinking. In solving complex problems, they saw that procedural thinking is not merely mechanics.

The artist begins by generating ideas. These can be within the artist's head, in written journals or on a piece of paper full of thumbnail sketches. Among them, the artist must choose the best way to communicate her or his vision. The next step is more detailed plans, a maquette for three dimensional work or more detail to some of the thumbnail sketches. In this way the artist is testing out every possibility and getting rid of the ones that don't work. (Amanda Ferris [Art])

Each of the subject areas has developed specific procedures for managing data generation. In some areas, such as writing, procedures remain flexible throughout the process.

There are many ways to stimulate the mind to generate data. Writing is one good method in English. Outlines are an excellent way to generate data. Freewriting to begin with gets everything out from behind the cobwebs in an uncritical way, which is valuable. Piecing the parts together, writing the thing, generates data into your own style. Everybody generates data differently, and it is a chance to activate the individual in you! (Steve Cobb [English])

None of our students lost faith in routines as they thought about problem solving in their subject areas. The most successful students saw routines as flexible tools in a process that required extensive revision.

In the area of English, the skeleton is the grammatical communication system that allows us to read, write and speak. Yet it is not the language system that is responsible for what is being read, spoken or written, rather it is only a common representation of what we may mean. (Dan Frazer [English])

Knowing the steps is not enough. Adjusting or creating steps to meet the need is what counts. Redesigning steps requires, above all, a clear sense of purpose gained by stepping back from the action.

TEACHING PROBLEM SOLVING

When students have created a new idea, they can begin to use that idea, experimentally at first, for practical purposes: to evaluate their own experience, to write a poem, to design a bridge, to solve the housing shortage. The kind of envisioning that begets a new idea may be largely internal to the mind, but thinking for creativity or problem solving soon must seek a place in experience. "How can I make this work?" becomes the question. Such questions produce new "experience," sometimes a scrawl on the back of an envelope and sometimes elaborate plans for making something happen. In seeking concrete form in order to change experience, thinking assumes a systematic, step-by-step structure.

The teachers who wrote articles in this section have all discovered ways to help students move from impulsive flailing to some planned approach that lets them understand and refine their creative problem solving as they learn about a content area. We have represented data generating processes in three phases, not because they occur in that order in the life of the mind, but because in that order their relationship is most recognizable (see Figure 4.1).

As students work on solving problems, we have seen that representing or modeling the problem is an essential step, at the beginning but throughout—as new information suggests alternatives. Setting up procedures that let students work systematically toward solutions is also important, even if disappointing results force them to redesign. Finally, we see setting up a framework for answers as another facet of the process. How will we know if our answers are any good? In solving any problem, we see these steps as simultaneous and mutually supporting.

We have assigned articles in this section to three categories which rely on these aspects of representing and working through problems. In each case, the students use data generating processes to create a solution—a product aimed at meeting a need.

Modeling a process: Designing a simplified version of the problem to define factors and steps, preliminary to running through calculations to find answers

FIGURE 4.1 Applying Plans to Problems: Data Generating Processes

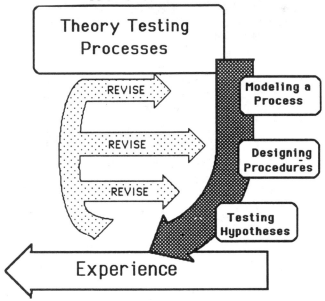

Designing procedures: Imagining a goal, then setting up different paths toward the goal with specific steps and a real product

Testing hypotheses: Designing a data generating process within an organization that will provide clear answers

As in earlier sections, stepping back to make revisions is essential to success. Finding a way to represent the planning process in concrete form gives students and teachers a chance to modify their approach. In the articles that follow, both the process and the product of student investigation can become the subject of class discussion and insight about data gathering.

Modeling a Process

Business management is often taught as a process of applying established planning models to different kinds of business situations. Walter Wheatley, Nick Maddox and Terry Armstrong have seen, however, that the mechanical application of planning models to hypothetical problems fails to activate the energy and vision business people need to solve problems in the real world. They have developed and refined exercises that activate the energy of vision already embedded in the purposes their students bring to class.

Clara Wajngurt sees writing as a technique for defining steps in problem solving before leaping to calculation. To gain control, her students write out an approach to any problem, then try the calculations. In written form, algebra problems become less opaque and discouraging. Variables become visible. A fresh approach becomes possible. She uses writing to help students design a new theoretical plan and then to develop further objectivity on their mathematical problem solving strategies. Writing also lets her students revise their theory of math competence—the way they see themselves.

Using a graphic organizer called a Vee map to guide the process of scientific thinking, Wolff-Michael Roth teaches his students how to conduct inquiry in Earth Science. They begin by focusing on a question and generating all the knowledge they already have about the subject at hand. Then, they design a new procedure for generating information that will help answer the question. The Vee map procedures lead them around the cycle described in this book, to the point that they question their own findings and develop new questions.

Rather than following a prescribed protocol for problem solving, Karl Smith teaches his students to design their own models for different kinds of problems. Working together, they create increasingly sophisticated models that account for an increasing number of variables. They can express their models in pictorial or algebraic form. After students have designed an approach, he lets them run through calculations and propose answers. Of course different versions of the problem produce different results. Then, his students use the "data" they generate to criticize and refine their original model.

Designing Procedures

For data to be meaningful, it has to be organized in ways that show its meaning. Jo Margaret Mano uses graphs with different structures to show students how to generate information that will answer real questions. Raw data have no worth. Organized in different ways, they convey meaning. Mano's students use graphics to organize and carry out original research on events in their own lives.

Testing Hypotheses

Robert Yager helped develop the STS (Science/Technology/Society) model of scientific investigation to show his students how to investigate important societal and scientific issues. Problems abound in this society. Why not involve students in inquiry that aims for useful answers? Yager's focus is local, but his students develop research skills they can take anywhere. STS motivates students to learn material they can use in solving problems they see as important.

Jack Matson makes his engineering class a crusade against the comfortable. What products would change the world? Imagine something truly worthwhile. When students have designed an innovative product, they then set out to design and produce it. This is a course on risk. Failure is applauded. Risk gives Matson a new standard for measuring the value of student work. Risk gives his students a reason to aspire and methods to use in design.

WALTER J. WHEATLEY, E. NICK MADDOX,
AND TERRY R. ARMSTRONG

Guided Imagery
in the Management Class

I first used imagery in the classroom several years ago as the focus of my doctoral dissertation. The results of my dissertation findings reflected that imagery is a very effective pedagogical technique that is well received by students. Today my colleagues and I use imagery, in some form or another, in almost every class we teach and every training workshop that we conduct. While most students are aware of imagery from its popularity in the sports world and its frequent incorporation in many television shows, they still are a little reluctant at first to experience it.

To overcome this minor difficulty, I introduce them to imagery by asking them to count the number of windows in their house. A couple of minutes later I ask them how many they counted. Six. Eight. Fourteen, if you count the patio door. When I ask them how they got their total, the answer is always the same. They took a mental walk through their house and counted them. What is interesting is that some walk inside the house and others walk outside the house. They are always amazed at how many other things they "saw." They will report seeing dust on the window ledges, things laying around the house, the grass outside needs cutting, etc. After this very painless introduction to the power of imagery, the students become game for many different learning experiences using imagery.

Basically, guided and non-guided mental imagery techniques are nothing more than having students relax and use their imagination. Applications of these techniques can be found in the areas of medicine, health, psychology, counseling, and even sports performance. Wherever there is a need to enhance personal well-being and performance, one will find the utilization of imaginal technology. Nowhere, however, is the use of mental imagery more prevalent than in the area of education. The value of mental imagery techniques to enhance the education process has been demonstrated in virtually every area of academic endeavor.

UTILIZING IMAGERY TECHNIQUES
IN THE MANAGEMENT CLASS

In the business management classroom, we have found mental imagery to be very effective in increasing the scenario building and goal-setting productivity of students. Another important skill taught in the business management classroom is decision-making. In testing the efficacy of imagery to enhance the decision-making process, we have found that imagery-trained students generated significantly more alternative solutions, more unique solutions, and more original solutions to decision-making exercises than non-imagery-trained students. We want to explain how we incorporate various forms of experiential imaginal pedagogical techniques into the management class in order to enhance the creative and imaginative skills of students.

Although specific procedures are limited only by the imagination of the instructor, we will discuss techniques that employ guided imagery and non-guided imagery. Guided imagery can be script specific (students vicariously project themselves into a formally prepared script) or can employ an informal script to promote an atmosphere where students will visualize a particular topic and then act upon it. Non-guided imagery techniques involve exercises designed to induce a relaxed environment which will yield a high level of new ideas and experiences. Both of these imagery techniques allow students to develop their creative and imaginative skills.

GUIDED IMAGERY TECHNIQUES

Guided imagery works like this: the instructor reads a script that encourages students to visualize themselves finding solutions to such topics as products of tomorrow, changes in customer demographics or any other business related area. During this delivery the students relax and try to envision images induced by the script. The value of guided imagery lies in the images conjured up in the minds of the students.

Formal Script Guided Imagery Training

Formal script guided imagery training allows a student to project him/herself directly into a script that has been prepared by the instructor. The experience for the student is very much like being an actor in a motion picture playing in their minds. The formal steps we use in the guided imagery process are presented below:

1. Tonesetting and Centering. We orient students to the training by explaining the basic format of learning and by asking that they take a few moments to center their thoughts and emotions in the moment.
2. Self-Induced Relaxation. We direct the students in a relaxation tech-

nique to induce a state of calmness and restfulness. A ten minute period of relaxation induction is sufficient with most students.

3. Free Imagery Practice. After centering and relaxation have been achieved, we present an open script to enable the students to experience how to evoke clear and vivid images in their minds.

4. Specific Script Presentation. At this time we present the specific script to the students in a clear and balanced manner. Students are instructed to visualize as vividly as possible the details of the script and to involve themselves cognitively and effectively in the process of guided imagery.

5. Free Imagery Practice. Following presentation of the specific script, we use a second free imagery session to reinforce learnings and perceptions gained from the script. A short relaxation period combined with some initial suggestion on focus helps the students to actively use this new information in their imaging.

6. Retrieval and Recentering. Upon completion of the imaginal process, we gently and slowly ask the students to re-focus their attention back into the moment and into the training environment. Imagery techniques create considerable relaxation and internal focus and it is important to recenter all students prior to ending the session.

7. Processing and Debriefing. At the completion of the training sequence, we allow an opportunity for reflection and discussion so that the students can review the training experience, their feelings about the experience, and any unusual or positive aspects of the training.

With a little practice, guided imagery sessions become very easy to conduct. The main point in this process is to allow the students to become comfortable with the relaxation process which is vital for the generation of vivid images. Some students will be uncomfortable with the process in the beginning. To overcome this initial resistance to participate fully in the guided imagery process, the instructor should fully explain the imagery process and the related benefits before any imagery sessions are conducted. It should be made very clear that an imagery experience is as normal as a common daydream. For those students who may refuse at first to try the imagery experience, simply have them close their eyes and relax during the session.

In addition to the relaxation process, a good script is vital if the vicarious guided imagery experience is to be a successful learning tool. Scripts are really relatively easy to prepare. Each script should begin with a relaxation scene, should include specific suggestions that will invoke images of the topic at hand, and should not include any terms that contain strong emotional content that might disrupt the state of relaxation. Here's a sample script designed for the enhancement of goal-setting skills.

Strategic Planning Guided Imagery Script for Goal-Setting

Close your eyes. Lie back. Shake out any kinks or tightness that you may feel. (Pause)

Pay careful attention to your breathing. Breathe in and out slowly and deeply. Feel how slow and deep breathing helps you relax. Now take a deep breath and hold it for a moment. Now, exhale very slowly. Feel the tension leaving your body. (Pause)

Breathe from your abdomen, deeply and slowly. Concentrate on your breathing. You are doing fine. (Pause) Now focus your attention on an imaginary spot in the center of your forehead. Look at the spot as if you were trying to see it from inside your head. (Pause)

When your eyelids become heavy and relaxed let them drop. Your eyelids are now relaxing. Sense how relaxed your eyelids become as you stop staring at the spot. Embrace this feeling of relaxation. (Pause). Let it radiate all through and around your eyes. Good. You are becoming very relaxed. (Pause)

Allow this feeling of warmth and relaxation to move out to your temples and across your forehead. (Pause) Your relaxation now radiates to your scalp (Pause), to the back of your head (Pause), to your ears (Pause), to your cheeks (Pause) and to your nose. (Pause) Very good. You are becoming very relaxed. Now relax your mouth (Pause) and your chin. (Pause)

As the tension leaves your face, relax your jaw muscles. Breathe real deep and let your jaw open slightly. Feel all the tension smoothly flow away. (Pause)

Now relax your neck muscles. Imagine all your tension flowing out the top of your head. Allow your neck muscles to totally relax. (Pause)

Let this feeling of warmth and relaxation flow down into your shoulders (Pause) and slowly into your arms and hands (Pause). Now let your back go completely limp (Pause), relax your chest (Pause), and now your abdomen (Pause). Feel the warmth and relaxation reach dow to the base of your spine (Pause). Good.

Now, let your hips go completely loose and limp. Allow the warm glow of relaxation to radiate to your thighs (Pause), down your legs (Pause), and down to your ankles (Pause) through your feet (Pause) all the way to the tip of your toes (Pause). Take a deep breath. You are doing very good. You feel very warm and free inside. (Pause)

You now feel completely relaxed. You have given away all of your tension. Take a moment to see if any part of you is not fully relaxed. (Pause)

Starting from the top of your head and working down find any part of you that is not completely relaxed. Then simply inhale a deep breath and send it into that area (Pause), bringing soothing, healing, relaxing, nourishing oxygen to comfort that area. (Pause)

As you exhale imagine blowing out right through your skin any tension, tightness, or discomfort. By inhaling a breath into that area and exhaling right through the skin, you are able to replace tension in any part of your body with gentle relaxation. (Pause)

When you find yourself quiet and relaxed, take a few moments to enjoy it. (Pause)

At this time I want you to keep your attention on the sound of my voice and on what I say. We are going to experience a guided imagery script that will enhance your ability to create better plans in the business world where you will soon be working. (Pause)

I am going to give you suggestions and instructions. As much as possible, visualize what you hear in a clear, vivid, and detailed way. Try to put yourself within the scene that is described as completely as you are able. (Pause)

Imagine yourself ten years in the future. You are the general manager of a very successful business. (Pause)

You are in a staff meeting with your managers discussing next year's objectives for your firm. (Pause)

Your sales manager tells you that, although sales are good, there is a need to add some additional product lines if you are to grow market share. In addition, something must be done to speed up deliveries. (Pause)

You are pleased to hear that the new high speed equipment is working well, offering a good productivity gain but your manager of manufacturing is concerned about some labor problems that might arise because of it. (Pause)

Zero defects has always been your firm's goal, but your manager of quality control has some reservations about the quality of the raw materials that have been received lately. You ask if maybe a change in vendor is necessary or is there a substitute material that your firm could use. (Pause)

Your personnel manager informs you that there has been a large improvement in safety programs but absenteeism is becoming a problem. There is discussion on how to deal with this. (Pause)

As you conclude the meeting, you thank everyone for all the hard work in achieving last year's goals. You encourage them to help in obtaining the new goals that have been set for next year in order to keep your company strong and growing.

We have found this script to be very successful in developing goal-setting in the business management course (Wheatley, 1985). Examples of such goals would include the need for a successful firm to generate adequate sales, realize a necessary rate of return on sales, have a high level of quality in its product, etc.

Since a guided imagery session is such an extremely relaxing experience, a feeling of calm and quiet will be experienced by both the instructor and the students at the conclusion of the session. Because of this, the instructor should allow a few moments for the students to adjust back into the present. During this time of peace and tranquility, the instructor should allow for an open discussion session regarding the imagery experience. The instructor will be amazed at the specificity and vividness of the images experienced by the students.

Informal Script Guided Imagery Training

Informal script guided imagery training involves a very less formal script which normally centers around one particular topic. We will give the students a chance to get relaxed and then ask them to visualize some current or future event. After a short period of visualization, we will then ask the students to create what they envisioned in many different mediums such as modeling clay, yarn, or colored pipe cleaners. Here we will discuss an exercise where we use colored pipe cleaners.

In order to facilitate the use of visualization techniques within a wide range of university classes, we ask the students to close their eyes and visualize a desired state. For example, we may ask them to visualize their career twenty years from now. Telling them to keep their eyes closed we ask them to get in touch with their feelings about this desired state and to pay very close attention to the colors they see. While they have their eyes closed we place a large number of pipe cleaners on a table (at least three pipe cleaners per student but often as many as five or ten with about 40 different color combinations.) Then we ask the students to open their eyes and come to the front of the room and pick up the pipe cleaners and create a sculpture which represents their vision. If someone comments they didn't have a vision we tell them that it isn't necessary, but to come up and get the pipe cleaners anyway and create a sculpture that represents the career they want in the future.

Once the students have completed their sculptures we have them share their sculpture and what they mean to the class. One example of the more popular sculptures that we have seen is one that is all green in the form of a dollar sign where the student will state that his/her career goal is to make a lot of money. Other popular sculptures will take the shape and colors of where student may want to work, for example blue waves symbolizing that they want to live and work near the ocean. There is generally a combination of nervous laughter and outright childish play but everyone quickly gets into the act of sharing their vision with everyone. Later we would have the students to write a career plan based on the insight they obtained from the exercise. Overwhelming student response to this combination of imagery and written exercises is that it always produces new creative insights for the career planning process for the students.

NON-GUIDED IMAGERY TECHNIQUES

As we mentioned above, non-guided imagery techniques can also be very powerful tools to enhance imagination and creativity skills. The techniques include the key ingredients of relaxation, no criticism, and processes that allow the students the opportunity to utilize their imagery processes to develop new and novel approaches to various activities. Two of our more favorite non-script imagery exercises are described below.

Preparing a Collage which Depicts You

Successful managers always know who they are, what they are like, and how they feel about themselves. A critical element in successful work groups is that the members of the group not only know this about themselves, but they pretty clearly understand these same things about all the other members of the group. In the classroom setting, there is not enough time for members of the work group to get to know what other members of the group are about as is done in the work world—i.e., through lengthy observation and personal interaction. Therefore, we have our students prepare a collage of themselves in order to allow members of the work group to get to know each other quickly.

The exercise is really quite simple. On a piece of paper or posterboard, we have the students tell a story of themselves through the use of words, pictures, shapes, lines or a combination of any or all of these or other means of describing yourself. The collage is brought to class where it is used within the work group as a tool to help others see the student as the student sees him/herself. Getting to know each other is an important step in group development. In addition, the motivating of employees, or group members in this case, can be accomplished when managers know and understand who their employees are and what their goals are.

The collage is a mechanism which also facilitates group acceptance. Feelings of peer acceptance are more apt to lead students to academic success as well as social success. After students get over their initial reluctance to do something they feel to be juvenile, they really get with the program. They comment on how helpful the collage exercise was in helping them to get to know themselves better. Most of the collages become prized possessions which the students will keep as permanent mementoes.

Flip Chart Exercises

Flip chart exercises are utilized to develop and reinforce many management concepts and theories ranging from leadership styles to management information systems design. This type of training is a projection technique which generates a lot of excitement in a relaxed atmosphere conducive to greater degrees of divergent thinking. The students are directed to think about the management topic just discussed and to incorporate the underpinnings of the topic in some form of images. These images are then consummated into a pictorial model or paradigm which the students draw on large sheets of flip chart paper. The flip chart papers are then taped to the classroom walls for all students to observe and to learn from. An example of a leadership model drawn on the flip chart paper appears in Figure 1.

In addition to enhancing imagination and creativity, several other learner outcomes are obtained from the flip chart exercises. The small group naturally provides a better stage for quality and quantity communication. Students are more apt to offer their opinions during group projects. Students feel more comfortable asking their peers about something they do not understand than asking the instructor in a large classroom. Each student feels more responsible and the motivational power of group membership is intensified. Becoming involved in group activities and cooperating, rather than competing, provides a learning experience that will yield considerable dividends for the students later on in their professional careers.

As with the collages, there is some initial reluctance on the part of the

FIGURE 1

students to engage in a "Sesame Street" type of exercise. Thus, we will normally visit with each team and give them some examples of images that they can employ to represent some facet of the activity. Once they become relaxed, the creative juices begin to flow and some truly remarkable work is accomplished. As with the collages, the students often take their flip chart exercises home with them as permanent mementoes.

INSTRUCTOR AND STUDENT REACTIONS TO IMAGERY PEDAGOGY

Instructors will feel such exhilaration with the use of imagery as a teaching tool that they will want to utilize this exciting educational device in other courses.

Guided imagery and other envisionary techniques are not teaching and training methods that are to be employed to the exclusion of other major pedagogies such as lectures, cases and simulations. They should be utilized in conjunction with existing teaching methods to enhance the creative and imaginative skills of the student. To date there is no evidence that suggests an area in which imagery cannot or should not be employed to enhance the education process. The use of guided imagery in the classroom is limited only by the imagination of the instructor.

When given adequate explanation of the process and what it is to accomplish, accompanied with practice, the overwhelming majority of students find it to be a very exciting and effective method of learning. Students respond that they are using imagery to prepare for exams in other classes and to mentally rehearse for class presentations and job interviews. Other students state that they find the relaxing element of imagery to be a very effective means of coping with stress. The most often reported use of imagery is in their career planning. Students will use imagery to vicariously experience their future life in various jobs in a variety of different geographical locations. One student responded that she was thinking about a job in a large city until she visualized herself driving in congested traffic conditions. Another student, who had grown up in the South, turned down a very high paying job offer with a firm located in a northern mid-western city after visualizing how harsh the winters might be. It is amazing how vivid and realistic these imaginal experiences can be for the students.

The education and training literature strongly suggests the efficacy of imagery as a means of improving the imaginative and creative skills in students. In this article we have discussed our use of imagery in the management class because of its inherent need for imagination and creativity. Other types of classes also offer natural environments in which to introduce students to such cognitive expansion techniques as guided imagery and other imagery applications. We encourage others to follow our guidelines and enhance their own classes through imagery.

REFERENCES

Anthony, W. P., Wheatley, W. J., and Maddox, E. N.. Better management through the mind's eye, *Association Management* 37, 11, (November 1985), 86–94.

Maddox, E. N. The effects of analytical versus creative: Imaginal problem-solving strategy and answer outcome expectancy on creative problem-solving tasks. (Unpublished Dissertation, The Florida State University, 1987).

Wheatley, W. J., Maddox, E. N., Anthony, W. P., and Coe, F. S., Enhancing education through the use of mental imagery. *Reading Improvement* 24, 3, (1987), 150–159.

Wheatley, W. J. Enhancing strategic planning through the use of guided imagery. (Unpublished Dissertation, The Florida State University, 1985).

CLARA WAJNGURT

Problem Solving
Through Math Journals

When it comes to mathematics, people are often classified into two basic groups: those who like mathematics and those who hate mathematics. Sometimes people who don't like mathematics feel they lack the ability to do mathematics. However, a more accurate perception could be that those who claim to lack mathematical ability simply accept that characterization of themselves. As a result, attitudes toward mathematics can influence class performance as well as career choice. In one of my courses I surveyed my technological mathematics students, who already have some idea of their future professional direction, regarding how to identify math anxiety. A typical response was

> If solving math problems makes the person nervous, panicky and causes him to frequently get wrong answers to simple math problems during class and on exams, then probably he is math anxious.

This kind of anxiety often leads to the development of emotional and intellectual blocks to mathematics, which finally lead the student to avoid mathematics in general.

In order to understand how to reduce these emotional and intellectual blocks to mathematics, we need to conceptualize the learning process. Conceivably, if any step of the mathematical learning process is not achieved, blocks to learning mathematics could result—especially as a result of the hierarchical nature of learning mathematics. Suppose a student is to learn a mathematical procedure, like solving an equation. The following four steps illustrate the way one learns mathematics:

Step 1: The student must *apprehend* the procedure by perceiving the objects of the situation—e.g., the terms of the equation: $2x + 5 = 11$.

Step 2: The student must *acquire* the method for perceiving the process which relates the objects of the equation (mathematical steps) and the method for attaining the knowledge needed after presenting the procedure (memorization of steps described in writing). The following shows the mathematical steps, along with the verbal explanation, for solving $2x + 5 = 11$.

Step 3: The student must *store* the method described in his memory, e.g., by solving similar equations: $3 + 2x = 43$.

Step 4: The student must *retrieve*, at a future time, the described method, by securing the needed information that has already been acquired and stored in his memory.

Particularly, the instruction can help students progress effectively through these four stages of mathematics learning by stimulating apprehension through working out the example on the board and by using writing as a pedagogical technique to help students understand the mathematical process described (step 1). Then have each student work out a similar example by following the step-by-step list of instructions described in writing (step 2). The instructor can help students store the described procedures by assigning problems for homework and can elicit retrieval of the described procedure by giving a quiz at the end of the week (steps 3 and 4). By understanding the various stages of mathematics learning and by using writing as a pedagogical tool to help students experience the mathematical learning process, the instructor will enhance the students' abilities to mentally organize the needed information that helps select a particular strategy which solves the problem. At the same time mathematics avoidance can be reduced.

WRITING TO SEE AND SOLVE PROBLEMS: THE MATH JOURNAL

A math journal is one concrete way for students to take the time to think out mathematics problems with confidence. This process not only strengthens students' writing skills, but also encourages their active participation in the learning process.

In this way, the journal has an overall aim to record and organize the student's thoughts into words. Does keeping a journal help students to further clarify their thoughts about the mathematical situation? Can this journal also serve as a vent for expressing mathematical anxieties and insecurities? I questioned students in my arithmetic and elementary algebra course (the prerequisite for the technical intermediate algebra class) about the pros and cons for studying mathematics through writing a personal journal. Most of the responses are exemplified by the following:

1. Math means understanding every step of the problem, writing deals with anything we think.
2. I enjoy writing more than math because you are always right when you write down your thoughts—not in math.

FIGURE 1 Writing to Solve Equations

Mathematics	Writing
1. $2x + 5 = 11$	1. Start with the equation
2. $2x + \cancel{5} = 11$ $\quad -\cancel{5} \quad -5$	2. Do your additions before you work on your divisions in order to isolate the variable. We add the opposite of "$+5$" to both sides of the equation (balance).
3. $2x = 6$	3. This will isolate the x-term.
4. $\dfrac{2x}{2} = \dfrac{6}{2}$	4. Divide by the number in front of (the coefficient) the x on both sides of the equation.
5. $x = 3$	5. This isolates the variable x on the left side and we have solved for x.
6. $2(3) + 5 = 11$	6. Check by substituting the value we received for x in step 5.

ACTIVATING TWO LANGUAGES FOR THINKING

These responses lead me to believe that mathematical comprehension involves more of a mental, visual perception of the structure of written symbols, than a free ability to explain the meanings of the symbols. As an example, consider the following four student journal entries that describe the process for solving the equation discussed earlier, $2x + 5 = 11$. The associated mathematical learning process exemplified the *acquisition* phrase.

Figure 2, Responses 1, 2, and 3 illustrate that writing helped the students to better conceptualize the mathematics problem. Particularly, the writing style and description of steps varies from each response. Figure 2, Response 1 describes the mathematical steps and verbal explanations explicitly. Figure 2, Response 2 is less verbal explanations in a second column. Figure 2, Response 3 lacks the mathematical steps but maintains the ability to clearly express his thoughts into words. Figure 2, Response 4 does not relate to the problem verbally. Most likely he became confused by the meaning of "verbal explanation." He illustrated the correct solution to the problem in the general case and the incorrect solution to the assigned problem.

Clearly, it seems that writing out the steps to the problem helped the students to better conceptualize the problem, organize their thoughts for selecting a strategy to solve the problem, and to solve the problem by carrying out the selected strategy which used, in this case, algebraic and logic skills.

FIGURE 2 Four student approaches to solving math problems: Acquisition and acquiring phases of mathematical thinking

Question: Describe in writing how you solve the equation:

$$2x + 5 = 11.$$

Show the mathematical steps along with the verbal explanation.

Response 1: Step 1: Add −5 to both sides of the equations

$$2x + 5 = 11.$$

$$\underline{-5 \qquad -5}$$

$$2x + 5 - 5 = 11 - 5$$

Step 2: Cancel +5 and −5 and add the numbers
on the right side of the equation.

$$2x = 6$$

Step 3: Divide both sides by 2

$$\frac{2x}{2} = \frac{6}{2}$$

$$x = 3$$

Response 2:

$$2x + 5 = 11 \qquad \text{Get 5 to the other side}$$

$$\underline{-5 = -5} \qquad \text{of the equation}$$

$$\frac{2x}{2} = \frac{6}{2} \qquad \text{Subtract}$$

$$\qquad\qquad\qquad \text{Bring the } 2x \text{ down}$$

$$x = 3 \qquad \text{Isolate } x \text{ by dividing}$$

$$\qquad\qquad\qquad 2 \text{ by both sides}$$

Response 3: 1) Subtract 5 from both sides
2) Divide both sides. By 2

$$x = 3$$

Response 4:

$$2x + 5 = 11 \qquad\qquad Ax \; B \Big/ C$$

$$\underline{-5 = -5} \qquad\qquad \underline{-B \; -B}$$

$$2x \, 5 = 11 - 5 \qquad Ax = (C - B)$$

$$\qquad\qquad\qquad\qquad \overline{A} \qquad \overline{A}$$

$$\frac{2x}{2} = \frac{6}{2} \qquad\qquad x = \frac{(C - B)}{A}$$

$$x = 4$$

234

WRITING TO DEVELOP A STRATEGY

Several days later I assigned another related mathematics problem in class. Solving equations had been assigned earlier for homework. I now considered the following four student journal entries, which exemplified the range of responses, to illustrate the *storage* and *retrieval* phases of the mathematics learning process.

In Figure 3, Response 5 describes the steps for solution both ways—mathematically in one column and verbally in the second column. Figure 3, Response 6 describes the solution mathematically but not verbally. Figure 3, Response 7 describes the solution verbally but not mathematically. Figure 3, Response 8 is confused about the solution in both the mathematical and verbal areas.

Although the problem explicitly stated to describe the solution "in writing," many of the students needed to "think through" the problem mathematically. Again, writing served to facilitate the process for solving the mathematical problem.

MOVING ADAPTIVELY BETWEEN LANGUAGES

Basically, in order to "think through" a mathematics problem, the student must coordinate previous experience, knowledge and intuition, which together determine a method that solves a situation whose outcome is not immediately known. The mathematical thinking process requires that the student have sufficient motivation and lack of stress and anxiety to allow progress toward a solution. As illustrated by the students' responses, the solution may evolve by translating thoughts into mathematics, or by translating thoughts into words. Whichever strategy the student chooses, the student in the mathematical learning process must learn to concentrate on the mathematical terminology itself, in a precise and orderly fashion; and then to produce for her- or himself a meaningful mental perception of the given mathematical concept—either in writing or in numerical symbols. It is as if one were learning a new language and insisted upon mentally translating the words of the new language into his native tongue. Mathematics thus requires special concentration and attentiveness by which every step is a mental operation. Although writing is a vehicle for comprehending the mathematics, eventually the student will need "to think" in mathematical terminology.

In general, if factors like mathematics anxiety interfere with the mental processes of perceiving mathematical symbols, of attaching literal meanings to these symbols, or of analyzing relationships amongst the mathematical symbols, a student's journal writing could virtually serve as a means for improving comprehension and confronting these insecurities and anxieties. Figure 4 is a journal entry written after doing a series of arithmetic problems

FIGURE 3 Four student approaches to solving math problems:
Storage and retrieval phases of mathematical thinking

Question: Describe in writing how you would solve the word problem: Three more than twice a certain number equals forty-three. Find the number.

Response 5: $2x + 3 = 43$ 1) write the equation umarial form

                $-3 = -3$ 2) subtract 3 form each side

$$\frac{2x = 40}{2 \quad 2}$$ 3) divided each side by 2

                $x = 20$

Response 6: $2x + 3 = 43$

            $-3 \quad -3$

            $2x = 40$

         $x = \frac{40}{2} = 20$

            $x = 20$

Response 7:   certain # $= x$

          $2x + 3 = 43$

    1) solve for x
    2) subtract 3 from both sides
    3) divided both sides by 2
    4) cancel out 2's do division
    5) $x = 20$

Response 8: $43 x = 3$ solves for x
         -5
         $40 \; -3$
         $40 \; -x$
         Print value of x
         X

         $43 = 2x + 3$ solve for x
         $-3 \quad\quad -3$
         $43-3 = 2x$

          $40 = \frac{2x}{2}$

          $\frac{40}{2} = x$

         Print value of x

FIGURE 4   Writing to Reduce Math Anxiety

<u>Question</u>: How do we help a person who has difficulty in writing a composition—is it the same with difficulties in math? <u>Yes</u>.

<u>Answer</u>: A person who has difficulty in writing a composition is trying to figure out the question. (To understand the question)—In order to be able to answer it and be able to write his thought down on a paper. and a person who has difficulty in a math problem has to figure out how to read the problem the ⸺ - correct way and resolve it. The way to help that person is to try to explain it to him the easiest way possible,—step by step and to try to figure out that person's weak points. He might ⸺ be able to understand the problem if you just help him act with what he is weak at, because what he is weak it is what will confuse ⸺ him or throw him off. Explaining step by step, is the best and only way in my opinion. One thing always leads to another. A teacher must understand the student first and then the student will listen to the teacher, because the teacher in that way will make sense to the student. the teacher is teaching exactly what the student wants to hear to comprehend.

in class and compares the process of solving similar mathematics problems to writing in general.

If students learn to think more clearly in terms of mathematical terminology, they will approach the subject with greater ease. In order to facilitate this process, translating the thought process into words will help the student to better experience the apprehension, acquisition, storage and retrieval phases.

One of my students summarized the situation for us:

> The only relationship between mathematics and keeping a mathematics journal is that by writing down how you feel, you will get your frustrations out when you can't solve a problem—and once you get your frustrations out, you can go back and solve the problem.

WOLFF-MICHAEL ROTH

Constructing Knowledge
from Science Laboratory Activities

Many students do not take science at the high school level because of lack in motivation and low achievement, both of which may be due to the discrepancy between school and real-life experience. In real-life, problems are messy, ill-defined, and call for true problem-solving. Individuals feel in control of their activities. They interact with the setting and generate problems in relation with the setting, thereby controlling the problem-solving process. On the other hand, in traditional science classrooms students rarely experience the source questions of inquiry, the challenges, or the surprises of real-life. Students are seldom in a position where they have to find and frame problems, something which they do outside schools on a daily basis.

In my high school, we view the science curriculum and science teaching in a different way. We think that science should be more like real-life, and the teaching-learning context should be more like an apprenticeship situation in a shop. Thus, we provide students with a context in which they can frame their own questions to answer through investigations. In the process of this inquiry, teachers are not only a resource, but also acting practitioners who model inquiry and reflective behaviors. As such, they can coach students to construct new levels of inquiry skills in the context of a research problem which the latter find of genuine interest and which, thus, becomes an authentic activity.

GUIDING STUDENTS TO REFLECT
ON KNOWING AND DOING SCIENCE

We must realize, however, that it is not simply the doing that fosters learning, but the *reflecting* on the *doing*. In order for students to make sense of the labs and to construct new knowledge through an inductive process, we have to help them to reflect on their own learning processes. To this end, we make use of two heuristic or discovery devices, the concept map and the Epistemological Vee (Novak & Gowin, 1984). The concept map is a graphic way of representing one's knowledge of a content area and is well-known to science teachers. The Epistemological Vee (Vee-map or Vee, for short) is a heuristic device that calls to the students' attention both the practical steps of doing science and the theoretical side of knowing science. Figure 1 presents our modified version of the original Vee.

The Vee has two sides which are in continuous interplay, the conceptual or knowing and the methodological or doing. This interplay between knowing and doing science can be understood in the following way: what we know at any one moment, the ideas and tools available to us, will affect the questions we ask and how we go about answering these questions. On the other hand, what we find out will affect what we will know at a later point, and in turn will affect our future investigations. The idea of using the Vee is to help students uncover these aspects of learning science. Thus, the Vee serves as a map through the process of experimenting: from what students already know, through questions and investigations, to new knowledge.

At the top of the Vee are the *focus questions*, and this is where knowledge production in many respects begins: questions generate the intrinsic motivation for children and scientists alike to begin a quest for new knowledge. New knowledge is generated by observing patterns in our environment. To recognize patterns, it is necessary to select specific *events* (point of the Vee) and objects for observation, and to make records of these observations. Our choice of these events and objects, however, as well as the choice of measuring devices, and the choice of data analysis techniques will depend on what we already know (*concepts*); the ideas we possess at the outset of a query will determine what and how much we will learn from the experience. Our observations will result in records of *data*, which we submit to *transformations* in the form of graphs or statistical analysis to facilitate the interpretation of the data. Based on these data and transformations we will formulate *claims* not only to new knowledge, but also claims to the value of our findings. This new knowledge modifies our prior knowledge in that we add new concepts, modify old ones, or re-arrange the relations between them. The relationship between the concepts and ideas we hold can be expressed by a network that links these concepts. Such a map, the *concept map*, thus expresses what we know at any one moment, and particularly how our thinking changed over the course of an experience.

We can conceptualize the Vee-map also in terms of the following list of general questions:

1. What do we want to find out about? (*Focus Question*)
2. What do we know about the topic? (*Concepts*)
3. How do we go about finding an answer to my question? (*Events*)
4. What did we observe and measure? (*Data and Transformations*)

FIGURE 1 Gowin's Vee as a Reporting Format

REPORTING MY INVESTIGATION

FOCUS QUESTION:
What do I want to find out about?

Interplay
&
Interdependence

CONCEPTUAL-KNOWING

METHODOLOGICAL-DOING

CONCEPTS: What do I know about the topic before the experiment?

1. What do I know about the topic?
2. Which words and ideas relating to my question do I know?

CONCEPT MAP:
How do these words and ideas interrelate?

1. How do these words and ideas interrelate?
2. How does my new knowledge relate to what I knew before?
3. Have I made all connections possible?
4. Have I established a proper hierarchy among the concepts (events & objects)?

CLAIMS: What can I make of my findings?

1. Based on my data and results, what is the answer to my focus question? What hypotheses can I formulate that would explain the phenomena I measured/observed?
2. How can this knowledge be used in practical situations, i.e., is this knowledge of any value? Are there any moral implications to my findings?
3. What further questions came to my mind? What questions did my project leave unanswered?

**DATA &
TRANSFORMATIONS: What did I observe and measure?**

1. Did I list data tables and observations?
2. Can I represent the data in form of graphs?
3. How do these data and graphs look like? Describe.
4. What type of errors did I make? What is the relative and the absolute size of the errors I made?
5. Can the graphs be described mathematically?
6. What statistics can I report? Mean? Error of the mean? Standard deviation? What is the meaning of these data, what do they tell me?
7. Is there any other way to report my data?

EVENTS: How do I go about finding the answer to my question?

1. How was my experiment set up?
2. What did I do?
3. What equipment did I use?

After Novak & Gowin, 1984.

5. What can we make of my findings? (*Claims,* of knowledge and value type)
6. How do our concepts and ideas interrelate? (*Concept Map*)

Although I will discuss the sections of the Vee in the order in which a student would proceed during an investigation, we always have to keep in mind that the two sides of the Vee are in continuous interplay; what we know at any moment affects what we will "see" and what we will see will change our ideas. Let us follow Jere and Daniel in their quest for new knowledge, using the Vee-map they constructed during one of their investigations as an example (Figure 2). I will illustrate each part of the Vee with a concrete example from the work of the two students. Figure 2 represents a student review of background knowledge in plant ecology prior to the research investigation. Figure 3 summarizes the research methods they used to conduct a Field study.

A PRACTICAL EXAMPLE OF USING THE VEE IN THE CLASSROOM

Jere's and Daniel's class was involved in an eight-week study of ecologically different micro-environments around the campus of our school. During their first project on the 10×3 meter site which the two had selected for their studies, Jere and Daniel had focused on the relationship between the types of plants and the amount of light available to them. This site was situated close to the lake which borders the school grounds. In their field notebook, the two students had recorded the questions such as "Why is there no vegetation on the middle part [of their plot] if it is fairly moist?", "Is there a relation between soil moisture and temperature?", and "Of all the water that plants use, how much do they give back?" For their next project, Jere and Daniel decided to answer a question which was an extended version of the second one recorded in their field book, namely "Is there a relationship between soil moisture and the air temperature and what kind of plants fit into this relationship?"

Focus Question: What do we want to know?

All scientific investigations begin with questions. A good question will lead to an investigation of natural objects and events or to the development of experiments through which the student-investigators find out about a (cause/effect) relationship. In the end, the students make specific knowledge and value claims based on an interpretation of their experimental results. Thus, by making a knowledge claim, the students have arrived at new knowledge (and new and different meaning for "old" concepts) through induction from experimental evidence.

Of course, there are different types of questions that students can ask or teachers can posit to guide an investigation. In our example, Jere and Daniel wanted to find out, "Is there a relationship between soil moisture and air temperature and what kinds of plants fit into this relationship?" (Figure 2). In the course of this investigation, the students recorded new questions, hypotheses, and observations in their field note book. From these records, Jere and Daniel generated new focus questions which they investigated later on during the term. For example, in claims 3 and 4 (Figure 2), they stated the hypotheses "as the water evaporates, the leaves and the other dead twigs catch the moisture condensation and this might allow it to fall back to the ground" and "there are different soils in our area and, some of them allow water to seep through it faster then other soils." From these, the two generated focus questions such as "What is the percentage soil moisture and organic content in different parts of the biome?" and "What is the relationship between the type of soil and the percolation rates of water?" which they investigated in subsequent experiments. In this way, the use of the Vee helped the students to continue and to sustain a research program over a period of eight weeks without ever asking for new ideas from the teacher.

On the other hand, if a teacher is interested that students find out a specific relationship—as is the case when students are starting in a new topic area—she can formulate a question that will lead to student claims which otherwise would be lectured and copied. For example, when I wanted students to find a pattern for the growth of yeast cells in an environment of unrestricted food supply, I proposed the question "What is the relationship between the number of yeast cells and the time since the culture was started?" In their self-designed experiments, all student groups arrived, on their own, at identifying qualitatively the exponential nature of the growth curve characteristic for such a situation. Older students of ecology would be led to identify quantitatively the mathematical relationship between population and time.

The point I want to make here is that a good question goes a long way, and often leads to generative source for even more questions. Questions are the key to knowledge gained through inductive methods, and students should be in the position to ask their own questions from an early age at school. Questioning is a natural process for kids, but is often quenched once they enter school so that class can proceed in a teacher-directed way. The Vee-map gives us the opportunity to turn back and begin teaching with the children's own questions arising from their natural curiosity.

Concepts: What Do We Know About the Topic?

We often do not realize that what we know determines what we can and will learn. More so, what we know determines what we perceive; determines what we consider to be important; and determines how we

FIGURE 2   Concept List and Map of Student Knowledge
Review of Concept Relationships

CONCEPTS: (What you know about the topic)

humidity	transpiration	growth
evaporation	wind	food
moisture	ground cover	photosynthesis
water	moist	condensation
plants	dry	heat
precipitation	wet	energy

CONCEPT MAP: (Make a map of the concepts you learned about)

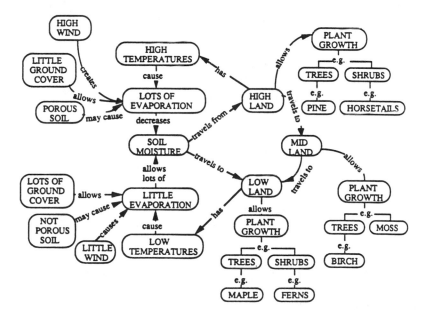

interpret what we perceive. Thus, what we already know becomes a filter through which we interact with our environment and which will determine what we will come to know. The use of the Vee allows to make this prior knowledge explicit.

Before beginning the investigation, Jere and Daniel asked themselves "What do we know about the topic of soil, moisture, and temperature?" and "Which words and ideas relating to our questions do we know?" Jere and Daniel began by brainstorming ideas, "What other ideas had been relevant in our biome?" Under the heading *concepts* they listed the words or concept labels which they already knew. Some of these concepts were irrelevant to this investigation—such as the word "photosynthesis" (Figure 2)—and they did not take them into further consideration. Other concepts, such as "evaporation," "moisture," and "wind" became key concepts during their investigation and were featured in both the *claims* section and on the final *concept map*. Both students used their field note books with the records of previous investigations, their text book, and other resources to generate further concepts which they had not yet considered.

Although Jere and Daniel did not use all of the words in their list in their investigation, I could observe that the generation of concepts and the associations to other concepts increased their search field for explanation of the data gathered during the observation phase. The list of concepts sometimes led Jere and Daniel immediately to the construction of a concept map through which they expressed the relation between the words they had listed. Once constructed, they expanded the concept map by introducing their new knowledge, constructed through the interpretation of and induction from the experimental and/or observational records. Most often, however, as in the present example, students expressed their understanding in terms of a concept map only after they finished an investigation. While generating their list of associated words, Jere and Daniel already began to think about and to plan their investigation.

Events: How Do We Go About Finding Out the Answer to My Question?

In the effort to find an answer to the focus question, students decide on the kind of observation to make and how to set up an experiment. They outline these planned observations and/or experimental procedures under the heading of *events* (Figure 3).

Jere and Daniel decided to measure soil moisture and air temperature at different points in their zone and to note the plants that were growing there. They began by asking themselves "What are we going to do to answer our focus question?", "How do we go about measuring the moisture of the soil?", and "What type of thermometers do we use for the temperature measurements?" They also planned to look up other information and mention a contingency plan in case the question they asked did not yield a satisfactory answer. For the present experiment on soil moisture, Jere and Daniel first had to find out how they could determine the moisture content of the soil. Both had considered to heat to dryness equal masses of different soil samples, and to determine the moisture from the loss in mass. However, after consultation with their teacher, they resorted to moisture determinations by employing an existing meter.

Interestingly enough, this sequence of having students first formulate a question of interest and then develop a way of answering the question gives them a sense of purpose for doing the lab. No longer do they just follow "cookbook recipes," the reasons for which most often was never apparent to them. Now they can and do take the responsibility for their own learning and develop a sense and purpose for the activities in class. Now they "own" their problems instead of receiving them from an authoritative source such as the teacher or the text book. The students then continue on to collect data and to transform them into various other representations.

Data & Transformations: What Did We Observe and Measure?

In order to establish a data base from which the student researchers can construct new knowledge, they will record (or, if interfaces for data acquisition are available, use a computer to record) observations relevant to answering the focus question. Different focus questions and different conceptual backgrounds again lead students to focus on different aspects of the events and objects we are observing. The data gathered during these observations could be descriptive-qualitative such as color changes in chemical reactions; the appearance of bubbles and steams in an experiment on the phase change from liquid to gas; or differences in the shapes and structures of plant and animal cells. On the other hand, the data could also be in the form of quantitative measurements such as reaction times; concurrent observations such as current and voltage measurements with the same resistor; or a student's breathing rate as it changes with the length of an exercise. The raw data collected during the observations often are not useful for deriving knowledge claims.

Rarely do researchers draw conclusions from raw data without organizing them in some form. The construction of tables, graphs, diagrams to represent the data in some organized fashion falls under the topic of transformation. Similarly, the calculation of central tendencies (mean, median, mode), variations (standard deviation, standard errors), and covariations (correlation, regression functions), also represent data transformations. These transformations are crucial to the kinds of claims we will make and they are also a function of the investigators' prior knowledge.

Jere and Daniel collected extensive data to answer their question. Initially, the two drew a map which included the levels of the area, ground cover, moisture levels, temperatures above, and tall plants in their biome. However, the map included such a wealth of information that it was almost impossible to distinguish any patterns. Jere and Daniel asked themselves, "How can we represent the data in a way that permits us to discern patterns?" They decided to first tabulate all their data which broke down moisture levels, temperature, and types of plant by the different areas in their zone (Figure 3). When they could not recognize specific patterns, they sought new solutions by asking questions such as "How can we represent

FIGURE 3   Student Analysis of Experimental Data

Methods for Finding and Interpreting New Information

CLAIMS

(Based on your data and results, what is the answer to your question. How can this knowledge be used in practical situation, i.e., is this knowledge of any value?)

1. We found that the moisture levels were lower at the top of the slope and higher at the bottom. This might be because the water seeps to the lower part of our slope.
2. There wasn't much of a distinct relationship between the levels of moisture and the air temp., however, it did appear that the higher the temp. the less soil moisture. This might be because the hot air creates evaporation faster and the air is less dense which might make it easier for water to evaporate.
3. There was a particularly moist part of our area which wasn't at the bottom of our slope. This might be because there was about 80% ground cover (refer to the scale on the map). What this might mean is that as the water evaporates the leaves and the other dead twigs catch the moisture condensation and this might allow it to fall back to the ground.
4. Relating to #3, another cause might be that in the wet area there was a plateau where the slope stopped. Yet another cause might be that there are different soils in our area and, some of them allow water to seep through it faster then other soils. Another factor might be that the evaporation rate (which would lower the soil moisture level) is faster when the wind blows. This is the same when we sweat.
5. As well, the temperatures were higher at the top of the slope than at the bottom (in general). This might mean that it is not only the water sinking to the bottom of the slope that makes it wet at the bottom but that the temp. is lower which might not create as much evaporation.

DATA & TRANSFORMATIONS:

(List your data, graphs, and descriptions of this data. Discuss the errors you possibly made, the statistics, the curve fits you achieved, etc.)

	Moisture levels	Temperatures	Plants
LOW AREA	3-8	28 C - 30 C	Maple saplings ferns, elm saplings cedar saplings, other shrubs
MID AREA	5-8 (particularly wet)	27 C - 30 C	Birch tree, oak tree, spruce tree, moss maple tree, dead ground cover, fungi
HIGH-MID AREA	3-6	28 C - 30 C	Tree stump, moss, birch tree, pine tree, elm saplings, lichen
HIGH AREA	1-4	29 C - 31 C	burr plants, scotch thistles, horse tails, maple tree, pine tree

SCALE

1-2 Dry
3-4 Damp
5-6 Moist
7-8 Wet

EVENTS: (Briefly describe the experiment you did).

1. Measure at different points of the slope soil moisture & air temperature
2. Observe and note the different types of plants in these areas
3. Draw charts, make conclusions
4. Read other info
5. If our results don't show any relationship, think up some other abiotic factors that might be responsible.

the data in tables or graphs?" and "Are there any other ways to represent our data?" These questions led them to plot the moisture levels against the levels of the ground (Figure 4) and against the temperatures in the soil. At this point we must not forget that the selection of a particular transformation is also dependent on prior knowledge. Teachers may need to be especially attentive and help students in acquiring new techniques for data transformation. Once the data transformations are completed, the students will turn to an interpretation of their data and will try to find an answer to their focus questions. On the basis of the map of the site, the data table, and the two graphs, Jere and Daniel derived the claims for this investigations.

Knowledge and Value Claims: What Can We Make of Our Findings?

From the data in their raw and transformed form, students begin to construct knowledge claims—claims about what they think the answer to the focusing question should be. In that, they are claims to new knowledge because they provide answers to questions, previously unknown. But knowledge claims also serve a second function as they can suggest *new* questions and hypotheses to be investigated in future investigations.

The knowledge claims are a function of how we interpret the question, how we choose to go about to get the data to answer the question, what kind of conceptual background we bring to the experiment/observations, and how we transform the data. I have often observed that different student groups arrive at different answers to the "same" focus question. This, however, is not a weakness but a strength of this method. What students find out during whole class discussions is that each group constructed the meaning of a question in a different way and thus found answers that responded to *their* question, not to *the* question.

On the basis of their data, Jere and Daniel made several claims that link the moisture levels in their area with its topology, the temperature above the ground, the type of soils, ground cover and evaporation. The two generated these claims by asking themselves: "What can we make of these findings?", "What is the answer to our focus question?", "What further questions and hypotheses account for our observations?", and "What is the meaning of the graph/data?" As they asked themselves this last question while looking at the plot in Figure 3, they came to the conclusion that "the moisture levels were lower at the top of the slope and higher at the bottom." Or, when they studied the graph in Figure 4, Jere and Daniel claimed that "There wasn't much of a distinct relationship between the levels of moisture and the air temp[erature]; however, it did appear that the higher the temp[erature], the less soil moisture." To explain a "particularly moist part of our area which wasn't at the bottom of the slope" the students drew on their prior observations/knowledge and reasoned that "this might be because there was about 80 percent ground cover. What this might mean is that as the water evaporates, the leaves and the dead twigs catch the moisture condensation and this might allow it to fall back to the ground." In this explanation they used the concepts "evaporation," "ground cover," and "condensation" from their list of related words, which express their knowledge before the investigation. The link which the two

FIGURE 4   Graph 1 of Students' Transformed Data

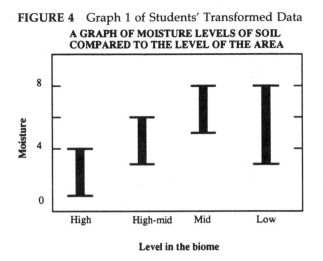

A GRAPH OF MOISTURE LEVELS OF SOIL COMPARED TO THE LEVEL OF THE AREA

Level in the biome

students made with prior knowledge became especially obvious when David explained that the effect of the wind on evaporation is "the same as when we sweat" (Figure 3, claim 4).

What is remarkable—and indeed is one of the aims of our approach to using the Vee—is that later questions which the students investigated were indicated in their claims sections of earlier reports. Thus, they hypothesized that the moisture levels might be a function of the type of soil and the seepage, which then turned into Focus Questions Three and Four. This in turn stimulated investigations into the causes of varying soil moisture in the different sections of their plot. The two boys did not address practical applications in this report, but these could easily be addressed in class discussions, or in a private session with the two.

At the end of an investigation, we ask such questions as "Is this any good?", "Towards what can this new knowledge be used?", or "Are there any applications for this new knowledge in our personal lives, the lives of our closer friends and family, the society as a whole?" The purpose of these questions is for students to think how their new knowledge links to their everyday life, to the society as a whole. With this activity we try to make the link between the classroom and the everyday life, the classroom and society as a whole. For example, after an experiment on the neutralization of acids, a student in the class remarked, "The value of this find is the fact that a weaker acid was formed. It is used for indigestion; the hydrochloric acid (strong) is turned into carbonic acid (weak) by taking sodium carbonate and burning up the carbon dioxide." At times, the value claims become almost philosophical as in the following claim of another student in the same class after an electrolysis of water experiment (which breaks water into its components, hydrogen and oxygen): "This experiment, by showing

FIGURE 5   Graph 2 of Students' Transformed Data

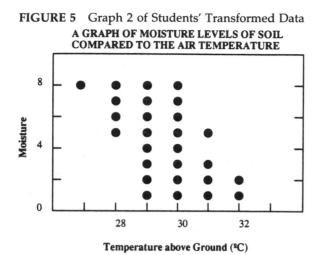

A GRAPH OF MOISTURE LEVELS OF SOIL COMPARED TO THE AIR TEMPERATURE

Temperature above Ground (ºC)

the fragility of water, shows us just how fragile our very existence is, since water is the basis of all of our lives." With the elaborations on such questions, investigations receive a purpose. And purpose is never value free, but intricately linked to our ways of thinking, feeling, and conceiving of ourselves. As Gowin (Novak & Gowin, 1984) pointed out, value claims and knowledge claims "ride in the same boat, but they are not the same passenger." After students complete their claims, they will express their knowledge in the form of a concept map.

Concept Maps: How Do the Words and Ideas Relate?

Once the knowledge claims are made, the students have to ask themselves, "How do the words and ideas relate to each other?" The relations between concepts are expressed. They will construct a concept map of their understanding, or they incorporate their new understanding into the existing maps of prior knowledge. In order to emphasize that they constructed new knowledge for themselves, the students can highlight the new sections of their maps which serves to reflect on the process of the inquiry as a constructive process of knowledge production. In this way, the students are in a position in which they can experience the excitement of finding new knowledge by practitioners of fundamental research. During whole class discussions, while trying to resolve the differences in their answers, the pupils also experience the negotiation processes so common among the members of a research community.

Concept mapping should be introduced to students before Vee-mapping so that they are already familiar with this procedure of expressing the relationship between the concepts, and in fact, the meaning of each of the concepts used. In the relation between two or more concepts, important generalizations (or principles) can be expressed in the map. As a whole, the maps constructed prior to the experiment/observation will express the theoretical framework which the investigators—here the students—bring with them to the events. The construction of maps after an experiment helps students to take a more reflective stance towards their work, making them think about how the concepts and the experiment are linked.

The construction of the concept maps constitutes an important part of the Vee-map, because they are an additional device for students to reflect on regarding what they learned. One student wrote in reflecting on her group's construction of the concept map on the Vee. "It [the concept map] kind of connected things together for me with respect to our experimenting with circuits," while another student in the same class noted that "the concept map was more difficult this time because I had never understood the connections between the words."

The map which Jere and Daniel arrived at after their investigation was quite elaborate and expressed in graphical form the claims they made (Figure 2). Because soil moisture and the topological features of their plot were their key concepts, the two began by connecting *soil moisture, high-, mid-,* and *low-land,* and by forming a proposition that expresses claim 1. Asking themselves, "Which features characterize each of the topological regions?" Jere and Daniel used the information on the plants from the data table and specified the plants that grow in each part of their plot. Knowing previously that water evaporates, they included this effect on the soil moisture. They then reflected, "What factors cause high or low levels of evaporation?" Again, they knew that evaporation was affected by wind ("This is the same when we sweat"), by temperature, and by the amount of cover ("How does this connect to the different levels of our land?"). During the present investigation they had learned that the temperatures were higher at the "high-land" than at the "low-land," which made them connect the temperatures to the topological features.

Summary

At this point we have not only come full circle, but at the same time covered a field in which all the parts are intricately interrelated and interconnected. The foregoing discussion should have made clear that our concepts, generalizations, and theories affect the questions we ask and the way we answer them. On the other hand, our experiences and the inferences we draw from them affect the knowledge we construct. Placing these processes on the Vee helps us and our students to view these relationships as one whole. The full circle from abstraction through practice to abstraction is externalized through the Vee and can be reflected upon. This cycling through experience and abstraction-reflection has been recognized as a crucial component to true meaningful learning (Schön, 1987). This cycle from abstraction-reflection through experience to abstraction-reflection which the Vee affords to the students is nicely expressed by Collins' (1990) metaphor of coming to know a new city: we learn to navigate a new city by repeatedly going through cycles of studying city maps (abstraction-reflection) and then plunging into the experience of the city by walking or driving through its network of streets.

EVALUATIONS

In spite of our concerns with assessment and with assignments of number grades we must not forget that all assessment necessarily requires some judgment and thus contains elements of subjectivity. We have found, as did others before us, that in general there is a good agreement among scorers of Vee-maps. However, there are many alternate ways in the construction of these maps that we have to remain flexible with the scoring of the Vees to do justice to a student's learning and way of expression. Over time, after scoring several sets of Vees, one can develop a set of criteria to evaluate consistently and quickly the work of a whole class. Because we emphasize collaboration in groups of two and three students, the actual number of Vee-maps to be marked is much smaller than the number of students we teach.

Students Evaluate the Vee

In my experience, the Vee-mapping technique has received an overwhelming positive response. In addition to the sections on the Vee as discussed above, I let students write short reflections regarding each lab, a sort of extension of the value claims, with a particular reference to each student's life. The following responses came from this source. Students realize that the Vee helps them to "keep the purpose of an experiment very clearly in mind"; or that the Vee organizes the whole lab experience as the following student who "found when working through a lab—I lost sight of how everything was connected and had to do some deep thinking to sort it all out. I guess, the process of doing the Vee was a real learning experience." Others feel that the Vee helped them to gain a better understanding of the research process, such as the student who feels that "I now have a clear understanding of how to do experiments or using the Vee-map kept thoughts orderly and focused. A great way to think through a problem." Positive responses have also related to the inductive process itself. Thus, students wrote "I think the lab work is challenging and that the answers to questions should come from the results of lab work, which gives some sense of accomplishment. The Vee greatly helps making sense of it all" or that "the combination of terminology and the visual [of the Vee] is necessary to get the sometimes abstract and complicated ideas in physics." To me, the following remark by a student, who had come with deep anxieties towards our science class a few weeks earlier, epitomizes the results of our approach to inductive learning: "This has been an exciting adventure in learning."

TEACHERS EVALUATE THE VEE

Teachers, too, show a favorable attitude towards the Vee, in particular those teachers, who subscribe to the same ideas that we do: students have to construct their own knowledge frameworks and learning proceeds through reflective practice on this process of construction. One teacher, who readily switched to a teaching strategy that allows students to ask their own questions, exclaimed "It works! A great way of letting them [the students] go off on their own and keeping them organized at the same time." Others agree with the teacher who found that the "Vee helped *me* to think differently about learning from labs" [emphasis added by the teacher].

I have used the Vee for years and I am quite confident that students who come to use this procedure over longer periods of time will become effective in constructing knowledge. In a direct comparison of college students in the junior and senior year with my grade 9 students, the latter out-scored the former on all questions asking for knowledge application, interpretation and comprehension of data. Lehman, Carter, and Kahle (1985) failed to report differences in achievement between students using Vee-maps and those who don't. However, the lack of an appropriate instrument may well be the reason for this finding.

CONCLUSION

In summary, we believe that students learn by finding answers to their own questions in an environment that resembles a traditional shop apprentice situation. Because the questions are their own, and because the activities are authentic, students construct knowledge inductively in a meaningful way. This construction of new knowledge is facilitated by employing the epistemological Vee which makes explicit prior knowledge and its interaction with the questions, procedures, and interpretation of the data and transformations. We believe with Wiggins (1989:46) that "One learns the power of the question only by seeing, for oneself, that important *facts* were once myths, arguments and questions." And we believe that "one learns self-confidence as a student only by seeing that one's questions, not one's current store of knowledge, always determine whether one becomes truly educated." The Vee is a device, a heuristic, that supports us in our work to help students feel empowered as makers of new knowledge.

REFERENCES

Collins, A. (1990). *Context, culture, and learning in the professions.* Presentation at the Annual Meeting of the American Educational Research Association. Boston, April 1990.

Lehman, J. D., Carter, C., & Kahle, J. B. (1985). Concept mapping, Vee mapping, and achievement: Results of a field study with black high school students. *Journal of Research in Science Teaching, 22* (7), 663–673.

Novak, J. D., and Gowin, B. D. (1984). *Learning how to learn.* Cambridge: Cambridge University Press.

Schön, D. A. (1987). *Educating the reflective practitioner.* San Francisco: Jossey-Bass.

Wiggins, G. (1989). The futility of trying to teach everything of importance. *Educational Leadership, 46* (11), 44–48, 57–59.

KARL A. SMITH AND ANTHONY M. STARFIELD

Building Models to Solve Problems

Modeling and problem-solving are inseparable, so much so that it is difficult to learn to solve problems without learning to model, and vice versa. We take the view that modeling is a more specific goal, that it is easier to learn to model, that it is useful to learn to model, and that incidentally one also learns a lot about problem-solving. Most problems are "solved" by constructing a representation (a mathematical expression, a graph, a manual or computer simulation program, a physical model, etc.). The process can be roughly described as (1) Formulating a model of a real system, (2) Drawing conclusions from the model, (3) Interpreting the model conclusions, and (4) Validating that the model actually works.

WHAT IS A MODEL?

We have asked hundreds of engineering students the question, "What is a model?" After giving them a moment to reflect, jot down their ideas and perhaps share them with a partner, we randomly select students to answer and we record the answers on a transparency. Students' answers from a recent class of third-year engineering students included:

- a representative system which simulates a situation
- a graphical representation
- a simplification-physical or conceptual
- a decision-making tool
- a means of testing a situation
- establishes parameters in which to work

Our role during this period is to guide the discussion, dignify all the students' contributions, and build on their understanding. Though they usually mention the main points about representation, simplification, abstraction, assumption, notation, algorithm, system, and generalization, one central feature of a model that the students seldom mention is purpose.

Information gleaned by asking students to reflect on their experience indicates they learn a great deal about problem solving by building models. Sara's experience in an ecological modeling course is representative:

> I think the biggest revelation I have had in this course so far is a very basic one, but it's difficult to describe. It's a new approach to problems, and a new way to use computers. I tend to have a brute-force approach to complicated problems—I begin at some entry point and slowly work through to an outcome. Then I begin again and make some different choices. The result is an array of outcomes, unless I have forgotten some possible choices. What I have learned is to collect the rules of the system, and build a picture of the system using those rules. Then it is easy to try different choices and view the outcomes, and more importantly it is easy to review the rules and change them or add to them. And it is easier to see which rules matter most, and which are less important. The difference between this approach and the old one is that I can more easily focus on the rules to the system, and on the problem itself. The mechanics are easy because they are built in, where before I took this course I tended to become so entangled in the mechanics that I couldn't see the system clearly.

We stress that learning in all disciplines involves constructing models, investigating ideas and developing problem-solving skills. These activities are not limited to students in science and mathematics. They are shared by all who have a desire to understand, to interpret and to explain. Business managers use market forecasting models, resource allocation models, and decision-making models. Airline pilots train in flight simulators, models of real aircraft cockpits. Weather forecasters develop models, to support weather prediction.

Our modeling courses concentrate on problem formulation, setting up models, and drawing conclusions from the models (see Figure 1). Students work in small, cooperative groups on a number of problems using a spreadsheet tool (or a more general modeling tool such as **PCSolve**) run on a personal computer. Students construct mathematical and computer models for each problem and then manipulate their model by varying its parameters and recording the effects to gain understanding of the physical, biological or social phenomenon being represented. Interesting problems are used to help students discover how to make assumptions, build a model and interpret their results. These are not courses in computing or mathematics. The problems presented to the students require formulation, solution, discussion, iteration and new solutions. They are problems which involve engineering, physics, biology, geometry and diverse others, including classics such as "How many ping-pong balls could you fit in this room?"—an example of the type of problem we set in an introductory course for first-year students.

WORKING COOPERATIVELY TO MODEL
AND SOLVE PROBLEMS

First year college students in Starfield & Smith's How to Model It course are organized into groups of three within the first 10 minutes of their first class. This arrangement surprises some of the students—however, most of them eagerly find the other members of their group and introduce themselves. A task such as the ping-pong problem is assigned and one copy is given to each group. Instructions to the students include: each group is to formulate one answer to present, make sure everyone participates, and make sure everyone can explain your group's answer.

While the students are working on the problems, we circulate among the groups, listening as the students discuss the problem with each other, occasionally intervening to ask a student to explain, and continually providing support and encouragement for the group work.

After we call the whole group back together, individual students are randomly selected (by asking each student to choose a number between 0 and 9 and using a 10-sided die to generate a random number). These randomly selected students give their group's answer and explain the method used to arrive at their answer. Several answers are requested and recorded on an overhead. Answers and methods are compared in terms of the formulation and assumptions. The usefulness of formulating an algorithm and using a notation system are discussed.

The final step in the cooperative groups involves the students processing their work in two ways. First they discuss how well they solved the problem, including their use of strategy and how each member feels about the group's answer. Second, they process how well they worked as a group—what things went well and what things they need to work on to function more effectively together.

DESIGNING, TESTING, AND REFINING MODELS

1. Building a Quick Model: A One-Minute Answer

Let's take a detailed look at the ping-pong problem introduced above. The classroom activity involves a quick, one-minute estimate by each individual followed by five-minute estimate by trios.

We ask the students to look around the room and take just 60 seconds answering the question: "How many ping-pong balls could you fit into the room?" The students are momentarily bewildered, but they soon start looking around the room, then at the size of the ping-pong ball, and begin doing either mental or paper-and-pencil calculations. Recent answers from a group of 17 high school students were:

10 billion; 12,000; 1 million; 500,000; 5 million; 100 million; 10 million; 300 million; 100 million and 12 million.

FIGURE 1   Ping Pong

TASK: Determine how many ping-pong balls will fit in the room. Record your method for determining answer.

COOPERATION: One answer from the group, everyone has to agree, everyone has to be able to explain the group's answer.

CRITERIA FOR SUCCESS: Best answer given available resources.

INDIVIDUAL ACCOUNTABILITY: Several group members will be randomly selected to present their group's answer and method.

EXPECTATIONS: Everyone participates, check understanding.

INTERGROUP COOPERATION: When finished compare answer with the answers of surrounding groups in an unintrusive way.

Not everyone gives an answer, particularly a numerical answer. Some give the answer, "a lot." Although these one-minute problems are difficult for students at first, we persist in posing them because we are determined to improve students' estimation skills.

2. Explaining Your Model: A Five-Minute Answer

The students are next asked to work with their group for five minutes to answer the same question, 'How many ping-pong balls could you fit into this room?' *and* to develop an explanation of how they arrived at their answer.

Students quickly formulate an approach and often divide the task—one student measuring the room, another getting a calculator, and the third measuring the ball. Students are intensely focussed during this time. We circulate among the groups, eavesdropping on their conversations, stopping to contribute or clarify, respond to questions (often by turning the question back or suggesting that they make an assumption and go on). When five minutes has elapsed, we call for the answer from each group.

Five-minute answers from each of the six groups of high school students mentioned above were:

20 million; 17 million; 15 million; 5 million; 27 million; 27 million.

Students are asked to compare the one-minute and the five-minute answers which are all displayed on the board or overhead. They often note, jokingly, that there are fewer five-minute answers and that every group obtained an answer. They usually observe that the spread is much less for the five-minute answers.

Since there is a range from 5 million to 27 million, we go on to explore their models to see if we can understand the differences in their estimates. Assumptions are usually considered first. Assumptions listed by the high school group were: room is an empty box, room is a rectangular box, no furniture or people present, ignore room irregularities, ping-pong ball is a cube, and furniture may account for some of the packing.

3. Presenting and Discussing the Alternatives: How Does Your Model Work?

We ask the groups, "How did you get it—did you construct a model? *If so, describe your model.*" Each group's model is recorded on an overhead transparency. Different groups formulate this problem in different ways and the range of answers is often due to their initial, often unspecified, assumptions. For instance, some groups estimate how many balls would fit on the wall at one end of the room, and then multiply by the number that would fit along the length of the room. Each of the high school students' groups estimated the volume of a ping-pong ball and the volume of the room, and divided the one into the other.

The group that got the answer "5 million" said:

let L be the length of the room, 28 feet,
let W be its width, 35 feet,
let H be its height, 10 feet,
and let D be the diameter of a ping-pong ball, 1.5 inches.

Then the volume of the room is

$$V_{room} = LWH$$

and the volume of a ball (treating it as a cube) is

$$V_{ball} = D^3$$

so number of balls equals

$$N_{balls} = \frac{V_{room}}{V_{ball}} = \frac{LWH}{D^3}$$

One of the groups that answered "27 million" volunteered that they used basically the same approach, except they used the volume of a sphere for the ping-pong ball.

$$V_{ball} = 4\pi \frac{r^3}{3}$$

We asked the students to explore the difference in the estimates due to the assumptions about the volume occupied by the ping-pong ball. They said treating the ball as a sphere would give an upper limit (since it assumes no space between the balls) and treating it as a cube would give a lower limit. Several students quickly constructed the ratio of upper limit over lower limit by dividing the two expressions

$$\frac{N_{balls(upperlimit)}}{N_{balls(lowerlimit)}} = \frac{\frac{3V_{room}}{4\pi r^3}}{\frac{V_{room}}{(2r)^3}} = \frac{6}{\pi} = 2$$

4. Deciding on a Model: How Good an Answer Do You Need?

Since the range of students' answers is from 5 to 27 million and assumptions about the ping-pong ball (cube or sphere) only make a difference of about 2 times, each group was asked to refine their model.

At this stage we typically try to establish the method that would give the best possible answer. We ask "How would you arrive at the best answer you can give to the question, 'How many ping-pong balls could fit in this room?'?" They think about this question and discuss it with their group before answering. One group recommends, "Measure the room and ball more accurately." Another group responds, "Fill a one-cubic foot box with ping-pong balls and count them; then multiply by the volume of the room." Someone in the back says, "Fill the room up with ping-pong balls and count them!" We ask if anyone can think of an approach that will give a better answer than that? After a few challenges, there is usually agreement that filling the room and counting will give the best possible answer.

As frustration rises, someone inevitably asks "Who cares how many ping-pong balls you can fit in this room?" We respond, "Thanks for asking the most important question!" How good an answer do you need? Is it worth the effort? How accurate an answer on the number of ping-pong balls you are willing to accept depends on how good an answer you *need*. Principally, it depends on the purpose of the model. You cannot really answer the question, "How many ping-pong balls could fit in this room?" unless you are told how good an answer is needed.

5. Putting it in Writing: Building a "Final" Model

For the final part of this activity each group was asked to formulate a two-hour answer and submit it in written report form. We stressed that their report address the question, "What is your model most sensitive to?" Each group implemented their model on a spreadsheet; systematically varied the dimensions of the room, the dimension of the ball, and the packing; clarified and tested their assumptions; and reported their findings. The following report from David, Mark, and Ernie is typical of first-year college students' two-hour answer.

> In order to arrive at this final answer, several assumptions had to be made. The radius of the ping-pong ball was determined by measuring the circumference at 4 11/16 inches and dividing this by 2π. The "2-dimensional packing" is allowing for adjacent balls filling in a portion of the space between balls—in fact this is an "effective radius," measuring half of the distance (along the horizontal component) between centers of adjacent balls. The same holds true for "3-dimensional packing", with the radius being derived from a formula for the height of a trapezoid (assuming that the vertices of the tetrahedron are at the centers of adjacent balls). This radius is then used as one-half the length of one edge of a cube, the "effective volume" of a ping-pong ball being the volume of that cube. The "trapezoidal area" is not entirely accurate, as it assumes that both the front wall and the straight line connecting the two vertices of the back wall are parallel, and they are not. The "area of remaining arc" was approximated with an isosceles triangle rather than an arc, with the error estimated at less than 1000 in^2. The column area assumes end walls perpendicular to side walls. The total number of balls is arrived at by dividing the total room volume by the "cubic volume" allowing for "3-dimensional packing." In our estimates, the margin for error in the result should be less than one million ping-pong balls. This could be improved upon given more time and more accurate room measurements. It is interesting to note how close the "effective volume" of a ping-pong ball is to its actual spherical volume. Most of the volume between balls is filled when suitable allowance is made for "packing." In higher dimensions, this "effective volume" would probably become even closer to the actual volume.

Further refinement of the model for the ping-pong ball problem is available, along with models for many additional problems, in our books *How to Model It* and *Building Models for Conservation and Wildlife Management*.

WHAT STUDENTS LEARN

Since reflection is an integral part of the process of building models to solve problems with students, we periodically ask students to step back and reflect, "What did *you* learn about modeling from this exercise?"

As the students contribute their insights, we typically look for and refine the following points:

1. Both the one-minute and five-minute exercises illustrate the point that a model is a partial rather than a complete representation.
2. Even a very rough answer is better than no answer at all. We encourage students to come up with the best answer within the available resources. Often a range (the answer is between _____ and _____) is better than a single number.
3. A model that is inadequate under one set of circumstances may be the best that you can do under another set of circumstances. It follows that the design of a model depends as much on circumstances and constraints (of money, time, data or personnel) as it does on the problem that is being solved. It also follows that the assumptions one makes depend on the circumstances in which one solves the problem.
4. A symbolic representation (choosing a notation and building a formula or formulae) is "clean" and powerful. It communicates, simply and clearly, what the modeler believes is important, what information is needed and how that information will be used.
5. Sometimes one uses models implicitly (without being aware that one is doing so); at other times one consciously or explicitly constructs or uses a model. An *explicit model* is an indispensable tool for solving problems and for talking about the solution.

Students have ample experience solving problems that have a unique answer, in other words, problems that have an answer—*the answer*—printed at the back of the book. Although these problems have a certain limited usefulness in the improvement of students' mechanical problem-solving skills, they are not appropriate for developing students' modeling abilities. The appropriate problems to assign for the development of students' modeling skills do not have a simple unique answer—their answers depend on the problem's formulations and assumptions.

Problems in the real world do not magically appear in a form ready to be solved. They are messy and often not clearly identified, or if identified, the label or identification may be incorrect or misleading. The principal problem is often figuring out what the problem is. In short, real problems (in contrast to text-book problems) are not naturally well formulated. Even after identifying the problem, much iteration is usually required to create a satisfactory solution. Students, however, often think that once they have *solved* the problem, that is, generated an answer, they are finished. And for them, the sooner the better—they won't reconsider their work unless forced to. The attitude engendered in students by problems with a single answer doesn't prepare them for tackling and solving the problems they will encounter in the world.

For several years we've been conducting a modeling course for upper division and graduate students in ecology, in which these students are teamed with first-year engineering, science, and math students. Interdisciplinary teams work together to formulate and solve the problems. During the process of building models together, the engineering students learn some biology and the ecology students learn some mathematics and computing. Kevin, a first-year engineering student, said of the modeling in an ecology course:

> The last concept found to be very important is the analysis of the model upon completion. To merely use the answer received in a model as a justifiable answer is completely contradictory because you have not used the model as a means of justifying your answer but rather as a tool that is assumed to produce correct answers. When one arrives at an answer, the structure of the model and its resolution and sensitivity are used to justify the answer that one arrives at. By analyzing your model and questioning the logic behind some of the subroutines, the modeler begins to further define the scope of the question and is thereby able to create a better model. Also in the process the modeler learns more about how changes within the model may have an effect on the final outcome of the model. Sometimes by just analyzing the structure of the model one can fairly accurately predict its outcome within even using values within the model. A good example of this type of analysis was the mathematical model predicting zebra and water buffalo growth in a preserve.

Sara, an ecology graduate student whose comments opened this chapter, continues:

> . . . this approach to models is the most important thing I have learned this quarter, in any of my classes. I am good at organizing things logically, but for several years I have been frustrated; the problems I want to be able to think about have grown too large and too complicated for my brain to be able to handle all of the interacting facets at once. I want to be thinking about the relevance of various factors and their interactions, but I end up struggling so hard just to keep them all straight that I can't also think about how they interact. Your course has shown me the obvious—how to store the simplest version of the interactions in a system so I don't have to worry about mechanics and my brain has room to think about the system itself—how it works, which parts matter most, what the effects of the parts I haven't added yet are, and what the implications of the whole thing are under various conditions. It sounds maudlin, but this has been a real revelation to me.

Our students' comments on our modeling courses indicate they learn much more than to ask the question, "Do I have the right answer?"

REFERENCES

Johnson, D. W., Johnson, R. T., and Smith, K. A. (1991). *Active learning: Cooperation in the college classroom.* Edina, MN: Interaction Book Company.

Starfield, A. M., and Bleloch, A. L. (1991). *Building models for conservation and wildlife management.* Edina, MN: Bellwether Press.

Starfield, A. M., Smith, K. A., and Bleloch, A. L. (1990). *How to model it: Problem solving for the computer age.* New York: McGraw-Hill.

ROBERT E. YAGER

Science and Critical Thinking

Failures with traditional practices in science courses are focusing new attention upon science education which treats science as synonymous with critical thinking. Many in this camp are part of the Science/Technology/ Society (STS) movement which is multi-disciplinary and bigger than science per se. Emerging results with STS initiatives illustrate the advantages of STS—advantages that alleviate many of the problems arising from a mastery approach. Others in this camp are constructivists who have helped popularize a new Constructivist Learning Model (CLM). Basic to CLM is the view that real learning occurs only when meaning is constructed by each learner. That information transferred by one person (e.g., teacher) to another is language transmission only. And, further, no learning results unless previous experience and internalization of it are very similar for transmitter and transmittee.

The National Science Teachers Association (NSTA) has recently adopted a position on STS which provides an operational definition and a description of the kind of graduates science programs should develop— i.e., persons who are scientifically literate. STS programs are characterized as those with many features in common. They are programs which:

- utilize student identification of problems with local interest and impact as organizers for the course;
- use local resources (human and material) as original sources of information that can be used in problem resolution;
- involve students in seeking information that can be applied to solve real-life problem;
- extend learning beyond the class period, the classroom, the school;
- focus upon the impact of science on each individual student;
- view science content not as something that merely exists for students to master on tests;

- de-emphasize process skills as the "special" skills used by practicing scientists;
- emphasize career awareness—especially careers related to science and technology;
- provide opportunities for students to perform in citizenship roles as they attempt to resolve issues they have identified;
- portray science and technology as forces likely to impact the future (NSTA, 1990).

All of these features also exemplify the CLM. STS and the CLM result in more student learning and learning that arises from personal experience and thought.

STS invites a broader definition for science. It must be more than the "agreed upon" basic concepts advanced by scientists and the glamorized skills they agree they use. George Gaylord Simpson has formulated a useful definition for science as we ponder appropriate science for students through age 18.

> Science is an exploration of the material universe in order to seek orderly explanations (generalizable knowledge) of objects and events; *but these explanations must be testable.* (Simpson, 1957, 1963; Brandwein, 1983)

Simpson's definition emphasizes the importance of personal experiences— i.e., the acts of exploring, explaining, and testing. All of these acts are things that all people can do; they tend to make science approachable for all—i.e., a human enterprise available now—not just after mastering a textbook, what a teacher knows, or a specialized vocabulary.

Simpson's definition of science also provides an obvious link to critical thinking. Critical thinking refers to an individual's ability to make reasoned choices and judgments that account for the key elements of decisions used in dealing with a problem. There exist many definitions of critical thinking; in general, all involve factors such as: (a) deconstructing a problem so that it can be analyzed more easily, (b) incorporating information about the most important elements that might affect a decision, and (c) selecting a perspective on a problem that is defensible in terms of some desired action. For example, Halpern uses critical thinking to describe "thinking that is purposeful and goal directed" (1984, p. 3). Kurfess (1988) defines critical thinking as an investigation whose purpose is to explore a situation, phenomenon, question or problem to arrive at a hypothesis or conclusion that integrates all available information and that can therefore be convincingly justified.

This may strike most teachers as a tall order. Few of us naturally think in terms of developing testable hypotheses and rarely are we able to make use of all the available information that applies to a problem or question of concern. As three decades of research on judgmental heuristics clearly demonstrates (e.g., Kahneman, Slovic, & Tversky, 1982), the application of such formal objectives to most everyday decisions is unlikely to be either necessary or appropriate. However, basic to the notion of critical thinking is an ability to examine the available evidence and to go beyond its apparent or immediate value by virtue of adapting a questioning perspective. Viewed in this light, critical thinking skills lead to a few simple questions: Is there another side to the story? What does that experience, possibility, or result have to do with me? Am I accounting for the big picture? Are there inconsistencies in the information I am given? All of these concerns are basic to science when viewed in an STS context and when the CLM dictates teacher and student behaviors in the learning process.

Some specific examples of STS teaching where critical thinking is central to science instruction may provide helpful examples. Following are illustrations provided by Lead Teachers in the Iowa Chautauqua Program that illustrate how student thinking is central to exemplary science programs and exemplary science teaching.

I. Kevin Keopnick
(City High School, Iowa City, Iowa)

One unit I have had success with has been one we do with the Basic Chemistry course on Issues in Nuclear Chemistry. Especially this year, it has been having an impact on students that makes me think about just how people learn. By accident we began the unit this year on the day the Gulf War began.

It seems to me that people need a reason to learn something. STS approaches seek to find that reason for particular groups of people. City High Basic Chem students are probably not going to be science majors in college. They are, however, going to be eligible voters within the next couple of years. This, it would seem, is the ultimate target-group for science literacy efforts.

The unit begins with questions posed to the group. First, "What do you know about nuclear energy?" All answers are accepted without discussion and recorded on the board. Responses typically include:

- "It comes from atoms."
- "It's dangerous."
- "It was wrong to bomb Hiroshima."
- "$E = mc^2$ . . . whatever that means."
- "You can make electricity with it."
- "The waste is dangerous."
- "It makes really big bombs."

Next, we ask, "What do you think you ought to know?"

- "What atoms are."
- "How bombs are made."
- "Who has the bomb."
- "How and when nuclear weapons are used."
- "Where nuclear power plants are located."
- "Where nuclear waste is stored."

Finally, we ask, "What do you want to know about nuclear energy?"

- "Is our electricity nuclear?"
- "Are there any nuke plants around here?"
- "What happens to the waste?"
- "Are there any bombs around here?"
- "Is Iowa City a target?"
- "How does Star Wars work?"
- "Why did we bomb Japan?"

We try to structure our unit each year so that students begin at the knowledge-level at which they come into the course, and progress from there. Certainly, there are some activities we do every year, but, in the last five years, the unit has never been the same twice.

In class, we read the *Science 84* article "To Cleave an Atom," view the NOVA video "Nuclear Strategy for Beginners," operate a computer-simulated nuclear power plant, discuss nuclear testing with a City High teacher who was witness to two blasts at Desert Rock, Nevada, and do some background reading and labs designed to provide students with analogies to atomic structure.

For the past three years, we have also added the annual Basic Chemistry Nuclear Film Festival. Extra credit is granted to students who come in after school to watch and analyze many of the wonderful films made about issues in the nuclear age. Some of the films include:

Amazing Grace and Chuck	*The Atom*	*Back to Chernobyl*
Butter Battle Book	*China Syndrome*	*Dark Circle*
Day After	*Day One*	*Dr. Strangelove . . .*
From Atoms to Quarks	*Hunt for Red October*	*Nightbreaker*
Nuclear Strategy for Beginners	*On the Eighth Day*	*Search for the Super*
War and Peace in the Nuclear Age	*Silkwood*	*Wargames*

This year the unit has been, at times, almost poignant. This morning, for example, one student asked why it was only American lives that were considered when the decision was made to bomb Japan. My lack of explanation then led here to the next question. "Why is it only American lives we consider in Iraq?" To me it is evident that my students are thinking—

perhaps more than ever before. Science classes are popular when STS approaches are used; STS requires student involvement and thought. Students cannot be passive recipients of information teachers present or textbooks include!

II. Ed Rezabek
(Glidden-Ralston Community Schools, Glidden, Iowa)

Focus on thinking and decision-making skills has been emphasized in basic science classes for the past two years at Glidden-Ralston. Traditional laboratory activities integrated with student planned problem solving are being compared for effectiveness and enhancement of these two skills.

Formerly students were introduced to concepts through exploration activities and demonstrations. They participated in concept development activities. Finally application and extension activities were suggested and discussed. The teacher was central to the learning cycle.

Now in an attempt to stimulate student thinking and decision making, I have tried to turn as many student questions and/or units of instruction into problem solving activities which are issue-oriented and designed totally by student/student research teams. My unit on water processing/treatment provides an obvious example. Traditionally the students were given a sample of contaminated water, a set of recipe-type instructions and then they went through a variety of worksheets or teacher suggested methods to clean up the water. The goal was to make it suitable for washing hands. After completion of the activities, discussion, debriefing, and explanation of procedures and results that took place the main focus was student absorption of teacher presented information.

In the new format, students are given the sample of contaminated water with the job of cleaning it up suitable for washing hands. In this mode no instruction sheet is provided. Preliminary discussion has to do with what the students already may know. Next students determine what methods they will want to utilize for their clean-up process by researching water treatment from literature, using resources in town to learn about city processing of water, and identifying any other resource that may be of use in their cleanup process. The students design and carry out their cleanup process with instructor approval and supervision. I serve as a facilitator of the process. When questions come up, I may actually provide direct instruction on a particular concept, (i.e., charcoal filtration and adsorption vs. absorption). Otherwise, the problems and success/failures that the students encounter are left for them to realize and to make adjustments. Whether or not the student plan is experimentally correct is not a priority. As a facilitator I can suggest and offer questions that allow the student team to rethink procedures that are possibly not safe, or suggest ways a given problem might be solved using alternative methods.

When the student research and experimentation are completed, each group/team will report to the rest of the class to be critiqued and questioned. Prizes are awarded for a variety of water quality criteria (quantity, quality, etc.). Students take the roles of reporting scientists and plan out their presentations using appropriate visual aids and media.

Evaluation techniques are varied when using this method of instruction. Some evaluation takes place in one-on-one discussion. Feedback from students is evaluated for progress during planning and experimentation. In many cases traditional testing is used; multi-choice items are constructed from student reports and problem solving procedures. I feel the main mode of evaluation is in the student reports of their research projects—not only are science concepts picked up, but evidence of thinking skills is apparent in terms of the type/amount of writing the students can do and the extensions and connections that the students begin to see. I have found that science approached using this method accomplishes much more than was ever anticipated. Students gain the knowledge needed to solve problems, use the processes of science, utilize/apply creative ideas in an atmosphere which causes little if any anxiety. Students are dealing with relevant issues which affect them and society. There is ample opportunity to use the skills and processes on other problems students encounter in every aspect of their lives. The attitude of the students is seen as very positive during the problem solving process. This in turn makes science more enjoyable and less apprehensive. The teacher many times learns along with the students and at the same time gains awareness as to the misconceptions students have.

In surveying 41 students, comparing recipe-type labs to student planned problem solving, 68 percent were enthusiastic and preferred the student planned approach as compared to 27 percent preferred the recipe/teacher directed approach. Two students indicated that they saw value in both approaches.

The following are comments from my students concerning methods of "learning about and doing science":

> "I like the student planned approach . . . because you get to try to figure out a way to solve the problem . . . and you learn from your mistakes . . . I feel like I learn more." (Eric Schumacher)

> "I think we should do more with situations that make us use our brain and no one elses." (Amy Morlan)

> "I would rather be in a lab activity where you tell us what to do . . . I feel that I then know exactly what is expected." (Jarod Schon)

> "We make the decisions and learn to work with others. There are no set rules . . . We make our mistakes and learn from them . . . I remember more because I can understand more." (Shannon Bunnell)

"Teacher planned labs-recipes are OK . . . But it's almost too easy." (Mandy Kroeger)

"I enjoy the student planned activities . . . This way you learn firsthand while figuring out ways to solve the problems. It makes you use group skills, study skills, and safety . . . I have a better idea of what works and what doesn't work." (Kevin Brant)

"I would rather do the recipe type activities because it shows everything to do . . . I am very lazy." (Emily Soyer)

"I definitely prefer to plan out my own experiment . . . not only do you find answers to questions . . . you come up with more questions and you make up the questions yourself. By allowing us to take this approach you realize that we are kids with imaginations and you allow us to use them." (Kari Lappe)

"Printed-recipe-instructions are good, because then you know you are doing it right. But . . . it isn't as much of a challenge." (Andrea Conner)

"Working in groups to solve problems is better . . . this allows you to make your decisions which the group thinks is best." (Eric Johnson)

III.   James Kollman
(Denison High School, Denison, Iowa)

One of the greatest benefits of STS education is the ability to get students involved and interested in the subject matter. I give students complete ownership of the selection of the issues they want to investigate. We begin by looking through newspapers and magazines for articles that have something to do with science. The students then brainstorm pros and cons of each issue. Criteria they use in selecting an issue include: Availability of resources, importance of the issue, ease in relating the issue to the classroom subject, and interest of the class in the issue. Using these criteria they are able to eliminate some issues as possibilities. AIDS has been a very popular issue; however, chemistry students find it difficult to relate AIDS to chemistry. Biology students see the AIDS issue as being a natural, and it has been used by my biology classes a number of times. Issues that have been identified by my students for research include: Hazardous Waste, Ozone, Chemical Warfare, Oil Spills, Recycling, Pollution, Poaching, Animal Rights, Acid Rain, Abortion, Steroids, Alternative Fuels, Atmospheric Chemistry, Toxic Waste, Food Chemistry, Alcoholism, and Nuclear Waste. While not all of these topics will be issues the classes deal with, they are a list to start from. Students begin to keep an eye on the news (both broadcast and print) to find new issues to use in class. They begin to realize that there is a link between their science class and what is happening in the world around them.

Since the students select the issues themselves, they have a built-in interest. When the topic was ozone, students wrote to the company that manufactures the foam products used by our lunch program to find out if the foam contributed to the depletion of the ozone layer. It didn't. They became interested in the manufacturing process of the foam and the chemical reactions involved. The gas laws had meaning to them because the gas laws related to their issue. An indication of how involved and interested students can get was demonstrated by a group of four boys who went out at 1:00 A.M. to collect water samples downstream from a local packing plant for their water quality study. When I asked them why they went out so late to collect their samples, they said: "We didn't want them to see us because we want to ask them some questions and see if they're giving us the truth. Besides it was more fun this way." This statement says a lot about STS. First it indicates these students had developed the idea that information should be examined and not taken at face value. In other words these students were demonstrating critical thinking. Secondly, they were having fun. We all know that if students enjoy what they are doing, they do a better job and STS really does make the science more fun. Students have asked me why all their classes or at least all their science classes can't be STS. Student comments have included this statement by Tina Bissen: "It started out as just a report, but then we really got into it." The students really get involved in their own learning by designing their own activities. This allows each student to approach the material in their own learning style and leads to greater student progress. In addition, the students experience less stress.

Upon completion of the research, students decide what to do with their information. They have gone to the middle and elementary schools and taught mini-lessons about the issue; they've sponsored poster contests, set up displays, and made flyers to pass out at local businesses to pass along their information. This stage of their research allows the students to do something with their information. It gives the students a chance to show off what they've learned and gives them an outlet for their concern. At the completion of the research portion of his study of ozone, Greg Gunderson said: "Some people hadn't even heard of the ozone layer. We wanted to make others more aware of what we found out." One action taken by this class was to set up displays showing products that were damaging to the ozone and alternative products that posed no threat to the ozone layer. Products for the display were donated by the local Hy-Vee Food Store. The reason for the display was summed up by Kellie Tech who stated: "Maybe people will think next time they buy some of these products." As the students gain knowledge about an issue, they take it to heart. It becomes a cause they feel the need to do something about. A year after the ozone project, I have these students coming to me with new articles they've found on the topic. I have never had students show such a long lasting interest in topics. In the fall of 1991, two chemistry classes identified the issue of chemical warfare as one they would like to research. One class began their research and the other decided on a different topic. With the outbreak of war in the Middle East and the threat of chemical weapons, this topic has become very important to both classes and I am swamped with articles each time chemical weapons are mentioned in the newspapers.

Since STS is student directed learning, it allows the students to have input into their own educational experience. Additionally, since STS is issue-oriented instruction, the material is relevant to the student and re-lieves some of the burn-out some students feel. As one student put it: "In most classes we have to memorize stuff that doesn't mean anything to me in my life." Students begin to make connections between their coursework in science class and their other classes as well. In researching topics like deforestation, students are able to link their study of the biological issues present with concepts from other classes such as economics, math, social studies, nutrition and health. In addition, they are frequently required to draw upon skills learned in classes such as language arts and math. To paraphrase a couple of current educational catch-phrases, what we are dealing with is "whole science," or "science across the curriculum."

With the students able to take ownership of their education, they are able to design experiences in their own learning styles and as much in depth as they choose. It has been my experience that students are not used to this type of freedom and are reluctant to take the reins, but as they discover that it is truly *their* research project they begin to expand their projects. My students have enjoyed educating the teacher. Often they will come to class excited about some new information they have found or that came in the mail, and really seem to enjoy it when I tell them that I didn't know that bit of information. I have gone from being the "expert" in my classroom answering all the questions (that I could) to having students ask me; "We're doing the research. We know more about the topic than you do. Why do we need you in here?" This is a very telling question. The question is indicative of the fact the students have begun to learn independently.

Along with independent learning, students developed the ability to analyze information and utilize critical thinking. Students begin to question the validity of information and the possible bias of authors; they begin to explore side-issues as they emerge and students actually search for ways to make connections; they become the teachers. As my students progress with their research projects, I stress they are becoming experts in their field of research.

Since formal education ends at some point in each student's life, isn't it important that we provide them with the skills necessary to be able to process information? Since students won't always have an expert or teacher available to help them understand the information they encounter, they must, at some point, develop the skills necessary to be able to continue to learn on their own. In traditional classrooms, we do a wonderful job of breaking down information into small, digestible bits and telling the students what is important and what they will be tested over without ever explaining why something is important or why it rates being a test item. STS provides students with the opportunity to sift through information on their own and make their own decisions about what is important based upon their criteria. Beyond teaching information, STS teaches information management, how to analyze data critically, and allows for the connections to be made between bits of information. Information is transient; scientific information is subject to change and revision. The ability to work with information is crucial and STS is probably the most effective way to teach students how to work with information.

WHAT STS TEACHING DOES TO STUDENTS

In each case the STS module arose from student generated questions. They identified the problem, helped with a division of effort and responsibility, sought out answers, analyzed available information, decided on tentative solutions, and moved to specific individual and group actions. In short students experienced science as critical thinking. They experienced science in the way that Simpson defined it. They became curious about something current and something in their immediate environment; they offered their own explanations and ideas; they investigated and tested these ideas; they shared their experiences and took some actions based on the process. In these situations critical thinking was not taught via steps like a recipe; nor were the important concepts presented "because they are important and you need to know them." The concepts of science were sought out because they were needed and useful. The skills were seen as important because they were used. They were not something that people called scientists used in someplace called a research laboratory.

Science, when it is viewed as critical thinking, can become the glue that holds the curriculum together. Rustum Roy, one of our national STS leaders, has called STS the glue that holds science together for most people and makes it useful.

Emerging results with STS in K–12 classrooms in Iowa illustrate its power in developing process skills in students. Figure 1 is an indication.

It is apparent that when science is taught with critical thinking as central that students increase their understanding and mastery of process skills dramatically.

Science must focus on three fundamental concepts—alternatives, objectives, and attributes; when it does the curriculum will have moved from a focus on what each student is to think and on to a focus on how they think. When this occurs, children will be empowered to take control over

FIGURE 1 Percentage of middle school students who demonstrate their ability to perform in fourteen processes of science areas while enrolled in traditional class sections versus students enrolled in STS/sections

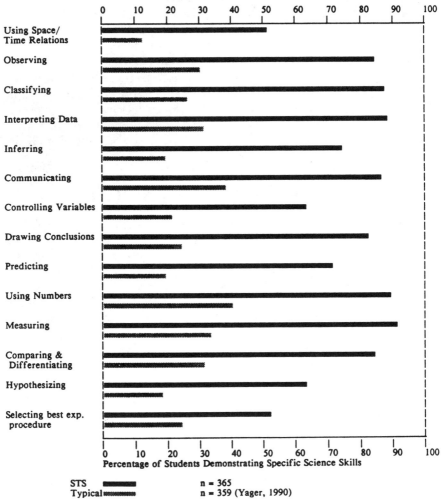

Percentage of Students Demonstrating Specific Science Skills

STS ▬▬▬ n = 365
Typical ▬▬▬ n = 359 (Yager, 1990)

their world in a meaningful way. Science instruction when viewed as critical thinking has the potential of changing a child's behavior from automatic thinking and use of general rules to decision thinking based on the structuring of problems and linking of facts with personal values. To move science and the nation's science teachers to assist in such efforts will not be easy. But it may be a necessity if true educational reform is to occur.

The research evidence is clear. Teaching science as concepts and skills which must be mastered before they can be used is an impossibility. All of us seem to learn from the experience itself. Real meaning has to be constructed by each person. Engaging students in problem solving activities is the way to get students to think and to practice basic science.

REFERENCES

Brandwein, P. F. (1983). *Notes toward a renewal in the teaching of science.* Chicago: Coronado Publishers, Inc.

Halpern, D. (1984). *Thought and knowledge: An introduction to critical thinking.* Hillsdale, NJ: Erlbaum.

Kahneman, D., Slovic, P., and Tversky, A. (1982). *Judgment under uncertainty: Heuristics and biases.* New York: Cambridge University Press.

Kurfess, J. (1988) *Critical thinking: Theory, research, practice and possibilities* (Report No. 2). (ASHE-Eric Higher Education Reports).

National Science Teachers Association. (1990). *The NSTA position statement on science/technology/society (STS).* Washington, DC: Author.

Simpson, G. G. (1957). *Life: An introduction to biology.* New York: Harcourt Brace Jovanovich.

Simpson, G. G. (1963). Biology and the nature of science. *Science,* 139 (3550), 81–88.

Yager, R. E. (1990). Instructional outcomes change with STS. *Iowa Science Teachers Journal,* 27 (1), 2–20.

Jo Margaret Mano

Maps and Graphics:
Developing the Critical Eye

The fear of quantitative methods, even of numbers themselves, both blocks many students' learning and shrinks their interest in subjects which require such understanding. A more subtle confusion surrounds the many types of graphics which present visual transformations of numerical data. In response to this problem I developed a teaching approach that aims to make numerical arguments more real, and thus more meaningful, by focusing a critical eye on concrete examples. Maps and Graphics: Measures and Symbols is a course designed to meet the needs of entering college freshmen in applied analytic skills, but the idea can be adapted for various contexts and different educational levels. Techniques traditionally used in applied geography provide the material, but the major thrust of the course is a critical study of *graphical language and integrity*. The core intent shifts away from dealing with numbers to focus on getting students to think about the ingredients of graphics and maps by discovering, questioning and using them.

The written word unfolds sequentially, piece by piece. In contrast, a visual story is perceived as a whole, and the coded messages must be extracted one by one. This incremental method of teaching starts with a specific graphic, then takes the puzzle apart to build understanding by examining intrinsic data characteristics. The maps and graphics course is structured to present a series of increasingly complex challenges, from basic concepts to methods of analysis and display, and finally to developing statistical hypotheses (Figure 1). Learning is reinforced by drawing, for construction generates real examples of abstract quantitative concepts. Maps and Graphics encourages students to investigate, evaluate, and *use* maps and graphics which have integrity.

A graphic with integrity should not only present data accurately, but also tell a story, provoke questions and supply potential information for future hypotheses (Tufte, 1983). Truthful presentation requires correctly scaled axes, clear labels and a display method which shows *how* the analysis has been done. To support and reinforce critical questioning, students are

FIGURE 1   Student Project Presentations

Maps and Graphics: Measures and Symbols		
Topic	**Content**	**Exercise**
Data sources	Finding and using U.S. Census data	Constructing a table from Census data
Data measurement	Scales of measurement, visual variables	Nominal, ordinal, and interval weather data
Data characteristics	Point, line and area discrete and continuous data	Interpolation of isotherms
Maps and graphic representation	Scale, symbols, projections co-ordinates	Topographic map profile section
Graphic integrity	Time lines, pie charts and histograms	Population pyramid and pie chart
Statistics and data description	Range, quartiles, deciles, and percentiles	Box and whisker plots
Statistical analysis	Central tendency measures, variance and standard deviation	Histogram, ogive, frequency polygon
Sampling techniques	Sampling types, reliability	Random sampling of air photo data
Mapping distributions	Dot, choropleth and isarithm methods	Population density map
Correlation and regression	Simple regression, residuals	Plotting regression line, finding residuals
Logarithmic and triangular scales	Population growth, soils, sector analysis	Economic sector analysis

asked each week to collect an example of a good or bad graphic from newspapers and magazines to illustrate the study topics. The idea of graphical integrity invariably generates an ethical argument. Students ask, "What is to stop me lying with graphics, now I know how it's done?" Nothing— but at least you can recognize graphic truth or falsehood. "How far can you go in emphazing your graphic message before it becomes a lie?" Class consensus draws the line as far as one's conscience will allow. The course builds an understanding of data characteristics and powers of expression by looking at a variety of graphics, with different levels of integrity.

The most important aspect of the course is the weekly practical exercise which uses and reinforces the ideas introduced with each subject. Most require only pencil and ruler, occasionally graph paper or a xeroxed outline map. The exercise is begun in the classroom and completed as homework. Asking students to address the crux of the issue, and choice of units or scales and other key elements in the classroom, while they feel free to ask for help, has proved important in building confidence in judgment. Each unit is viewed as a series of choices in reliability and correct graphic depiction, with student input a serious consideration in arriving at a solution. The corrected weekly exercises serve as both a means to identify errors in construction or concept, and as a series of reference examples for the student. This concrete experience helps to make the topic memorable, for students have frequently commented that the physical act of making the graphic helps them understand and retain the ideas illustrated. The semester project is a research paper integrating graphics in analysis and presentation.

The first purpose of the course is to get students to think about the reliability of information. Data sources and their reliability are discussed by collecting student ideas on where information originates, followed by a critical evaluation of how reliable that information might be. Is the *National Enquirer* as trustworthy as the *New York Times*? Are population statistics from third world countries as dependable as those from more developed places, and why? The vast storehouse of U.S. Government data is then demonstrated by a library tour, which also serves as a good introduction for identifying research sources as students begin searching for material on their individual projects.

INVESTIGATING DATA WITH GRAPHICS

A first challenge, introducing scales or levels of measurement, asks students to consider that data vary in quantitative strength, determined by type, which require different graphic translations. The idea that nominal, ordinal, interval and ratio data are essentially different in the quality and power of their expression helps students to evaluate and identify graphics which confuse these intrinsic data characteristics. In introducing these abstract ideas, they are made more concrete by tying levels of measurement to the symbols, or visual variables, used to depict them in maps and graphics. Visual variables include the variations of color, shape, value, size, and texture of symbols. Color and shape should only be used to show nominal (name or kind) differences. Size, value (lightness or darkness) and texture should be used to show ordinal (more or less than) variation. Contrasts in color intensity and figure advance/retreat work together to produce a visually based hierarchy—simply stated; darker, larger objects *look* more important. *USA Today*'s daily colored weather graphics provide vivid examples of the use of visual variables to illustrate levels of measurement. Dotted or dashed areas of nominal data (snow or rain) are combined with colored ordinal (colder to warmer) divisions of similar temperatures. The recorded temperatures used to make the map are based on an interval scale.

After discussing examples of these concepts, the students do the exercise shown in Figure 2. The answers for one of the four weather stations are shown at the bottom. The concept of months being divided into those

FIGURE 2 Levels of Measurement

Data used to produce maps and graphics have characteristics which must be taken into account to prevent "lying" or distortion in graphics. Data may be *qualitative* (different in kind) or *quantitative* (different in kind and/or amount). Quantitative data (temperature, rainfall, population totals) can be measured more precisely than qualitative data (hot/cold, wet/dry, dense/sparse population) which is only different in *name*. Data can be described even more precisely by using a four level hierarchy. The four levels (or scales) of measurement are *nominal, ordinal, interval* and *ratio*.

Nominal data are at the lowest, qualitative level of measurement. Things are distinguished by *name* (land/water). The next three levels are quantitative.

Ordinal data can be *ranked* (higher/lower), using the idea of greater than ($>$) or less ($<$).

Interval level data use *equal units* as intervals on the measurement scale (contour height lines or Fahrenheit (F) and Celsius (C) temperatures).

Ratio level uses equal intervals and *starts at a true, physical zero* or base. The Kelvin (or degrees Absolute) temperature scale is an example.

This exercise uses mean monthly temperature for 4 sample weather stations to demonstrate scales of measurement. Temperatures are in Fahrenheit. *Nominal* scale will be used to divide the months into vegetation growth (G) and no-growth (NG) months. Growth months average above 50°F and no-growth below 50°F. *Ordinal* scale is used to rank the months from hottest to coldest. (Assign the same rank where there is a tie. You may have two thirds and no fourth, the following rank would be fifth.) *Interval* scale will be used to graph the mean monthly temperature on the Fahrenheit and Celsius scales. For each station determine the nominal, ordinal and interval level. Draw the interval scale on graph paper, and connect the dots for each month with a hand-drawn line. Set up your exercise using the format below.

Q. How would you change the graph to show *ratio* scale? Start at −273°C.

Weather Station: Portland, Oregon

	J	F	M	A	M	J	J	A	S	O	N	D
	39	42	46.5	52	56.5	62.5	66.6	66.5	61.5	54.5	47	41.5
Nominal	NG	NG	NG	G	G	G	G	G	G	G	NG	NG
Ordinal	12	11	9	7	5	3	1	2	4	6	8	10

Interval

```
F°                                              C°   (You will have
68                                              20   to include more
                                                     numbers in
50                                              10   the vertical
                                                     scale for some
 3  _____   0   stations)
    J   F   M   A   M   J   J   A   S   O   N   D
```

too cold or warm enough for plant growth as an example of nominal scale presents few difficulties. Ranking the months is only problematic if there is a tie, and comparing ranking to placement in a race illustrates this idea. This is the first time in the course students have to confront graph paper and the choice of scales for the axes, so most student queries are about the interval scale. While the concept that graphic integrity requires that axes must be evenly scaled is discussed in class, the students have to think through what this means in practical terms as they complete the exercise. The students realize they have to think about the range of data so that they can scale the vertical axis to fit on the graph paper, and the need to space the months out evenly on the horizontal axis. The four weather stations have different ranges, so they discover that keeping the same vertical scale allows comparison between the stations. Varying the vertical scale because plotting points may be easier distorts the comparison. Early in the semester, scale bothers a substantial number of students when it is expressed in an abstract form (1:25,000). By the end of the course, very few cannot draw correctly scaled axes, labelled with a ratio, as they see the reason for shrinking the data to fit available space.

Students ask, "Are these real data?" Yes, they are. This generates the inevitable question, "How useful is a monthly average in knowing about the weather?" Not much—but it does provides a means of comparing different climates in the world. Students appreciate that averages are a crude measure and generalization (grouping into categories) clarifies, but loses individual data values. The sample student responses to the exercise shown in Figure 3 reveal how thinking through the construction, and repeating the approach makes the concept a reality.

Having manipulated data to make their own graphics, students are then asked to think about and evaluate graphical integrity with a deeper understanding of the ingredients that make up the most prolific media graphics choices in their weekly collection: time lines, bar graphs and pie charts. Edward Tufte's book *The Visual Display of Quantitative Understanding* provides both inventive methods for evaluating graphic truthfulness and wonderful examples of lesser known, powerful graphics. It is the major text, supported by readings from a variety of cartographic and statistical sources. He suggests graphics with greater explanatory power; for example, box and whisker plots can portray the ranges and quartiles of statistical data, *and* sample size by varying box width.

DISCOVERING AND EVALUATING HYPOTHESES WITH GRAPHICS

Statistical analysis is kept deliberately graphic. Concrete examples of ogives and polygons show how line slope and direction create meaning in graphs. The final group of topics focuses on the use of graphics to generate display and test relationships between variables. Scattergrams are used as

FIGURE 3 Levels of Measurement: Student Responses

How did the exercise make you think about different levels of measurement?

The exercise did help me *understand* the measurements (nominal, ordinal, interval) better. This exercise called for three levels so I had to understand them to use them.

Having us organize them [levels of measurement] in those ways made it easier to think in those terms.

The exercise did help me think about different levels of measurement because I had never thought about the different levels as individual. I had never broken down this kind of information into its subject types. I always processed it as is.

I found out that some measurements were more involved than others. It helped me understand the difference by the practice of making the graphs.

This exercise helped me *think* about different levels of measurement, and I had to come up with a scale with the proper intervals . . .

It helped me [understand] because I had to do it four times.

The exercise forced me to use each level, therefore self-explaining and making them more familiar.

I can see how many differences there are when you view something . . .

the introduction to the ideas of dependent and independent variables. Finding the "cause" (independent) to put on the X axis and "effect" (dependent) for the Y axis is not easy, for spurious relationships might be assumed from co-variations of unrelated items. Plotting the related cause and effect between such constants as latitude and the range of yearly temperature gives a general upward trend of points as higher latitudes tend to have a greater temperature range. This leads to the question: "Can we make a hypothesis that relates them?" Such an upward trend would suggest a positive correlation between increased latitude and increased annual range. The regression line that approximates this trend minimizes the distance between all the points and the line, and provides a way of predicting the expected relationship. Yet not all observations will fall on the line, for other factors, such as altitude and distance from the ocean, also affect annual temperature range. The vertical distance between the regression line and a specific point will show how much each real observation differs from its predicted relationship. These "residuals" may provide information for modifying the hypothesis. For example, the modified hypotheses would state: annual temperature range increases with increasing latitude, *and* increasing distance from the ocean.

FIGURE 4 Regression Exercise

Use the paired values in the table to construct a scattergram. Think about the relationship between the variables. Be sure to put the *independent* and *dependent* variables on the correct axes. Use the key numbers to identify the points as you plot them on the graph paper. Using the *semi-averages* method, for each column calculate 1) the mean, 2) the mean above the mean, 3) the mean below the mean, and then draw an approximate regression line between them. *Then* answer the questions.

Percentages for voter registration and voter turnout on election day for selected cities are given in the table below.

City	Voter Registration Rate	Voter Turnout Rate
1. South Bend, IN	96.4	85.2
2. Minneapolis, MN	92.5	58.5
3. Scranton, PA	90.4	80.3
4. Duluth, MN	85.1	74.9
5. New Bedford, MA	82.4	74.6
6. Topeka, KS	81.9	69.3
7. Omaha, NE	79.8	66.8
8. Memphis, TE	84.7	50.1
9. Peoria, IL	87.4	64.9
10. Boston, MA	74.0	63.3
11. Birmingham, AL	39.1	13.8
12. Chattanooga, TE	70.7	46.6
13. St. Petersburg, FL	69.7	59.5
14. Hartford, CT	70.7	34.1
15. Baton Rouge, LA	64.7	47.8
16. Little Rock, AR	61.2	46.9
17. Norfolk, VA	43.6	22.4
18. Jacksonville, FL	54.9	46.9

Mean _____   Mean _____

a) What type of relationship is shown? _____ correlation.

b) Identify one city with a higher than expected turnout rate. _____
   What other factor(s) might explain this residual?

c) Identify one city with a lower than expected turnout rate. _____
   What other factor(s) might explain this residual?

The related exercise is based on voter registration and election day turnout and requires only graph paper to plot an example of simple regression (Figure 4). The first step produces a scattergram which seems to imply that, in general, the greater the registration rate, the higher the voter turnout. The graphic answer (Figure 5) shows the plotted points and pre-

FIGURE 5   Student response

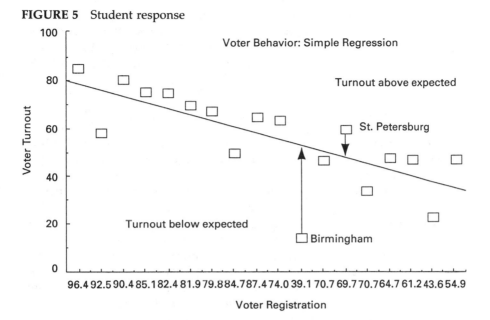

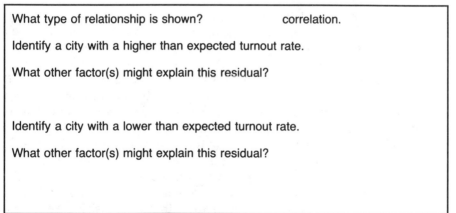

What type of relationship is shown?   correlation.

Identify a city with a higher than expected turnout rate.

What other factor(s) might explain this residual?

Identify a city with a lower than expected turnout rate.

What other factor(s) might explain this residual?

dicted relationship as a line, with samples of student suggestions for the "oddball" residuals that do not fit. Even where students forgot the correct term to describe the upward slope as a "positive" relationship, the synonyms they used: "direct," "true" and "real" showed they understood the *concept*; that the number of voters who registered influenced the number who turned out to vote. The few students who misinterpret the slope as negative revealed they thought that you registered *after you voted*, and thus had confused cause and effect. Even this mistake provided material for thought, and the opportunity for a subtle civics lesson!

The variety of explanations for turnout above or below the expected rate show that students appreciated the range of different reasons that could cause such variation, from weather to hotly contested races, to a rather perceptive "understanding the politicians"—cited as a reason for turnout both above *and* below that predicted.

USING GRAPHICS: STUDENT PROJECTS

As a semester project, the students make a short presentation of their research paper, which must contain at least three original graphics. Topics are outlined early in the semester, so that input can be given about the topic scope and relevant graphics. The students have often commented that this assignment is both the most challenging and most rewarding assignment. "I was very pleased we had the project in this class. Not only did it give me the opportunity to learn how to use graphics within a paper, it exposed me to the many interesting topics presented by my classmates." "Having to use graphics in the project meant I had to keep looking for the right numbers to do it." "I had to send away for my data to Hershey Corporation. The stuff they sent was hard to turn into graphics."

Students are often frustrated in their search for higher level data, and then find themselves limited in the types of graphics they can construct. Having learned a wide selection of graphic techniques, they are reduced to using the simpler types of maps, time-lines, bar graphs and pie charts because of the type of available data. Advice about alternative possibilities while the project is in its early stages results in more effective graphics. It is also an opportunity to reassure students that the scarcity of data in a desired form is not unusual, and graphic options are often limited. This is confirmed by the sample of types of media graphics the class has amassed by the end of the semester, for there are few innovative graphic examples.

The subjects students have chosen to research have covered a wide spectrum, from AIDS to illiteracy, from garbage recycling to sports statistics, from teenage pregnancy to car performance. One student chose to contrast the swimming team's performance with local rivals (Figure 6). The first range bar graphic shows she learned the New Paltz team posted the fastest 50 meter meet time, and while some rivals' times varied widely during the season, Marist's swimmers' were consistent. The second graphic reveals the home team's performance could be related to their greater practice yardage, and all teams swam more in January than February. Another student undertook primary research in cataloguing the amount of toilet paper rolls used in selected dormitories during a week. His conclusions found that female suites used over twice the amount of male suites, but was forced to admit that his research design was flawed since male students were borrowing rolls from female floors, and record-keeping was

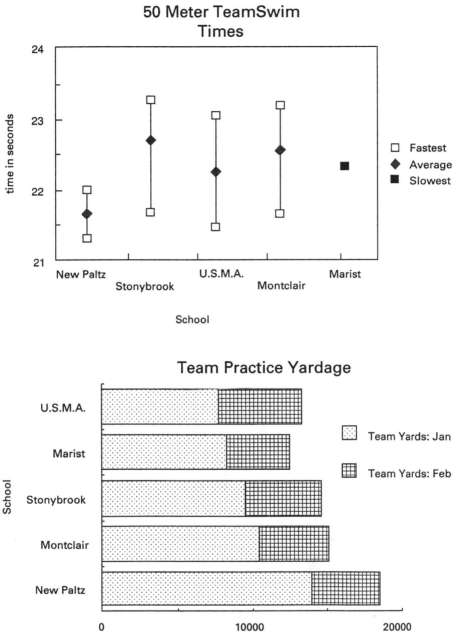

less than perfect: both factors illustrating research problems in more academic areas.

In a more serious vein, a student working on a project to assess off-campus calls in a new telephone system, sampled a 24 hour period and used computer generated graphics (Figure 7). He was not surprised to find the highest number of calls were made from 12 to 6 P.M. He suggested these were predominantly business calls, while the substantial amount in the evening from 6 P.M. to midnight were probably made by students. Analyzing the calls made within New York State to different area codes, he had to use a logarithmic scale to compress the total number of calls on the left-hand axis. This graph shows that local calls, the last two bars on the right, were briefer on average than those to places further away. Although he could only rank the calls by distance from zone 0 to zone 6, he decided to try rank correlation in the third graph. While the graphic shows no correlation, the computer software insisted on inserting a regression line. This graphic led him to two interesting conclusions: first, callers talked longer to places further away (potentially more expensive calls) and second, computer graphics can force you to lie if you can't suppress unneeded functions.

STUDENT EVALUATIONS

Students have been asked to evaluate the course in three ways—a course specific questionnaire, a department comment sheet and as part of a college wide evaluation. Individual comments have stated it was "a fun course," "much more useful than required idiotic courses," "doing the exercises was much better than listening to endless lectures in other courses," "it provided a good base which could be used in any area of study," "introduced a new perspective," "turned a college requirement into a worthwhile and interesting course," rated it "a very good experience," and stated "I really enjoyed the exercises," and "I am no longer fooled by graphics, and can tell the good ones from the bad."

Perhaps the most interesting comment, from a student initially uneasy about the numerical content, was "I thought this course was going to be all math. We didn't do any math the whole semester!" This statement suggests that the graphic focus had successfully disguised the real learning of mathematical and analytic skills as a method of critical thinking.

The major premise behind this course is the students' understanding of quantitative concepts through practice and practical applications. The approach aims to free students from "math anxiety" to view methods as useful tools, rather than unfathomable mysteries. Encouraging students to develop a critical eye focuses on an important skill in the expanding graphic media: the careful assessment of visual communication. The content also appeals because of its relevance and usefulness. Opportunities for thinking

FIGURE 7 Student Graphs of Telephone Usage

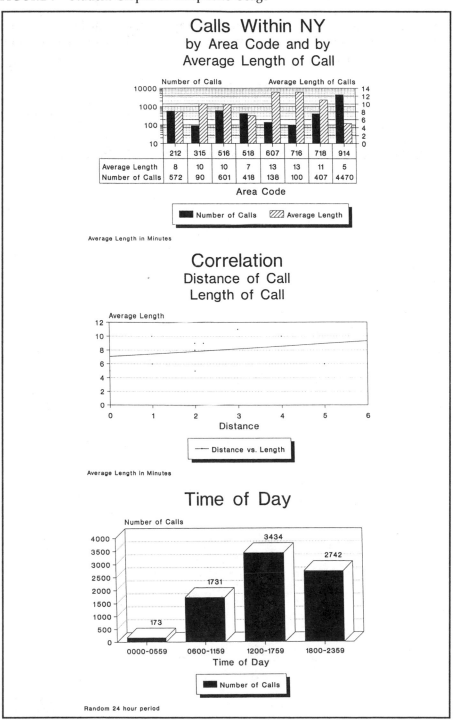

Calls Within NY
by Area Code and by
Average Length of Call

	212	315	516	518	607	716	718	914
Average Length	8	10	10	7	13	13	11	5
Number of Calls	572	90	601	418	138	100	407	4470

Area Code

■ Number of Calls ▨ Average Length

Average Length in Minutes

Correlation
Distance of Call
Length of Call

Distance

— Distance vs. Length

Average Length in Minutes

Time of Day

Time of Day	Number of Calls
0000-0559	173
0600-1159	1731
1200-1759	3434
1800-2359	2742

■ Number of Calls

Random 24 hour period

graphically will increase in the future as computer use is further integrated into the curriculum. The wise understanding of graphics forms an integral part of such learning.

REFERENCES

Tufte, Edward (1983). *The Visual Display of Quantitative Information* Cheshire, CT: Graphics Press.
See also
Tufte, Edward (1990). *Envisioning Information* Cheshire, CT: Graphics Press.

JACK V. MATSON

Planning Failure
in Engineering Design

Pretend you are a student who just signed up for Innovative Engineering Design. Innovation is potentially easy because you have what it takes: a mind to generate good ideas and the willingness to try them out. It is the natural process of exploring your interests and creating new and different variations. However, it can be impossible if you do not believe in yourself and do not follow through.

Let's face it, the world may not be ready for your terrific ideas. Many faces are arrayed against you. Society is surviving quite nicely without whatever you have to offer and will resist change.

Consequently, an innovator's life is filled with failure. You are exploring the unknown where trapdoors, blind alleys, and society's obstacles will cause you to make mistakes, blunders, and omissions. For any innovation, there simply are an irreducible number of failures. It turns out that the key to successful innovating is in the understanding of failure.

Your strategy needs to become one of accelerating the innovation process and compressing the time it takes to get through the failure mode. So what are you waiting for? The first class in Failure 101 is about to begin.

FAILURE 101: FIRST CLASS

Have you ever failed? Taken it personally? Had anxiety? Felt rejected?

I need to convince you that you need more failure in your life. Why? The more you fail, the more you succeed.

Here are some examples. Stockbrokers need 300 steady customers to be successful. They acquire customers by making cold calls on the telephone from lists of prospects. The statistics are for every 250 cold calls they will land one customer. Therefore, to be successful, a stockbroker must make roughly 75,000 cold calls and be rejected 74,700 times.

Inventors have even worse odds. They must accumulate 1000 ideas and sort out 100 of the most promising. Of the 100 ideas, on close examination only 10 will be feasible. And of the 10 ideas just one will make it in the marketplace. For the inventor to be successful he must tolerate 999 rejected ideas out of one thousand.

Professors must deal with similar statistical realities. Four out of every five grant proposals are rejected; two out of three manuscripts for publication are returned to the author. To be successful in academia, a professor will accumulate five to ten major failures per year.

Have you ever skied? Were you humiliated by the experience? The beginning skier if he is smart will take lessons. The instructor teaches a contacted technique called the snowplow in which the legs are twisted in a "V" position to slow the skier down and cushion any fall. You learn how to fall (fail), get up, and repeat the experience. Then you are ready to attempt the ski lift. As you transcend upward, you notice it is not stopping at the top. You must jump off. But you fall and the operator must stop the lift and scrape your body off to the side, another failure. The next challenge is the bunny or beginners slope. You fall your way down the hill while six year olds use your body as a mogul. Yet, after each wipe out, you pick yourself up, brush yourself off, and eagerly test the next piece of slope. These failures have turned you on; you have an appetite to learn. Why? Successful skiers have the attitude, "Wipe me out; failure turns me on." They know the more they fail, the more they succeed.

The benefits of failure are many. Failure eliminates boredom and apathy. When it occurs, you want to find out why and press to understand. Failure makes you humble. It is hard to be arrogant and egotistical when failure is a constant occurrence. You feel reconnected to the rest of humanity through your bumbling and mistake-prone existence. Failure makes you more reliant. The late General George Patton remarked, "Success is not how fast you get to the top, but how high you bounce off the bottom." Like the skier, you fall and bounce back up ready to attack the next challenge.

Failure accelerates the learning process. Inside each failure is a partial truth. As these accumulate, a foundation of understanding is developed upon which success is built. Lastly, failure makes you more creative. Central truths emerge during periods of failure which lead you in new creative pathways.

You can trust failure and depend on it. On the other hand, success is a transient condition. It fools you into thinking you really understand what is going on, which leads to apathy, boredom, and eventual failure. I once saw a message on the bulletin board of a high tech musical instrument maker which read,

FAT CATS DON'T INNOVATE

which sums up the true meaning of prolonged or too much success.

Actually success and failure are synonymous, both are experiences. The only difference is in how you perceive your experiences and react to the outcomes. For example, you take your friend's Mercedes-Benz out for a spin and dent the fender in a five car pileup on the freeway. In one scenario, you call your friend and relate the bad experience of denting the fender. Or you tell him you were in a horrible five car accident and all that happened to the Mercedes was a dent in the fender! His reaction to the first scenario would be anger, and to the second scenario relief. So change your perceptions of failure and success.

Life is an adventure, an experiment. You are your own Chief Experimentalist. Think of your life in terms of odds and the law of averages. You select a mate by dating many prospects, take a job by making many interviews. All but one prospective mate and employer end up as failures as information you feed back to yourself to make you wiser and more mature.

Life itself developed on earth in a statistical manner. The first forms mutated through errors in the replication of genetic material. Most mutant forms of life were unfavorable and died out. But the one in a million mutants was positive, reproduced, and changed life forms. Through this process of failure life on earth evolved. Today the process of mutations continues in all species, as a living testament to the power of failure.

In reality there are only two ways to fail in an ultimate sense: quit, or not try. I guarantee you will succeed if you are willing to fill your life with failure.

In this class, you will only succeed if you are willing to fail frequently and intensely. As you will experience, that is the creative pathway to engineering. Design. Here is your course syllabus.

Cive 4311 Innovative Design (Failure 101)

Design in the narrowest sense is the use of equations to size physical structures, as in the design of a building. Design in the broadest sense is the use of your creative talent to innovate new products and systems. This course is dedicated to this proposition. You will have the opportunity and freedom to explore all ramifications of design, including concept, development, and the entrepreneurial aspects.

You (alone or with a team) will design an innovative something of your own choosing. You will produce at least a prototype and proceed to search for customers. By the end, you are expected to have customers (people willing to buy your design).

Course Outline

I. Concepts of Creativity
   Idea generation
   Success and failure
   Serendipity and surprise
   Einstein, Da Vinci, and dreams

II. Entrepreneurship
   Risk
   Intelligent fast failure
   Strafe and chaos
   The Art of the Deal
III. Design concepts
   Innovativeness
   Kansei "feels just right" design
   Stupid, lousy, and bad design
   Art, literature, and design
IV. Design Therapy
   Partial Reinforcement Effect
   Paradox Revisited
   Freud and design
V. Protecting Your Ideas
   Patents
   Copyrights
   Trademarks

Texts

1. *Mindfitness*, Matson
2. *Protecting Engineering Ideas and Inventions*, Penn

ORIGINS OF FAILURE 101

In the mid-1980s the University of Houston converted to the core curriculum, which meant that even engineers had to acquire a taste for liberal arts. In the Engineering College, each department was to offer two senior level knowledge integration courses. The theory was that no new information was to be presented, but that the previously acquired knowledge was to be synthesized. I was assigned to teach these courses by default. No other faculty member volunteered and I was not doing much at the time. I was in an on-the-job sabbatical trying to figure out what to do next with my professional life.

My first impulse was to make the courses into projects. The students could design a road, bridge, building, or sewage treatment plant and I would bring in sociologists, economists, and others to round out their integration of knowledge. I formulated a proposal and prepared to meet with the University Core Curriculum Committee who had to approve the contents of these courses.

At the meeting an obstreperous English professor vehemently objected to my proposal as a sham because I had not considered the most creative impulses of mankind found in the arts and literature. I thought he was wacky and so did the Committee as they voted sixteen to one in approving my proposal.

Later upon reflection I had to agree with him. I had ignored the subject of creativity entirely. I met with the English professor over the summer and intensely studied the subject of creativity. I decided both courses would be devoted to creativity that fall.

The first course was a total disaster. In my ignorance I attempted to teach the rules of creativity. "Students, here is the step by step process by which you become creative," I intoned. No response. Blank stares. Later on I realized that the creative process does not work on a set of rules, instead it defies and circumvents the rules.

I did have one modest success the first year. My desperation was so great that I decided to give a 140-question questionnaire from a magazine on rating a person's creativity. The risk was that the students would perform poorly, be shown to be not creative, and the results would be devastating. But I was desperate. The students did well on the quiz, scoring average or better. I was encouraged. My department chairman was not; he publicly wondered when something positive was going to happen. Privately I wondered the same thing.

During the second year I made my first marvelous discovery. One evening I watched my son building a structure with wooden popsicle sticks. I joined in on the fun. The next week I took a pile of sticks to class and instructed the students to build the tallest structure. Quickly they transformed themselves into six year olds playing with the sticks. At the end of the period I measured the height of the structures. A revelation occurred. The students with the tallest structures were those who played a lot with the sticks before they decided on a particular design. Those who had an idea immediately and spent the period building invariably came up short. I coined the early play by the successful students, "intelligent fast failure." They were going through all potential combinations quickly and settling on the best before starting full construction. I tried out the sticks on other students, and verified that those who accelerated the failure process early produced the best structures.

Using popsicle sticks became a fixture in the classroom. I could quickly transform the students into a creative mode by dreaming up a new stick project, and they became intellectual six year olds. I extrapolated the lessons of the sticks to every creative endeavor. Intelligent fast failure became the operative phrase for creativity. After a year of stick projects, I summed up my batting average with the students: roughly one third went through significant transformations and understood the concept of creativity; one third passed through the course treating it like any other course with not much impact; and one third actively opposed my efforts to elicit creative behavior. During my next year I focussed my attention on the dissenters.

I thought up a concept with the acronym BAD, which stood for Bold Acts of Defiance. The students would have to demonstrate through a project a denial of my teachings to free themselves in a creative way. BAD backfired badly. Most of the class agreed to put me on trial for impersonating a professor. The remaining students, three women, decided to defy me by not defying me and called themselves "The Undefiant." They defended me at the trial. I pleaded not guilty by reason of insanity, but the plea was rejected. In a lengthy pseudo legal process I was found guilty. As evidence the students cited one failed project. It involved using the senses other than sight. I had darkened the classroom and given them four different materials to identify: wood shavings, corn flakes, uncooked grits, and scented kitty litter. Once they tasted the kitty litter and found out what it was, a group bolted the room and reported me to the department chairman. Perhaps the verdict was just.

The next year, my fourth, a brainstorm the size of a hurricane hit me. Why not reward failure? Those who fail the most get the highest grades. That instruction would put the dissenters in a bind. If they dissented by failing, they were doing what I wanted.

I set up a series of failure assignments. With the popsicle sticks they had to design the worst and most stupid consumer products. They responded with hamster hot tubs, hand held barbecue pits, kites which flew only in gale force winds, etc. Next I surprised them by instructing them to go out to the street and attempt to sell their junk. To my utter surprise most were able to sell their products. They harassed prospective customers so much the people paid small sums of money to get rid of the students.

The students had outsmarted me through their brush-off sales techniques. In the subsequent course I changed the instruction to go on the street and court as many rejections as possible. If someone appeared to be interested in buying, they raised the price, downgraded the junk, or ran away. Mission accomplished. They had quickly learned that failure was no big deal and could even be fun.

Other exercises followed. There was "Dress for Failure Day" when each student designed an outfit guaranteed not to net them a position in a job interview. Then they constructed a "Failure Resume" based on the real failures in their lives. Here is my failure resume:

Resume of Failures

Jack V. Matson
Doctor of Philosophy
Professional Engineer
Failure

Educational Failures

1952	Placed in "Bunny" slow readers' class in the fourth grade
1954	Lost election for class vice president by a wide margin
1957	Cut from basketball team after first tryout
1966	Dropped out of law school
1971	Flunked doctoral screening exam

Vocational Failures

1956	Could not handle first job as pin spotter in bowling alley
1961	Fired from summer job as a bottle washer at a distilled water company
1965	Terminated first try at an engineering career with an oil company
1970–71	Resigned from second and third jobs as an engineer—couldn't fit in
1977	Asked to leave academia
1983	Laid off the employees at my engineering company and closed its doors

These seemingly frivolous exercises contained some serious messages. The students realized they had creative abilities even if these were displayed in failure modes. And failure became a normal part of the practice of creativity. The failure resume exercise made each student realize failures were significant factors in his life.

To my amazement, the students showed little resistance or defiance to expressing their creative talents in the negative direction: the most stupid, worst, and dumbest. I coined the term "Negative Creativity" to define this phenomena.

NUTS AND BOLTS OF FAILURE 101

The course has a fundamental purpose: the students must design a product, and by the end of the fifteen week semester have potential customers. The first three weeks are taken up by the failure exercises. Then they must use their creative abilities to innovate. That is a tough assignment.

Idea generation comes first. They go through standard techniques such as brainstorming, and graze newspapers and magazines for good ideas. They also use "Negative Creativity" by thinking up the worst ideas to solve a problem. They bring to class several of their best ideas and worst ideas. Interestingly, the creative content of the worst ideas is generally much higher than in the best ideas. We look for ways to combine the best with the worst to produce more unique ideas. We call the idea formulation stage CHAOS (Creating Havoc Accelerates Outrageous Success).

The next stage is the testing of the ideas; it is called STRAFE (Success Through Rapid Accelerated Failure Engineering). The strategy is to accelerate the rate of failures and compress the time it takes to find out what works and what does not. Intelligent Fast Failure is the operative phrase. The students try to experiment with their ideas simultaneously, working on each idea in parallel, as opposed to sequentially in which an idea is pursued until it fails then another idea is tried.

Another four weeks pass and the frustration levels rise as nothing seems to have worked out. The semester is more than half over with no tangible progress. We go into a design therapy phrase in which each student recites his failures and his classmates offer suggestions. The air crackles with new and fresh ideas. Enthusiasm is renewed only to be crushed when the new ideas do not work out for most of the students.

In the final weeks of the semester a desperate sort of atmosphere hangs over the classroom. The final stage of compromise is in progress. The realization dawns that good, even great ideas are not working out but something has to be produced. Creative compromise of ideals produces a final product. Over ninety percent of the students come through. To get there, they average five major failures during the semester.

The course ends mercifully for some, too soon for others. For the final grade, we peer review the projects. Each student grades every other student, and I use these grades as a strong advisory. Actually, there is never much difference between my evaluation and the students. Another chapter of Failure 101 has been written.

WHAT I HAVE LEARNED

The following is a list of six essential elements required for the creative process to bloom in the classroom.

1. Atmosphere

The mood in the classroom is playful with surprises. Guest speakers will show up without warning. Some mind tingling exercise will be tossed out to them. They experience the role surprise and serendipity play in the innovation process.

The classroom is turned upside down in some ways. We use the boo rating scale for evaluation. Boos are good; the louder the better. They are encouraged to cheat fair, to borrow ideas from others but acknowledge the sources. They learn that taking ideas from others is a time honored tradition in the world of creativity and innovation. They can work in groups or individually. I prefer groups of two for idea cross-fertilization reasons, but that is their choice. The bottom line measurement of the atmosphere is whether they achieve the state of the six year old intellectual in every class.

2. Freedom

Freedom is everything and in important ways the only thing to the creative mind. My colleague, John Leinhard, suggests innovation is the quest for freedom; and that innovators need to fly free. Yet freedom in the classroom is the most difficult goal to achieve. The students are totally conditioned to be prisoners, and declarations by me that they can take off their shackles do not release them from mental bondage.

Freedom gradually takes shape through the failure exercises, as the students realize they indeed have the freedom to fail. Fear gradually subsides and is replaced by a playful joking and relaxation of tensions.

3. Passion

Failure 101 is not a simulation; it is the real thing. A number of students (small in percentage) have pursued their projects after the semester ended. The students own their ideas, and this ownership should produce a burning desire to test and experiment. Mark Twain put it this way, "Success is going from failure to failure with enthusiasm." The students who "get it" light up and show emotion; that is my best indication.

4. Courage

Kit Carson said it best, "The cowards never start, and the weak die along the way." The students summon up the courage to break away from preconceived notions of education and display their creative impulses risking defeat and failure. Innovation simply does not exist without the courageous actions of the innovators.

5. Rebellion

I explored rebellion in my experiments with students. I have much more to learn. Frederick Nietzsche was quoted, "Rebel against conditions in which you repeat only what you have heard, learn what is already known, and imitate what already exists. Only then can life be more than a decoration." Leinhard put it this way, "I doubt the genius if he is not in trouble." Rebellion is a channel for creative acts, and as I have shown can be used to advantage.

6. Effort

Michelangelo, the creative genius of the Renaissance, spent months working on bozzeti (buds), small wax figurines, going through the painstaking trial and error process of figuring out what he wanted to do. I tell my students all promising creative ideas degrade to hard work. Details must be probed, for the Gods reside in the details. Effort is the bottom line.

STUDENT RESPONSE

Rap (to the appropriate background music)

If you are down on your luck
And sick of regular class
Professor Matson says, "come into my grasp!"
Failure 101 is my way
To feel real alive, I have to fail today.
If at first you don't succeed
Dr. Matson will tell you what you need
You try and try until you are out of breath
Your ultimate goal is a big fat F!

Or, as another student put it:

If at first you don't fail, try, try again.

DOWNSIDE OF FAILURE

As you witnessed, productive failure is difficult to implement in the classroom situation. You want control, but must give it up. You want order but must encourage disorder. You want certainty but must learn to provide surprises. You want creativity to fit nicely into the schedule, but it turns out to be a messy process.

The students will question your IQ and motives. The kindest students will consider you eccentric and the unkindest will call you a lunatic. They will be emotional and uncontrollable at times, and you will have to let it be that way. Some classes will be disasters because your experiments will fail. But you are the role model and must put yourself on the line periodically.

Do not do as I did, and attempt to take an entire course and turn it upside down. Begin by injecting concepts of failure and creativity into lectures and homework assignments. For example, alert the students before the lecture begins you will cleverly teach something wrong, and for their homework assignment they must find it. You will be amazed at their attentiveness in looking for your intentional failure, and at how much they learn in this negative creativity mode. Or develop a problem in which their goal is to fool you in as many ways as possible.

Lastly, enjoy and savor those moments of ecstasy when the light bulbs flash on and illuminate everyone's minds. One time I gave an assignment to build a bridge entirely of bananas. The bridge which could support the most weight would be the winner. Well, bananas are squishy and burst when weight is applied. But one group of students built a banana bridge which supported thousands of pounds. They froze the bananas first! They nor I will ever forget their innovative concept, so simple yet so unexpected. Yes, successes such as this one are a pleasure to be enjoyed occasionally.

Acknowledgements

To my students and friends who participated in the experiments; and to Art Mortell for an injection of fresh ideas on failure.

Biographical Sketches

PHILIP M. ANDERSON is an associate professor in the Department of Secondary Education and Youth Services at Queens College/SUNY. Recipient of a Ph.D. in curriculum and instruction from the University of Wisconsin-Madison, he previously taught in the English Department at Ohio University and the Education Department at Brown.

TERRY ARMSTRONG is an associate professor of management at the University of West Florida. He has served as editor of the *Organization Development Journal* for three years and has published six books and numerous articles in the areas of applied social science and organization development.

CAMILLE BLACHOWICZ is professor of education at the National College of Education of National-Louis University. Along with her research and work in staff development, she has had extensive experience as a classroom teacher, as an intermediate team leader, and as a reading specialist in grades K to 8. She is co-author of the basal reading series, *Scott Foresman Reading: An American Tradition*, and co-author of *Reading Diagnosis for Teachers: An Instructional Approach* published by Longmans.

ROBERT E. CANNON received his B.A. degree in biology from Earlham College in 1968 followed by M.A. and Ph.D. degrees in biological sciences at the University of Delaware. He has been at the University of North Carolina-Greensboro for 18 years, and is an associate professor of biology and assistant dean of the College of Arts and Sciences. He

teaches microbiology courses and is a private pilot.

GEORGE W. CHILCOAT teaches social studies methods in the College of Education at Brigham Young University in Provo, Utah.

JEANINE COGAN is a psychology graduate student at the University of Vermont, with special interests in women's studies and creative thinking.

INGRID G.. DAEMMRICH teaches writing and literature in the Department of Humanities-Communications at Drexel University. A specialist in compositional and literary theory, she has published numerous studies in her field. *The Handbook of Themes and Motifs in Western Literature*, co-authored with Horst S. Daemmrich, is used as a reference guide by students throughout the world.

DIANA MAYER DEMETRULIAS is professor and dean of the School of Education at California State University, Stanislaus. Prior to her university teaching and administration, Dr. Demetrulias was a high school teacher of English and mathematics. She is the author of several monographs, including a *Phi Delta Kappa* Fastback in teacher education, and of 40 articles in professional journals. Her areas of interest include teacher education, creativity, equity, and computer education.

CHARLES R. GAROIAN an assistant director of the Palmer Museum of Art, taught studio art and art history in secondary schools for 17 years prior to coming to

Penn State. While in the public schools, he developed unique mixed media strategies for teaching critical thinking in the visual arts. His current responsibilities at the Palmer Museum consist of program development and outreach. A mixed media performance artist since 1970, he has performed, lectured, and presented workshops at the San Francisco Museum of Modern Art, the Cleveland Museum, and the Hirshhorn Museum and Sculpture Garden in Washington, D.C. His performance piece, *S/Laughter*, was recently presented at the Painted Bride Art Center in Philadelphia.

Louis H. Henry is professor of economics and directs the Academic Honors Program at Old Dominion University in Norfolk, Virginia. He earned his degrees from King's College and the University of Notre Dame. He received the Joint Council on Economic Education's National Teaching Award in 1986.

Jannett K. Highfill is an associate professor of economics at Bradley University, Peoria, Illinois. She did her undergraduate work at Wichita State University, and received a Ph.D. from the University of Kansas in 1985. Her recent publications are in the areas of international trade, applied microeconomics, and economic pedagogy.

Kenneth Holland is professor of political science at Memphis State University. He has a University of Chicago Ph.D. and has authored several books, including *Writer's Guide: Political Science* (with Arthur W. Biddle) and *A Vade Mecum for American Government*. His major field of research is the judicial process, and he has contributed a number of articles to scholarly journals and edited works.

Gary Isenberg received his B.A. in psychology from the University of Vermont and currently counsels emotionally disturbed teenagers in Boston.

Richard Jenseth is assistant professor of English at Lehigh University. He has been working on problems of understanding in crossdisciplinary and crosscultural texts with respect to cultural conflict and cultural identity.

Kim M. King received her Ph.D. in sociology in 1985 from the University of North Carolina at Chapel Hill. She is an assistant professor of sociology at Hiram College in Ohio. Her graduate schooling included intensive training in teaching and she has had many published articles in *Teaching Sociology*. Her substantive interests and research include deviance, the family, youth, sociological theory, and qualitative methodology.

Herbert Leff is a psychology professor at the University of Vermont and specializes in creativity and metacognition.

Jonathan F. Lewis, an associate professor at Illinois Benedictine College, received his Ph.D. in sociology from the University of Oregon in 1982. He has published articles on teaching in the journals *Teaching Sociology* and *The History Teacher*.

E. Nick Maddox is an associate professor of management at Stetson University. He has co-authored a book entitled *Envisionary Management* and has written several articles dealing with the utilization of imagery in the decision making process. He is active in the World's Future Society and the Organizational Behavior Teaching Association.

Jo Margaret Mano (Ph.D. Columbia, 1985) was born in Britain and came to the United States in 1964. Since 1980 she has taught in the Geography department at SUNY, The College at New Paltz. Her teaching and research fields include cartography, Geographic information systems, remote sensing, urban planning, and geographic education.

JACK V. MATSON teaches engineering and innovative entrepreneurship at the University of Houston, aiming to give failure a more respectable name. Twenty percent of his students may continue the business they develop in his course after they have completed it. "The 'best' grade in this course is an F," he has said, "and that's no joke."

DONALD MEEKER formerly headed the Department of Business at Newbury College in Boston and now writes and gives workshops on creativity in education and business.

ANN NEVIN is an education professor at Arizona State University (formerly at the University of Vermont) and specializes in collaborative consultation and pedagogical theory.

GREGORY RUBANO teaches English at Toll Gate High School in Warwick, Rhode Island. During 1978–85 he was also a methods associate in the MAT Program at Brown University. He received a B.A. from William and Mary, an M.A.T. from Brown, and is currently completing a Ph.D. in curriculum and instruction at the University of Connecticut.

MICHAEL W. SMITH teaches undergraduate methods and graduate courses in response to literature at the University of Wisconsin-Madison. Both his teaching and research have been greatly influenced by his 11 years of experience at Elk Grove High School, Elk Grove Village, Illinois.

KARL A. SMITH teaches in the Department of Civil and Chemical Engineering and ANTHONY M. STARFIELD teaches conservation and wildlife management, both at the University of Minnesota. They have collaborated for several years in teaching systems modeling to engineers, conservationists, and teachers and collaborative learning to teachers at all levels. With A. L. Blaloch, they wrote *How to Model it: Problem Solving for the Computer Age* (New York: McGraw Hill, 1990).

JULIE A. SPRINGER is coordinator of the National Teacher Institute, education division, at the National Gallery of Art. She holds B.A. and M.A. degrees in art history and has written articles and book reviews for both art history and education journals.

ELIZABETH J. STROBLE, an assistant professor of secondary education at the University of Louisville, teaches graduate and undergraduate courses in models of teaching, English methods, and curriculum construction. In a previous appointment at Northern Arizona University she also served as associate director of the Northern Arizona Writing Project.

THOMAS W. RISHELL has taught mathematics at Cornell University since 1973. Born in Chicago, he grew up in Ohio, graduated from Youngstown State University in 1962 and received a topology Ph.D. from the University of Pittsburgh in 1970. He has taught or worked as a research associate at Pittsburgh, Dalhousie, Tokio Kyoiku Daiguku, and the University of Oregon.

WOLFF-MICHAEL ROTH, after completing undergraduate and graduate degrees in physics in Germany, began teaching secondary courses in Canada, including science, mathematics, computer science, and physical education, grades 7 to 12. After receiving his Ph.D. in science education from the University of Southern Mississippi, he served as the head of the Science Department at Appleby College in Ontario, then became assistant professor of education at Simon Fraser University.

HOWARD TINBERG is an assistant professor of English at Bristol Community College in Fall River, Massachusetts. He has published articles in *College Composition and Communication, Teaching English in the Two Year College, English Journal,* and elsewhere. His abiding concern as a teacher is to find ways of merging theory and practice.

CLARA WAJNGURT teaches mathematics at Queensborough Community College in Bayside, New York, and is also currently serving as acting grants officer at the college. She has been conducting mathematics anxiety workshops at the college each semester and is sensitive to the needs of her students. Dr. Wajngurt has a doctorate in mathematics—number theory—from the City University of New York Graduate School.

ROBERT YAGER has been on the faculty at the University of Iowa for over 30 years. He has served on the national STS advisory board, UPSTEP (a model science teacher education project), Iowa ASSIST (an in-service delivery system), and the Iowa Honors Workshop (leadership development for the architects of exemplary science programs) and currently serves as the regional director for STS, networking for Iowa, Missouri, Minnesota, Nebraska, and Kansas.

WILLIAM V. WEBER is an associate professor of economics and the director of the Office for Economic Education at Eastern Illinois University. Dr. Weber has published in a variety of journals, including *Economic Inquiry* and the *Journal of Economic Education,* and is an author of economic textbooks and supplements.

WALTER J. WHEATLEY is an associate professor of management at the University of West Florida. He has co-authored a book entitled *Envisionary Management* and has written several articles on improving the education process with imagery. His current projects include writing and illustrating a series of children's books applying imagery to the learning process.

ROBERT ZELLER is associate professor of English at Southeast Missouri State University, where he teaches writing. He received his B.A. from Duke University and his M.A. and Ph.D. from Pennsylvania State University. He has published on Australian literature as well as the teaching of writing.

Selected Bibliography

ARTICLES OF GENERAL INTEREST

Alexander, P.A. & Judy, J.E. (1988). The interaction of domain specific and strategic knowledge in academic performance. *Review of Educational Research*, 58:4, 375–404.

Bransford, J.D., Sherwood, R.D., & Sturdevant, T. (1987). Teaching thinking and problem solving. In J.B. Baron & R.J. Sternberg (Eds.), *Teaching Thinking Skills: Theory and Practice*. New York: Freeman.

Bruffee, K. (1986). Social construction, language, and the authority of knowledge: A bibliographical essay. *College English*, 48(8), 773–90.

Clarke, J. (1987). Building a lecture that works. *College Teaching*, 35(2), 56–58.

Clarke, J. (1989). Designing discussion on the inquiry cycle. *College Teaching*, October.

Clarke, J.H., Gilbert, G., & Raths, J. (1989). Inductive towers: Helping students see how they think. *Journal of Reading*, 32: 86–95.

Clarke, J. (1991). Using visual organizers to focus on thinking. *Journal of Reading*, 34:7, 526–34.

Donald, J.G. (1983). Knowledge structures: Methods for exploring course content. *Journal of Higher Education*, 54(1), 31–41.

Ennis, R.H. (1987). A taxonomy of critical thinking dispositions and abilities. In J.B. Baron & R.M. Sternberg (Eds.), *Teaching Thinking Skills*. New York: W.H. Freeman and Company, 1–26.

Ennis, R.H. (1989). Critical thinking and subject specificity: Clarification and needed research. *Educational Researcher*, 18:3, 4–6.

Flower, L., & Hayes, J.R. (1984). Images, plans and prose. *Written Communication*, 1(1), 120–60.

Gagne, R.M. (1980). Learnable aspects of problem solving. *American Psychologist*, 15(2), 84–92.

Larkin, J., McDermott, J., Simon, D.P., & Simon, H.A. (1980). Expert and novice performance in solving physics problems. *Science*, 208 (20 June 80), 1335–42.

Larkin, J.H. (1979). Information processing models and science instruction. In J. Lochhead & J. Clemmons (Eds.), *Cognitive Process Instruction*. Philadelphia: Franklin Institute Press.

Mayer, R. (1989). Models for Understanding. Review of Educational Research, 59:1, 43–64.

Nisbett, R.E., Fong, G.T., Lehman, D.R., & Cheng, P.W. (1987). Teaching reasoning. *Science*, 238, 30 October, 625–31.

Perkins, D.N., & Simmons, R. (1988). Patterns of misunderstanding: An integrative model for science, mathematics and programming. *Review of Educational Research*, 58(3), 303–26.

Perkins, D.N. (1988). Thinking frames. *Educational Leadership*, 43(8), 4–11.

Perkins, D.N., & Salomon, G. (1989). Are cognitive skills context bound? *Educational Researcher*, 18:1, 16–26.

Presseisen, B. (1988). Avoiding battle at curriculum gulch: Teaching thinking and content. *Educational Leadership*, April, 7–10.

Sternberg, R.M. (1987). Questions and answers about the nature and teaching of thinking skills. In J. Baron & R. Sternberg (Eds.), *Teaching Thinking Skills: Theory and Research*. New York: W.H. Freeman and Sons.

BOOKS

Ausubel, D. (1968). *Educational Psychology: A Cognitive View*. New York: Holt Reinhart and Winston.

Barell, J. (1991). *Teaching for Thoughtfulness*, White Plains, NY: Longman.

Beyer, B. (1987). *Practical strategies for the teaching of thinking*. Boston: Allyn & Bacon.

Biddle, A.W. (1985). *Writer to Writer*. New York, McGraw Hill.

Biddle, A.W. & Holland, R.M. (1987). *Writer's Guide: Political Science*, Lexington, MA: D.C. Heath & Co.

Biddle, A.W. & Bean, D.J. (1987). *Writer's Guide: Life Sciences*, Lexington, MA: D.C. Heath & Co.

Bloom, B.S. (Ed.) (1956). *Taxonomy of Educational Objectives. Handbook I: Cognitive Domain.* New York: McKay.

Bruner, J. (1986). *Actual Minds, Possible Worlds.* Cambridge, MA: Harvard University Press.

Chase, W.G. (Ed.) (1973). *Visual Information Processing.* New York: Academic Press.

Clarke, J.H. (1990). *Patterns of Thinking: Integrating Learning Skills with Content Teaching.* Boston: Allyn & Bacon.

Bobrow, D.G., & Collins, A. (Eds.) (1975). *Representation and Understanding: Studies in Cognitive Science.* New York: Academic Press.

Costa, A. (1991). *Developing Minds: A Resource Book for Teaching Thinking.* (2nd ed.) Alexandria, VA: ASCD Publications.

Daemmrich,

Fulwiler, T. (1987). *Teaching with Writing.* Upper Montclair, NJ: Boynton Cook.

Fulwiler, T. (1987). *Writing to Learn.* Upper Montclair, NJ: Boynton Cook.

Fulwiler, T. (1989). *The Journal Book.* Upper Montclair, NJ: Boynton Cook.

Fulwiler, T. & Biddle, A.W. (1993) *A Community of Voices: Reading and Writing in the Disciplines,* New York: Macmillan and Co.

Gardner, H. (1983). *Frames of Mind: The Theory of Multiple Intelligences.* New York: Basic Books.

Gentner, D., & Stevens, A.L. (1983). *Mental Models.* Hillsdale, NJ: Lawrence Erlbaum Associates.

Halpern, D. (1984). *Thought and Knowledge: An Introduction to Critical Thinking.* Hillsdale, NJ: Lawrence Erlbaum.

Holland, J.H., Holyoak, K.J., Nisbett, R.E., & Thagard, P.R. (1986). *Induction: Processes of Inference Learning and Discovery.* Cambridge, MA: MIT Press.

Johnson, D.W., & Johnson, R.T. (1986). *Learning Together and Alone.* Englewood Cliffs, NJ: Prentice Hall.

Jones, B.F., Palincsar, A.S., Ogle, D.S., & Carr, E.G. (1987). *Strategic Thinking and Learning: Cognitive Instruction in the Content Areas.* Alexandria, VA: ASCD Publications.

Kolb, D. (1977). *Learning Style Inventory* (Manual). Cambridge, MA: McBer and Associates.

Kolb, D. (1984). *Experiential Learning: Experience as the Source of Learning and Development.* Englewood Cliffs, N.J.: Prentice Hall, Inc.

Kuhn, T.S. (1970). *The Structure of Scientific Revolutions,* 2nd ed. Chicago: University of Chicago Press.

Lochhead, J. & J. Clemmons (Eds.), *Cognitive Process Instruction.* Philadelphia: Franklin Institute Press.

Marzano, R.J., Brandt, R., Hughes, C., Jones, B.F., Presseisen, B., Rankin, S., & Suhor, C. (1988). *Dimensions of Thinking: A Framework for Curriculum and Instruction.* Alexandria, VA: ASCD Publications.

Neimark, E. (1987). *Adventures in Thinking.* New York: Harcourt Brace Jovanovich.

Newell, A., & Simon, H.A. (1972). *Human Problem Solving.* Englewood Cliffs, NJ: Prentice Hall.

Nickerson, R.S., Perkins, D.N., & Smith, E.E. (1985). *The Teaching of Thinking.* Hillsdale, NJ: Lawrence Erlbaum Associates.

Perkins, D.N. (1986). *Knowledge as Design.* Hillsdale, NJ: Lawrence Erlbaum Associates.

Resnick, L. (1987). *Education and Learning to Think.* Washington, DC: National Academy Press.

Simon, H.A. (1975). *Models of Thought.* New York: Yale University Press.

Smith, Karl (1990).

Sternberg, R.J. (1985). *Beyond IQ: A Triarchal Theory of Intelligence.* Cambridge: Cambridge University Press.

Sternberg, R.J. (1986). *Intelligence applied: Understanding and increasing your intellectual skills.* San Diego: Harcourt Brace Jovanovich.

Vygotsky, L. (1986). *Thought and Language* (A. Kozulin, Trans.) Cambridge, MA: MIT University Press (original work published 1926).

Whimbey, A. & Lochhead, J. (1982). *Problem Solving & Comprehension* (3rd ed.) Philadelphia: Franklin Institute Press.

Whimbey, A. & E.L. Jenkins (1986). *Analyze, Organize, Write.* Hillsdale, NJ: Lawrence Erlbaum & Associates.

Wilson, J. (1963). *Thinking with Concepts.* Cambridge: Cambridge University Press.